THIS BOOK IS IN MEMORY OF GORDON,
FRANCES, AND ELIOT ELLEFSON.

DEDICATED TO THE PEOPLE
OF JACKSON, MINNESOTA

A Jawbone book
First edition 2019
Published in the UK and the USA by
Jawbone Press
Office G1
141–157 Acre Lane
London SW2 5UA
England
www.jawbonepress.com

ISBN 978-1-911036-51-7

Unless otherwise stated, all photographs used
in this book are from the author's collection.

Printed in China

1 2 3 4 5 23 22 21 20 19

CONTENTS

FOREWORD
BY JOEL MCIVER

Rock'n'roll eats its young. Very few musicians reach a significant level of success within the industry without losing something, whether it's their minds, their health, their material possessions, or simply their humanity. I've been navigating the murky waters of heavy metal for a couple of decades now, and I've yet to meet anyone who hasn't disappeared into the rabbit hole.

One notable exception comes to mind, though: David Ellefson. Whether in or out of Megadeth, the titanic metal band which he still anchors after all these years, the man has held onto his fundamental decency as a human being. You're going to love this book, his third so far; as with the previous two, Ellefson has a ton of wisdom to share, and he's generous about sharing it.

I first met the man at Winter NAMM in California in 2008. He was out of Megadeth at the time and working for Peavey, at whose stand we talked about bass guitars. As I chatted with him, I wondered to myself if I was revealing any fan-boy nervousness; as a teenager, I'd been a huge fan of his bass playing, spending hours figuring out his bass parts. I'd even seen Megadeth play at the UK's Donington festival in 1988, unaware that Ellefson was at a particularly low point at the time. Twenty years later, as I talked with him at NAMM, my impression was that this was a genuinely good guy in an environment populated with damaged people.

Two years after that, I met Ellefson at the first Big Four show in Poland. We talked bass again, and this time my focus was on staying coherent despite rather too many shots of free backstage vodka. (If he noticed my intoxication, he was polite enough not to mention it.)

Back in the UK, I dropped him an email suggesting that we work together on a book. I'd recently written the memoir of Glenn Hughes, and I knew that Ellefson's autobiography would be an eye-opening read. He was keen, so we recruited a literary agent and got started. The book, *My Life With Deth*, came out in 2013 and was a critical and commercial success. I remember holding the first copy and casting my mind back to that Donington gig in 1988. We had both come a long way …

A life and career as productive as Ellefson's can't be contained in a single book, of course, and I'm delighted that Ellefson has compiled a second volume of autobiography with his talented business partner, Thom Hazaert, at the helm. Enjoy *More Life With Deth*; if more of us heeded the lessons within it, perhaps the rock'n'roll world would be a better (and safer) place.

PREFACE
BY DAVID ELLEFSON

Welcome back for *More Life With Deth*! The idea for this book was presented to me by my record-label and coffee-company partner, Thom Hazaert (more on him later), as I came home from a Midwest coffee tour with an *Ellefson Family History 1600s–1979* under my arms. That history seemed to conveniently mark the beginning of this new archive of my life.

As I had contemplated writing another autobiographical book at some point, and the family history seemed to set the stage to commit these next chapters of my life to print, this book both prefaces and moves past my first autobiography, *My Life With Deth*, which was published in 2013. That book contains a broader-stroke overview of my early days growing up in Jackson, Minnesota, moving to Hollywood after high school, co-founding the rock group Megadeth, and much more. With this book, I thought it important to look back on the decade since I rejoined Megadeth, our triumphs and tribulations, alongside several new and exciting musical adventures that came about both organically and unexpectedly.

Additionally, this season of my life has led me to new creative and business endeavors that I've long sought to explore. Some of these include my EMP Label Group, Ellefson Coffee Co., a booking agency, a nonprofit organization, continued record producing, writing and recording with other acts, and even an artist-development and management firm.

I hope you enjoy these new pages as much as I have enjoyed living and sharing them with you all!

INTRODUCTION
BY THOM HAZAERT

I first met David Ellefson in the 2000s, in his time away from Megadeth, when he was working as an artist rep for Peavey. Over a decade later, we reconnected, almost certainly by divine confluence, and since then have ended up partnering on pretty much everything: record labels, a coffee company, clothing lines, a merchandise company, instruments, beverages, magazines, and now this book. (Seriously, it's like *Spaceballs*.)

Originally, the book would have been me ghostwriting with him, but as it developed, we discovered that my color commentary and 'outsider on the inside' perspective gave a different angle to the story. So we went with it. And while I had a bit of hesitation—and a few moments of *who the fuck am I?*—with David's support and glowing feedback on my initial contributions, my inner attention whore got its way, and I am now privileged not only to be a part of the story, but to be able to help tell it.

While I started my journey into this business of music as a writer, the winds of change that Klaus Meine sang about have blown me all over the damn place—management, A&R, marketing, running record labels, even brief forays into film direction and production. But wherever I ended up, I have never been far from my humble beginnings as an eager observer of the rock'n'roll condition. And Megadeth, my favorite band for the last thirty-plus years, have never been far from my heart.

For my birthday in 2016 (November 8, if you want to send a gift), David sent me the *Peace Sells ... But Who's Buying?* deluxe boxed set, plus a copy of his book *My Life With Deth*, inscribed with the words, *Thom ... Thank you for being part of my life's journey.* Little did we know how prophetic those words would prove to be when, just two years later, I ended up not only talking him into doing a follow-up to that book but writing it with him.

I am eternally grateful to David, his amazing family (and mine), and the rest of our team, for the opportunity to participate, and support, the amazing legacy that is David Warren Ellefson.

And now, without further ado, we present our feature attraction ... *More Life With Deth.*

REINVENTION

1.1 NECESSITY: THE MOTHER OF INVENTION

Monday, February 8, 2010.

'Hey Dale, did you hear I re-joined Megadeth today?' I said enthusiastically to my dear friend and F5 vocalist, Dale Steele.

'That's great!' he replied. 'Now get prepared for when it ends again, because last time, you weren't.'

It was a sobering moment of reality amid the global celebration of the triumphant reunion of 'Dave & Dave,' together once again in Megadeth. And the truth is, Dale was right.

At the time, I was forty-five years old, and I had skillfully rebuilt my life and career in the years since Megadeth came to an abrupt ending back in 2002, when Dave Mustaine's arm injury brought about an enforced hiatus for the band. There is a proverb that states, *'As iron sharpens iron, so one man strengthens another.'* Dale Steele was practicing this very spiritual principle in his accurate assessment. In other words: learn from your past and be alert as well as prepared.

I met Dale when I produced his band NUMM in Minneapolis, just a few months after Megadeth disbanded. I was still in a career and financial free-fall after the band ended, and I had reached out to literally everyone I had ever met in the business, asking for a job or a job lead or just some way to get back on my feet again. We had made a lot of money over the years as a band, but we still had debts, outstanding bills, and unrecouped positions with labels, publishers, and merchandisers. As with any business, sometimes you stay in business simply to preserve your business. Unfortunately, that was over now, and I had to move on.

By way of a mutual friend and booking agent from my hometown of Jackson, Minnesota, I was introduced to Bob Pickering of Oarfin Records. Bob suggested I produce Dale's band, and I did just that a few weeks later. Dale was a hustling kind of guy with great drive and determination to be a rock star. His ability to write lyrics and melodies on the spot in the studio was impressive to me, and we stayed in touch.

Unfortunately, after shopping the NUMM demos around the industry, I came up with zilch for the band. For the first time, I realized how difficult it is to get other people in the music business to believe in your project, because they are all busy trying to get someone to believe in theirs! My experience with Megadeth showed me that without a cheerleader at the helm, it is tough to break down the doors of obstacle and get anywhere in the entertainment business.

•

In early 2003, Dale moved to Phoenix to abort NUMM and join forces with me, guitarists Steve Conley and John Davis, and drummer Dave Small, in a new band venture that was coming into place called F5. Dave came up with the name after watching the movie *Twister*, an F5 being the strongest category of tornado.

The band was fun and easy, and it renewed a sense in me of why I started playing bass in the first place. We would jam at Steve's house in Glendale, Arizona, several times per week, and the songs seemed to effortlessly write themselves. I had rediscovered the magic of what a band can become when you allow everyone to do their own thing and let each of us gel our parts together intuitively in the creation of the songs.

In Megadeth, it was mostly Dave who wrote the songs, taking on the role of *master composer*. F5 was a refreshing new approach. I felt invigorated, like I was part of a team, excited to go to rehearsal every day, to write and record new material.

In F5, we utilized the dropped-D half-step tuning. This was a departure from the standard A440 tuning we always used in Megadeth. Subsequently, new ideas were flying everywhere. As many composers will tell you, altered tunings can bring a new sound to an old instrument, opening up fresh new inspiration in much the same way the feel of a new guitar can awaken the creative juices.

I was so excited that I began to sift through old cassettes, demos, and CDs at my house for song ideas I had catalogued from as far back as the Megadeth *Countdown To Extinction* era and the 1991 *Clash Of The Titans* tour, when each day I was brimming with novel lyric and music ideas. Much of that creative thrust stemmed in part from my awakened senses in my first years of sobriety, as well as from how Megadeth had really started to gel as a group, with Nick Menza and Marty Friedman participating as full-fledged band members.

While many of my creative contributions had made it onto the *Countdown* album, there were still some ideas lingering behind. Sometimes, an idea is really good, but it's just not right for the collection of songs on an album at that exact moment in time.

Now, in F5, I didn't deem myself *the boss*, but I was at least an equal fifth of the band. I really relished the creative forces that occurred naturally between the five of us. In fact, as much as I *could* have appointed myself the leader, I felt it best to try to keep a democratic approach to everything with the band. I was especially keen not to dampen or hinder the group's creative output. Over the years, I've learned that a boss or leader is often needed to keep uniformity and direction, but this can be a double-edged sword when trying to keep unity with creativity.

Initially, F5 had a much harder and more 'metal' sound than that of our 'radio rock' debut album, *A Drug For All Seasons*. Our initial compositions were heavy, rowdy, and fun. A different sound would be shaped during the preproduction and final production stages of the album, however—and here's how that process morphed into the album.

Through mutual friends, I was introduced to Steve Smith, who was then a senior vice president at Clear Channel Radio, and who looked like Sammy Hagar's doppelgänger. He had shoulder-length curly blond hair, drove an $80,000 convertible Lexus, and had turned the home theater of his million-dollar Scottsdale mansion into a first-class, state-of-the-art recording studio.

Steve was a cool guy, and the two of us bonded over our love of both music and the music industry. He lived five minutes from me in a swank, gated community. (He was only several blocks from the Mustaines' old residence, too, and at one time they had lived in the same gated community.)

When Steve first brought me to his home studio, his engineer, Ryan Greene, was mixing an album for local Arizona pop-punk favorites Authority Zero, who were also part of Steve's mini-empire of Phoenix-based music. Ryan had also engineered the demo sessions for Megadeth's *Countdown To Extinction* back in 1991, as a staff engineer at the EMI Music Publishing studio next to Le Dome, a sophisticated celebrity nightspot restaurant on Sunset Boulevard in West Hollywood. I hadn't seen him since then, and it was wonderful to reconnect with him.

A few weeks later, Steve asked if he could come down to an F5 rehearsal. I warned him that where the band rehearsed was in a strip center of grungy car garages and mechanical workshops in Mesa. This was a far cry from the luxuries of Scottsdale, but he wanted to hear what we sounded like as a live group. I agreed to have him drop in for a listen.

F5 were loud. We were good musically, and we were believable in our delivery. We were like a locomotive of pure metal. Our songs were heavy, and the guitars were shredding.

Steve's first critique was that every song was in the same key, C# minor—and he was right! We'd written so many songs in such a short time together that we hadn't even thought about it. Steve suggested we change it up a bit from song to song, to help give some them variety. We subsequently followed his suggestion, and he then invited us to start recording at his studio.

Now, I have worked with enough producers and record-label A&R people over the years to know that if you don't have a clear direction in your artistic endeavors, someone else will. In this case, I was hungry to get back in the game, and I knew that Steve could at least get F5 and me through the door again. Like I said before, without a cheerleader at your side, this game of music just doesn't happen. And now Steve was our cheerleader.

In our first rehearsal at Steve's, we set up on a sort of 'showcase stage' he had built in the main room of his studio. I had been on a similar type of stage years earlier, when Megadeth auditioned for managers and agents in Los Angeles—Capitol Records and so on—so I was comfortable with the process. You turn up, get on that stage, and show them your stuff.

I felt confident that F5 would deliver, but as we started playing, Steve began to offer more and more critiques to the group, which didn't always go down well. The other guys in the band were essentially local musicians: they had not had the same big world experiences I had in my eighteen years with Megadeth—and even before Megadeth, when I cut my teeth in the business working the Midwest music circuit, prior to moving to Hollywood in 1983. So, at this point, I stepped up as the bandleader and spokesperson on all matters F5. But I could tell that this was causing a rub within the band.

Our guitarist, Steve Conley, already felt a bit resentful. A few months earlier, he had booked a gig for us at a heavy metal-bar in Phoenix he had played frequently called Joe's Grotto. It was a comfortable home for him, and it was where he felt the band should have debuted. But now we were being swiftly diverted into becoming a radio-rock band, and I could tell that he didn't appreciate our songs being ripped apart for the sake of commercial appeal.

In that sense, Conley is a true metal guitarist. And, in hindsight, he was probably right. He has good instincts on metal music, and he had been down this radio-rock road before in his previous bands. In fact, I'd seen him playing in one of those bands, Lifted, at Joe's Grotto a year earlier, and I liked them so much that I shopped their demos to the A&R staff at Roadrunner Records, as well as the president of RCA in New York. It was by this process that I came to know the steep hill a new band had to climb in order to get noticed by record labels, back in the modern rock/nu-metal climate of the time.

Truthfully, I should have given Conley's insights a bit more validation. But I got cold feet about the Grotto gig, and I pulled the show back. This was mostly because I felt it might be too small for someone like me to debut a new band. I was a seasoned metal musician, accustomed to performing in arenas and stadiums. This was my first real band away from Megadeth in almost twenty years, and I wanted everything to have the right look, so I chose the more slick and professional industry approach espoused by Steve Smith.

The sessions at Smith's studio got tense, and the band began to question my authority and vision for the group. Drummer Dave Small said I was 'wishy-washy' and couldn't commit to a course of action. The truth is, I wanted to protect my reputation. It takes years to build a reputation and only a few dumb moves to ruin it. So I held strong to my working relationship with Steve and the course we had set for the group.

RYAN GREENE (PRODUCER) ❝*Back in 2003, I was in Scottsdale, Arizona, working on a record, and I ran into David Ellefson at a mutual friend's house/studio. Steve Smith* *had one of the most elaborate home studios I've ever seen. Steve and I were talking one night, and he said he was producing a new band David Ellefson was in called F5. I mentioned to Steve that I had done all the preproduction for Countdown To Extinction, and next time he sees David, ask him to stop by and say hi.*

David came by the next day, and after catching up for a half-hour, he asked if I'd be interested in co-producing, engineering, and mixing his new project. We were all excited to move forward. It wasn't the smoothest session I have ever been a part of—we were constantly changing arrangements and developing the sound of the record; David and Steve wanted a heavy-sounding record but radio-friendly, and A few of the other band members had different thoughts—but by the time we were done, I felt like we all did a great job. 🙳

As amazing a debut album as we had made—and we even invited in radio tastemaker friends from KUPD FM, Phoenix's huge rock station, to hear the first songs from the album—the record *was* too slick. When we finally debuted the band in 2005, my core thrash-metal fans cried foul.

Ironically, at the same time, Dave Mustaine was preparing to release a new Megadeth album called *The System Has Failed*. It was reportedly not originally intended as a Megadeth album, but rather as a solo effort. Then, once the record and publishing companies got word that Dave's hand injury had healed and he was ready to get back to business, they wanted a Megadeth album, not a solo record. This would be the first Megadeth album in twenty years that I had not participated in.

The System Has Failed won over the fans, while *A Drug For All Seasons* was seen as more of a slick modern-rock radio record—the exact sound that had turned away a legion of die-hard Megadeth fans in the late 1990s. Sure, F5 gained fans as we toured to help build the name, but at that time there was a shift in metal music, which was going back to its thrash roots, as championed by new bands like Lamb Of God, and the radio-metal genre was led by the likes of Disturbed and Godsmack. My fans wanted to hear thrash from me, not more radio songs.

I kept my eye on all things Megadeth that year, especially their ticket and record sales, as well as the fans' reaction to the group continuing on without me. It was unnerving and uncomfortable, but I knew I had to stay the course. Eventually, I just stopped looking at the press and went on with my life.

There was something about this new season I was in that was both invigorating and scary. I knew it was something that would help me grow as a man and as a musician, away from my comforts in Megadeth. I had a hunch that it would eventually lead me back to the band in a much stronger way for everyone in the decade that followed.

I would soon learn the many lessons of this discipline to be true to myself, and that in itself would ultimately help bring us all back together. For now, however, I was on a new journey in the wilderness, my only compass being prayer, faith, family, and my musical instinct.

1.2 CLIMBING THE CORPORATE LADDER

It was early 2005, and the F5 album had been released. Megadeth were on tour in support of *The System Has Failed*, and all the recent legal wrangling to dissolve our business interests together was behind us. I kept up my bass chops on Megadeth songs mostly because I still loved the music, and because I was getting requests from fans and even music-store clinic opportunities to play those songs. Even though we had suffered a breakup, it never felt like my time with Megadeth was over forever.

This was the beginning of a new season of growth for me; rather, and one that would ultimately change my life forever. Around this time, I enrolled in online college to finish my Bachelor of Science degree in Business Administration, which I had begun through the University of Phoenix back in 1997. While the U of P satisfied my appetite for continued higher education, the Megadeth concert tours of the time were too long and too grueling for me to be able to keep up with my homework as well. This was complicated further when I sought time off at home on breaks between tours. My two children, Roman and Athena, were young toddlers. I did not want to be holed up in my office doing homework, missing critical family time with my kids.

In October 2002, just a few months after Megadeth disbanded, I had taken on an artist-relations marketing position at Peavey Electronics, the largest privately owned musical instrument and amplifier manufacturer in the USA. Peavey was based in Meridian, Mississippi. I already used and endorsed Peavey's bass amplifiers, and when I reached out to my friend Tony Moscal about my need for employment after Megadeth ended, he walked me into a position with the company.

Tony was a marketing whiz with experience of hiring rock stars. Uriah Heep keyboardist Ken Hensley had worked under him during his tenure at St. Louis Music, where Ken became the artist-relations manager for iconic instrument and amplifier brands such as Alvarez, Ampeg, and Crate.

I first became aware of Ken when I saw Uriah Heep open for KISS at the Met Center in Bloomington, Minnesota, in February 1977. That was the first major concert I attended, and I instantly became a Heep fan. Years later, I gained great respect for Ken's courage to join the ranks of the corporate landscape and land on his feet in the music business in a new capacity after his years of rock stardom wound down away from his band. And now, ironically, here I was, following suit.

Even though the whole thing felt surreal, and my time outside of Megadeth felt like more of a hiatus than a breakup, it felt good to be part of a vibrant corporate workforce. I learned new things and I met new people. I suddenly felt grown-up, and I quickly realized that I was very fortunate to land the gig, having come out of being a rock star. Thankfully, I had the contacts in the music business that the job required, and it was a good fit on both sides.

One thing seemed clear: the move up the corporate ladder. At some point, this ascent would require me to obtain a proper education— and a degree to sustain it. My role in artist relations was just the front door of the corporate world, and if I wanted to stay in this realm, away from making a living as an artist, educational accolades—along with a corporate résumé—would help me climb the business ladder.

So there I was, back in school. I learned about the very things we were doing at Peavey every day. Fortunately, Peavey was a very large, international conglomerate, and through my work I learned about marketing, manufacturing, sales and international trade, this being a time when many musical instrument products were starting to be manufactured outside the USA, with China becoming the leading nation for musical instrument exports.

•

It was also during this time that I joined two other upstart bands, both of which were the musical brainchild of French–German guitarist Peter Scheithauer, whom I had met through our mutual friend, Helstar vocalist James Rivera. James had sent me demos of a project called Killing Machine featuring drummer Jon Dette, who would later go on to play in Slayer and Anthrax. Once I was introduced to Peter (whose birth name is Pierre), he mentioned that he had written another record, which he was calling *Temple Of Brutality*. The album would feature WASP drummer Stet Howland and Virginia vocalist Todd Barnes. I was invited to join both bands, and I did so, sight unseen, and jumped on a plane to Fort Myers Beach, Florida.

Upon my arrival, I went straight into the studio to meet the guys and cut some tracks with Stet, Todd, and Peter. We had a blast! *Temple Of Brutality* was fun, loud, and rowdy, but it also had a thrash-metal vibe about it. Peter had convinced a local businessman to invest his money in the band. He was good at this sort of unsigned musician 'fundraising,' and the investor, Karl, enjoyed every minute of the ride. Although it is not something I have ever set out to do, finding an investor is probably how the record business began—a musician in need is a slave indeed! We didn't care. We had a lot of fun, as well as making some waves with the album, and Temple Of Brutality ended up doing some regional touring on the East Coast of the USA the following year.

Simultaneously, Peter and I recorded the Killing Machine album at famed heavy-metal producer Bill Metoyer's home studio in the San Fernando Valley. I brought in former Megadeth drummer Jimmy DeGrasso to join the session, alongside James Rivera on vocals and current Body Count guitarist Juan 'Of The Dead' Garcia.

Although we made a slamming record, Killing Machine never toured. Peter seemed to be good at getting money from investors and overseas record companies, but as much as we wanted to play some shows, it never seemed to be in the cards to do so. I guess that was okay by me. My Peavey work was going well, and I did not want to disrupt that. With college studies also on my plate, it was actually nice to just make records, wake up each day, work from my home office, and be available for my family. There was a newfound balance to my life. I was content.

1.3 MOVING PICTURES

One of my key roles as a Peavey contractor was to develop marketing campaigns using their equipment and well-known musical artists. I hired my dear friend and photographer Fran Strine as my field rep and began to gather media content for my roster of Peavey artists. One day, Fran rang me about a fun new band project: an act where he was the singer. They were called Iron Steel.

One of the hot new artists with Peavey around this time was Dragonforce. While the members weren't necessarily permitted to participate in side projects, the bassist, Frédéric Leclercq, had written an album of really heavy but largely parodic songs, hence the moniker Iron Steel. While Frédéric flew largely under the radar, the rest of the band (now with me on bass) were mostly well-known guys. The press around the band ramped up during the winter NAMM show January 2009—NAMM being the National Association of Music Merchants, a sales tradeshow where musical-instrument manufacturers display their offerings for the coming year. Fran set up some red-carpet events nearby, which were silly but fun. That band only did one live show, in Atlanta, which I elected not to participate in due to my schedule. But it was always fun to be musically active with friends.

I would later participate in Fran's hit Netflix film *Hired Gun*, to which I gave an interview about my life as a band member, as well as my experience as a hired musician, upon my return to Megadeth in 2010. I also narrated an independent film Fran created called *Battlefield Of*

The Mind, about PTSD and our nation's war veterans. For that film, Fran asked me to play bass on some songs for the soundtrack that were composed by Mike Mushok from Staind.

While I had watched Staind come up the ranks behind us in 1999, I never knew the impact Mushok's guitar playing had on the group. I soon discovered that Mike essentially *was* the sound of Staind's music. A year or so later, Mushok would play guitar on tour for Jason Newsted. Again, it was fun to get to know musicians in different genres and age groups, rather than from just their celebrity. I'd always rather know someone for their craft than for their fame. These were yet a few more tentacles that reached into new musical forays, fostering new friendships by simply saying *yes*.

FRAN STRINE "*My earliest recollection of Megadeth is that I used to tour around as a lighting guy for a circuit band called Hit The Deck, and the bass player was a huge Metallica fan. There used to be a place in Atlanta, on Marietta Street, called the Metroplex, where all the underground thrash and punk bands would go. Mike Flowers, the bass player from Hit The Deck, was like, 'There's this band Megadeth, that Dave Mustaine is in. He used to be in Metallica. We've gotta go see them.' It was on the Killing Is My Business tour. My God, it was insane. People were climbing off the walls. It was a small shithole place with chicken wire in front of the bar, 'cause people at the bar used to throw bottles at the band and stuff.*

That was my first time hearing Megadeth, and I was blown away. A few years later, of course, Peace Sells comes out, and they play two nights in a row at the Metroplex. I went both nights. Jesus Christ, man, I was just blown away. Years later, I became a photographer for Metal Edge, Circus, Hit Parader—all that stuff—and the first time I met Ellefson, and Megadeth, in a working environment, Megadeth did a song for a movie the wrestler Goldberg was in, Universal Solider: The Return.

Capitol Records hit me up—I was in Atlanta, and Megadeth were going to play 'Crush 'Em' and a few more songs at the Georgia Dome, for WCW's Monday

Nitro. *They called me and said they needed pictures of Megadeth with Goldberg, and they asked me if I was available, so I went down and shot some photos, and that was the first time I met Ellefson.*

So then Megadeth goes on hiatus, and one day I get a call from him, out of the blue—I had no idea who it was—and he was like, 'Hey, it's David Ellefson.' And I was like, 'Whoa, from Megadeth?' I was just a little taken aback. He was like, 'Yeah, yeah, yeah. I'm at Peavey—I'm the artist-relations guy now. I know you used to shoot photo and video stuff for Peavey, and I was wondering if you were still interested?' I was like, 'Yeah, absolutely.'

He would send me on assignments with Nickelback, Chimaira, Three Doors Down, Machine Head—all the metal bands were using 5150 [amps] at the time. Dave would occasionally come to Atlanta for Peavey stuff, and by this time we had done a couple NAMMs together and gotten to know each other.

So Dave comes to Atlanta, we were out late, and I was driving him back to his hotel, and we were both starving. I asked if he'd ever been to Waffle House. He was like, 'Never,' so I said, 'I gotta take you.' So we go to Waffle House, and it's, like, midnight—there's not many people there. He tells me to just order for him, because he doesn't know what to get. He's sitting where he can see the grill, and there's this really big guy cooking our food, and it's August, in Atlanta, so sweat is just pouring off of him onto David's food on the grill. And he looks at me, just three shades of white, like, Really? And I tell him, 'Relax, it's just part of the experience.' Then the guy comes by mopping the floor, and he's inching closer and closer to us, with the dirty mop bucket, dirty black mop-water with eggshells and garbage in it. And he asks if we can move our legs so he can mop under us. And this is while we were eating. Dave just looks at me, like, Are you kidding? And this guy is mopping under us, sloshing this dirty mop-water all over us, our table, our food. And we both just burst out laughing.

That was David's first, and probably last, Waffle House experience. But we became good friends through all that, and we worked together a lot, and continue to. Obviously, when Ellefson went over to Peavey, he brought over all the cool guys.

He had that clout: 'Oh Dave's over there? It must be legit.' Peavey always got that reputation of being kind of shitty gear and shitty amps. And I think David helped change that.

Everything he did was amazing. The marketing campaigns he would do were second to none. And he was able to get, like, Paul from Slipknot to come over to Peavey; Nickelback, when they were giant; Three Doors Down. He kept A-listers around that product, and we see what happened after he left. I attribute a lot of Peavey's success to David.

So I was on tour with Five Finger Death Punch, Ivan had gotten arrested on a flight for being drunk and obnoxious, and by the time we got to Singapore, after doing the Soundwave festival, I was looking at my life, thinking, I'm gonna be fifty years old—do I really want to be touring with all these metal bands? I'd been doing it for twenty years. I had found a really nice place in Northern California that I loved, and I was never home. And I was like, What can I do to get me out of this deal?

I'd done a couple of documentaries in the past, including Battlefield Of The Mind, *which David narrated for me. He's got a great speaking voice—that's why I called him. And, oddly enough, he'd done some voiceover stuff already, so I was like, Fuck … this is perfect.*

Anyway, I was sitting in Singapore, in the back of the bus, and I was like, Fuck, I gotta find my way out of here. I'd seen a movie called 20 Feet From Stardom, *about backup singers, and I knew there had been some movies about session guys, like* Standing In The Shadows, *and about Motown and Muscle Shoals, but nothing really contemporary. So, that was the idea: I was going to go home and hit the ground running. And we got financing right away. One of my friends, Todd Paulsen, threw all the money at us and said, 'Get to work.' I was so fortunate.*

I got David when Megadeth was coming through the Bay Area to play the Warfield Theater. I had just happened to call him that day, and I said, 'Hey, you got a couple hours to come and be in my movie? I know that you've been a hired gun.' He was like, 'Absolutely!' And that's the thing about David: he's been such a great champion of mine since day one. And he's never said no to anything that I've asked him to do. That's one of the things he said to us on set: 'Always say yes.'

David loved the idea of Hired Gun, and when I called him and we did a screening in San Francisco, at the Alamo Drafthouse, it was just beautiful—I needed somebody to come be my Q&A host, so naturally I called him. 'Man, I hate to ask you, and I can't pay you. But I can fly you in and put you up in a hotel.' And he said, 'Yes, of course. I love the movie, and I'd be glad to be a part of it.' So it was David and me, with Matt Pinfield as the moderator. There was a great energy, and the Q&A went on for roughly an hour. Then David went out, took pictures with fans, and signed autographs. Some things just never change, man.

I'll tell you one thing: when I met David for the first time, I was kind of disappointed. For the same reason I was disappointed when I met Alice Cooper, who was my hero. There's some part of me that wanted him to be the 'Looking Down The Cross' and 'The Conjuring' guy, and instead I met a soccer dad. The same thing with Alice: when he came in the room, I wanted him to have a dead baby in his hand and a knife through the heart. Instead, I got this complete gentleman who warmed me over in about two seconds. 🗩🗩

When *Battlefield Of The Mind* debuted at the Whisky in Hollywood, I got up and performed a couple songs with the house band. One of the sponsors of the event was a boot company who gave us all a pair of military-grade boots. It seemed odd until I took that pair of boots to Paraguay a couple days later. I was taping another independent film called *Landfill Harmonic*, which portrayed a sentiment of hope inside a village where young children literally lived in a landfill. With the help of a luthier and musical mentor, the children formed an orchestra and performed on instruments made from garbage. I was flown to Paraguay to visit the children and film my segment, which required me to wade through the garbage in the landfill. Ironically, the boots I got at Fran's film premier were perfect for the task! The tapestry of life never ceases to impress me.

I must say that the *Landfill Harmonic* film was extremely touching. The film moved all of us in deep and emotional ways that I'm happy were captured on film. Upon completion of filming for my segment, the director and I sat in a local café in the nearby city of Asunción, where we discussed the film's ending. My segment opened up a new opportunity that seemed obvious—that the hook to the film's climax would be for the kids in the movie to come onstage and perform with Megadeth.

A couple of weeks later, I ran the idea by Dave, and he was one hundred percent onboard. It helped that no sooner had we discussed the idea than we were boarding a Lufthansa flight in Europe. There was a nice little promotion for the film in the airline magazine, so talk about good timing! The director, who had happened to be a neighbor in Scottsdale, organized a GoFundMe campaign to secure the necessary funds to fly the orchestra up to the USA. The orchestra joined Megadeth onstage in Denver. We filmed the movie's climatic part, Dave announcing them onstage with us as we broke into an epic version of 'Symphony Of Destruction' with the orchestra at our side.

The whole experience was so wonderful and moving. The film's producer, Alejandra Becerra Newell, was a native of Asunción. This was her baby, and to see the children onstage with Megadeth brought tears of joy to everyone's eyes. It was a crowning moment of my career to be able to give back something so special to those who have so little. In a strange way, their joy at being happy with little cannot help but rub off on those of us who have been so financially blessed with comforts and first-world problems.

Landfill Harmonic premiered with the full red-carpet treatment for Megadeth in Asunción during our tour of Latin America in 2016. As we were escorted to the gigantic cinema, the mayor and other high-ranking officials greeted us, and the tear-jerking, feel-good movie played to a packed house of fans, friends, and the media.

A touching moment for me came after the film premiered, when I saw Dave nestled in with a couple of the orchestra members, who were set up to perform inside the mall's common area for the fans and media to witness. I found it touching, knowing Dave's childhood and upbringing, that he kindled the experience with these children as a fond comfort around his music. It always amazes me how our songs can build bridges across so many channels. Over the years, it continues to bring a smile to my face that Megadeth's music has found a real home in the hearts of the Latin America audiences.

In a strange way, that is my role in Megadeth: to bring people together in new ways that only I can, with my heartfelt 'Minnesota Nice' upbringing. It makes me eternally grateful to my family and the things they taught me about kindness, generosity, and an eagerness to offer a smile and a helping hand. Who knew that those Midwest qualities would travel down to a land so far away in South America, so many years later, as a member of Megadeth!

1.4 NEW BANDS, NEW ADVENTURES

I had realistic expectations about all my band efforts post-Megadeth. Not because I didn't believe in them, but because I knew the way the business worked. The business had really changed since I helped start Megadeth many years before. In fact, once Megadeth disbanded in 2002, I swore I would never put together another band ever again, because I knew the odds of success are akin to that of a Cinderella story. Yet the bug to play the bass and hang with musicians never left me, despite my financial and fatherly duties to provide for my family. I think those urges are just part of being a musician.

There was something else that gnawed at me, too. I had turned down some pretty significant offers back in 2002, and I struggled to not beat myself up over them. The first was when the Alice Cooper camp called me to ask if I'd be interested in touring with them that summer. 'Are you kidding?' I said. 'Of course I'm interested!' At that exact moment, however, my friends at Fender Musical Instruments, with headquarters ten minutes from my home in Scottsdale, contacted me about a new position they were creating inside the company: product manager for bass amps. Although I felt a bit unqualified, I knew it was wise to look at the bigger picture of where the job like that could lead me.

My head swirled as I considered the options. Fender made it clear that if I accepted their job, I would be done playing music full-time. I would be expected to report to the office Monday through Friday as a full-time salaried employee.

I told the Cooper camp that I had this Fender opportunity on the table, and if they could bear with me a few more days I would be able to give them an answer, *yes* or *no*, but that I would really like to tour with them if possible.

While I struggled to make my decision, Alice's camp called to let me know they had to move forward. They elected to have former Quiet Riot bassist Chuck Wright be their new bassist. Within a day, Fender alerted me that they too had elected to hire another guy for their position. I was crushed, having lost both gigs in the matter of a day. I was defeated.

My dear friend, former Megadeth guitarist Al Pitrelli, has had a lot of experience as a sideman guitar player over the years. He advised me to say yes to *everything*. In fact, just a few months earlier, when the *World Needs A Hero* tour was winding down, Al had invited me to play bass with him and Trans-Siberian Orchestra, who were going out across the USA later that month. Because I was badly run down physically from the stress of the Megadeth tour that year, and thinking we would be opening up the Megadeth recording fund to begin a new album early in 2002, I had elected to pass on Al's TSO tour op. Unfortunately, Dave then hurt his hand and dissolved Megadeth, and the album never happened.

Life at this time was like a domino effect of one bad thing triggering the next, all because I was declining offers as they were coming to me. It's funny—the phone stops ringing quickly when you say no to things. In the same way, it keeps ringing when you say yes!

I would kick myself more than a few times over those decisions—or maybe lack of decisions. TSO grew exponentially after that and have become one of the top grossing box-office draws year on year. I was definitely feeling the effects of not saying yes, just as Al had advised.

Truthfully, I was scared of my direction in life at that point. I had grown up in the comforts and discomforts of Megadeth from when I was a young man of eighteen years old to a young adult in his late thirties. I guess it was no different to anyone else facing a major job or career transition. But I would learn that often it is these tough life lessons that help us grow. I began to believe that if something is meant to be, it will keep presenting itself until we learn the lesson. The Buddhist philosophy supports this, and I believe so too does the Christian faith of relying on God and prayer to see us through times of uncertainty.

•

I would soon learn to heed Al's advice and begin to say yes to more things. As a result, my life began to explode with opportunity. My life today is a prime example of taking action based on faith. But back in 2002, I was lost in a whirlwind of thoughts and fears.

In many ways, I was unsure whether I wanted to continue as a full-time touring bassist away from Megadeth. I'm a guy who starts bands because they are my gang, my tribe. Until then, the only 'sideman' experience I had ever had was when, as an eighteen-year-old living in Minnesota, I took a job playing bass for a local group based in Estherville, Iowa. It was a job—I traveled and got paid well for my time—yet it never really felt like *home*.

All these years later, I was facing a similar dilemma. I was afraid I would one day wake up on a tour bus with regrets that I had missed my family and watching the children grow up. So I opted to hold out and investigate a bigger picture beyond the life of a touring musician. It was difficult, because deep inside every musician is the desire to create music, go out on tour, and rock with the fans from the center of the stage. Now, this decision required a new discipline to go and look beyond my own selfish desires; it required seeking something that would serve the best interests of my family.

I also didn't know what my next musical step should be. By this point, I was quite well known as a thrash-metal bassist, and if I chose to play with artists in other genres, I knew my fans would cry foul. I realized how valuable my name as a brand had become. Fortunately, my Peavey position was solid, and it provided a nice income. I was finally ready to put on the bass and do some more musical exploration. F5 certainly helped me get over that musical hump and get back in the game, as did Killing Machine and Temple Of Brutality.

One day, I got a call from Salt Mine studio owner Don Salter, my dear friend from Mesa, Arizona, about recording with Soulfly, the band featuring former Sepultura vocalist and songwriter Max Cavalera. Soulfly were undergoing a lineup change, and Don thought I would be a good fit as the band's new bassist. This time I said yes when the phone rang and Gloria Cavalera—Max's wife and Soulfly's manager—invited me to join the band at the Salt Mine to record tracks for their new album, *Prophecy*.

Soulfly were stylistically closer to my Megadeth fan base than F5, and they were already very well established internationally as a band. The first time I saw Max perform was with Sepultura, when they played with Megadeth at the 1991 Rock In Rio festival, and the buzz on the band was *massive*. They were from Brazil, and as the heavy-metal royalty of the region, Max definitely brought a South American passion with him into Soulfly.

My participation in the new Soulfly album was an exciting new venture for all of us. Working with Max and his new lineup—completed by guitarist Marc Rizzo and drummer Joe Nunez—provided yet another breath of creative air for me. As Marc said one day, 'This is about the most casual metal gig there is.' And he was right. Max is an incredibly creative artist, and he let his band intuitively follow his lead. Whenever I asked him for any sort of direction on bass parts, he would simply reply, 'Whatever you want is fine.' It was liberating and fun!

A couple of months later, I was invited to join the band to film the video for the album's title track, shot at Zion National Park in Utah. But because I didn't want to jeopardize my job at Peavey, I chose not to join Soulfly as a full-time touring member. I did perform on a handful of select dates with them over the next couple years, however, and I also recorded some bass on the follow-up LP, *Dark Ages*.

The Cavaleras were very gracious to me, and I learned that *that* is what saying yes can yield: a mutually beneficial musical collaboration for years to come. After all, when the phone rings, they aren't calling you to say no!

MUSIC

2.1 TAKING CARE OF BUSINESS

Rule #1: Don't quit.
Rule #2: See rule #1.
DUKE ELLINGTON

By 2006, I was starting to feel very comfortable stepping out and participating in a wide variety of musical opportunities. My natural response when the phone rang at this point had become an automatic yes. I had come a long way from where I was just a few years earlier. I've heard it said, *Courage isn't the absence of fear, it is taking action despite the fear.* Based on that saying, I decided to take action.

For me, experience was the key to turning that corner of confidence. The more I said yes and got involved in new things, the more confidence I gained. I always knew I had the bass chops to play most anything that was put in front of me, yet I'd been handicapped by my ego. Pride and image management can be a real stumbling block for growth and success.

For me, most of that centered on the thought that I had grown up in the thrash-metal culture, and how that culture defined me, at least in my mind. This is pride: what I think *you* might think about me.

Although I was sort of a 'man without a country' as a sideman, it had its perks. From 2002 to 2006, I had played on a myriad of albums in a wide variety of musical styles. Initially, this was at the urging and invitation of Don Salter, who brought me out to his Arizona studio. Don was one of my early post-Megadeth cheerleaders, and he continually encouraged me to work as a producer and network with other musicians. To him, being a rock-star musician is cool, but being a *working* musician is even cooler. Plus, why not work doing something I liked: music?

Around this same time, my good friend Billy Smiley would regularly invite me to Nashville to play bass on Christian and singer/songwriter records that he was producing. Billy was in a massive Christian hard-rock group called Whiteheart, whose early lineups had also featured producer/guitarist Dann Huff, who produced the Megadeth albums *Cryptic Writings* and *Risk* in Nashville. Dann had introduced Billy and me to each other in 1999, on my final day of overdubbing bass on *Risk*. Looking back, I always saw a greater significance to our introduction. Now, just a few years later, he would be helping me get back in the game again.

In 2006, I began participating in the well-known Rock'n'roll Fantasy Camp organization, my first one being the tenth annual event in Las Vegas. I was the token 'metal guy,' representing a genre the organization had never really included in its camps before. Up until this point, the rock camps were largely aimed at male customers in their fifties and sixties, and they utilized mostly classic-rock artists, with celebrity rockers like Roger Daltrey and The Monkees as the headline draw. However, the tenth annual camp brought in younger and more current musicians, including Mark Slaughter, Slash, Nicko McBrain, and me.

MARK SLAUGHTER ❝*I have been friends with David Ellefson for many years—almost our entire careers—and we'd always run into each other, both professionally and personally. I mean, it's crazy, it's very incestuous, the other side of this whole industry.*

We hadn't talked for quite a while, and then I run into David again when we're both counselors at Rock'n'roll Fantasy Camp. I had done it before, so I was pretty seasoned—I knew what to do, coming from my teaching background—and David was kind of like, 'What am I doing here?' So he just kind of asked if he could hang out with me. I think that's the first time we got to really start hanging on a personal level, more so than the phone calls we had to each other, trying to figure out the industry that we're both in. Obviously he was out of Megadeth for a while, and we spoke and kept in touch. But he's a smart guy—this isn't a typical musician, he uses his brain.

So, anyway, we're at Rock'n'roll Fantasy Camp, and I'm jamming with my band, and David calls me and goes, 'Dude, you have to come over to room three: Nicko is here, and he wants to jam.' So I go into room three, and Nicko is there, and we had all the MTV cameras there. So we get in there, I put on a guitar, and Nicko's looking at me, like, 'What the fuck are you doing, man?'

All of a sudden we start knocking out 'Run To The Hills'—I'm playing guitar, and he's looking at me, and when we're done he walks over to me, slugs me in the arm, and he says, 'I didn't know you fucking played, man. That was fucking great!' Before that, he just knew me as a snot-nosed kid, singing for Vinnie Vincent. **"**

Following the success of my first Fantasy Camp, I was invited to be a counselor at the Hawaii event. This in turn was to be followed by a month-long US tour opening for Extreme and King's X. This really helped me build up my repertoire of rock cover songs. I used to play covers all the time, growing up in bands in Minnesota, and this was a fun way to revisit those songs once again.

Then, on a completely different note, I became an elder for my church back home in Scottsdale. Our first task was hiring a new pastor, whose name was Jon Bjorgaard. As the elder team, we conducted a conference call with Jon. Quickly, Jon and I connected over our passion for music by both rock'n'roll and contemporary Christian artists.

Upon Jon's arrival in Scottsdale, he stated his vision for me to start a new contemporary worship service at the church, and he wanted to call it MEGA Life, based upon the scripture verse John 10:10.

By now, I had performed on a number of Christian records in Nashville, and I had attended several large worship conferences that featured popular artists such as Paul Baloche, Chris Tomlin, and more. While being a worship pastor was certainly out of my wheelhouse, I already knew that the answer to Jon's questions was *yes*. I understood the discipline of just getting on board with what the Good Lord may be bringing into my life, so I held auditions and began the MEGA Life church as an evening worship service. My wife took care of the hospitality, and my kids served as the ushers. I often hired musicians from outside the church to sit in with me, including drummer Troy Lucketta from Tesla. I was used to playing with top-level professional musicians, and I thought it might be a treat for the church to see my rocker buddies with a good heart for service participating in our new endeavor.

The MEGA Life church thrived, and today it has its own campus, hosting two services every Sunday morning. I handed off my duties as worship leader to a new team when I re-joined Megadeth in 2010, but occasionally I sit in and play bass when I'm home and off tour for extended breaks. I find it refreshing to share this musical camaraderie with other in-town musicians, and sometimes it's nice to just play music for music's sake.

•

It was around this time that a good friend of mine, music-business attorney Mark Abbatista, rang me about an idea he had to start a heavy-metal supergroup that he wanted to take to South America. As Mark and I chatted, we conjured up a band with me on bass, ex–Judas Priest singer Tim 'Ripper' Owens on vocals, former Megadeth member Jimmy

DeGrasso on drums, and Sepultura's Andreas Kisser on guitar. We called this band HAIL! out of our love for all things metal.

We debuted our supergroup in Chile, where we performed six shows in five cities up and down the coast. Big bands like Megadeth don't usually get to perform outside the larger metropolis areas, yet with HAIL! we could go into the more remote places. Here, the fan enthusiasm is incredible. It was fantastic to have created and identified another terrific musical outlet, and as a group we also got to see these amazing cities and fans across Chile.

The idea worked so well that we took HAIL! on the road across Europe over the next several years. We did full tours of Scandinavia, Greece, Turkey, and more. It was the type of act that we could take into smaller towns and cities, and the fans loved it because it was a *plug'n'play* type of band. No semi-trucks for the equipment or heavy touring staff to support it. Instead, it was four musicians and Abbatista just rolling in, rocking out, and melting faces at each show.

We had a lot of laughs and good times during those years. Our setlist was comprised of all cover songs, which helped me continue to build a strong repertoire of metal songs. I had played original music for most of my adult professional career, and now it was fun to learn some industry-standard cover songs, so I'd be able to jump in and jam on demand.

Things were really starting to heat up for me musically at this point, and I was thrilled to be back out in front of my fans, playing metal again—especially with notable musicians who were all on a similar cachet of notoriety and credibility. It was encouraging to see the fans eat it up!

In 2007, I was privileged to meet and play bass for one of my childhood heroes, guitarist and songwriter Randy Bachman of the seminal 1970s Canadian rock band Bachman–Turner Overdrive. Randy and I met at NAMM 2007. He was invited to perform a couple numbers at a party Peavey was hosting in the downstairs club at the Hilton. Because I trusted his musical abilities, I quickly called on Jimmy DeGrasso to play drums at the gig, since I knew he would nail it. I could count on him to walk in and do it with no rehearsal—and he did. By this point, I was used to working with musicians who could come in, sight unseen, and play without any rehearsal or soundcheck. It's fun and invigorating to be around guys at this level of musicianship.

That night, we played Randy's big hit with The Guess Who, 'American Woman,' and BTO's 'Taking Care Of Business.' I was elated. BTO's album *Not Fragile* was the first hard-rock album I'd ever heard. It was the one that got me into playing bass—the reason I got into music in the first place. That was 1974, when I was ten years old, and now here I was, in my forties, playing bass to a song I worshipped on my turntable as a kid. What a wonderful life!

A little while later, Jimmy DeGrasso called me about another killer gig he was doing. He was playing drums for Ronnie Montrose, the famed guitarist whose first album featured the then-unknown vocalist Sammy Hagar. Ronnie had started his career in the Edgar Winter Group back in the late 1960s, before going solo in the early 1970s. His self-titled debut is a record of *legendary* status to rockers of my age. Now, Ronnie needed a touring bassist, and when Jimmy called, I was definitely ready to say yes!

JIMMY DEGRASSO (FORMER DRUMMER, MEGADETH) ❝*David Ellefson, we met in the early 1990s when my band, Suicidal Tendencies, was opening for Megadeth on the Countdown tour. I used to run into him a lot during the tour, and he was always pretty friendly and down to earth. But I guess when you're from Minnesota there are no other options.*

We would continue to run into each other for years to come, on tour or at trade shows. I was asked to join their band several times over a few years—I mean no disrespect to anybody, but that is the truth. We started playing together in June of 1998. The first show was in Fresno, at an outdoor amphitheater. I only had three days to learn twenty-two songs and start the tour. No rehearsals. Twenty-minute soundcheck. Geez, thanks. This later turned into an ulcer.

Anyway, we did that band until the spring of 2002, when Dave Mustaine quit. After that, we all went on to do other things. Marty went to Japan … Al joined TSO and went back to the East Coast. I started a business, and so did David. I took a few years off from playing because I had been touring since the early 80s, and I was just over it. Then, a few years later, Ronnie Montrose called me to play with him.

I had known Ronnie for years, because he had produced some Y&T demos back in the day. At some point we needed a bass player. Ronnie told me to find one. Oops. Don't let the inmates run the asylum! I called David and told him to learn the first two Montrose records in five days. No rehearsal. See you in Florida. Payback is a bitch.

This music took him way out of his element. He was a thrash-metal bass player who was used to playing very, very fast and on top of the beat. I just told him to relax and slow down—watch me and I'll watch Ronnie. Think slow and then make it even slower. It worked out great. **”**

Our first show, which was also my audition for Ronnie, was at a theater in St. Petersburg, Florida. I had learned and prepared the songs from the setlist in advance. Upon my arrival, Ronnie gave me only one rule: *Just play the songs as they are recorded, but when we hit the solo section, I'll see you later, and I'll start playing some signature licks to help us all meet up for the ending chorus.*

The gig was musically very stimulating. It was just me, Jimmy, Ronnie, and his vocalist, Keith St. John, who sounded so much like Sammy Hagar it was scary. Jimmy even remarked to me one night, 'I didn't even know you could play bass like this, because I'd only heard you play in Megadeth before.' Obviously, this was a pretty big departure from what Jimmy had heard me do in Megadeth. I took it as a big compliment from a friend and professional for whom I had great respect and admiration.

The second and third shows we played with Montrose that week were opening for Def Leppard. As it turns out, the Leppard guys also grew up as *huge* fans of Montrose, and they were the ones who invited him to perform on the shows. As we arrived at the first arena show, singer Joe Elliot and guitarist Phil Collen came into our dressing room. They were like little kids with Ronnie, asking him fan questions. Then, being a huge Def Leppard fan, I started letting Joe and Phil know I grew up on *their* records. It was like three generations of musicians— everyone fan-boy-ing on each other's music and careers!

JIMMY DEGRASSO ❝The Montrose gig was a lot of fun. Ronnie was kind of a unique guy but always fun to play music with. We traveled the world and did dome great gigs, both big and small. And David learned to play slow. We did some gigs opening for Def Leppard in arenas that were very cool. I ran into Joe Elliott a few years ago, while I was opening for them in some other band. Joe remembered those gigs down to the details. He said he has the board tapes of them, so I'll have to get a copy of those one day.

Right around this time, David calls me and goes, 'I got a call to back up Randy Bachman from Bachman–Turner Overdrive at the NAMM show.' He laughs. I'm like, 'Sure, let's do it. Here we go again: no rehearsal and just go up and play.' Of course, we both grew up in the 70s, and we knew all these songs. But to play them with the original guy who wrote them, with no rehearsal, is a little daunting, to say the least. It was a far cry from 'Holy Wars.'

'David, just play slow. It will be fine.'

It's just that David drinks so much coffee, and it makes him very excited. Now, he has a coffee company. For the record, he still hasn't sent me any of his coffee. But I digress. When we play together, you can see me give hand signals where I *wave my hand back toward me, which means pull the feel back, or I'll push my hand out, which means let's pick it up a bit. We don't discuss these things, ever. It's just a mutual understanding we have of each other, which is really special.* 🙶

I continued playing with Ronnie for the next several years, doing mostly weekend gigs like casinos, bike rallies, the St. Louis Rib Fest, and other classic-rock festivals. Honestly, it was one of the most fun gigs I've ever done. The songs were fun, upbeat rock'n'roll tunes, and each night after the gig I'd go back to the hotel with a huge smile on my face, because of the great vibes of the music and the band.

I'd say a high point of the gig was the Hollister Bike Rally in northern California, where another childhood hero of mine, guitarist Pat Travers, was also on the bill. During the encore of Ronnie's set, we would play his hit song, 'Bad Motor Scooter,' and I would play an extended feature bass solo. On this particular night, Ronnie invited Pat to jam on that song with us. During my bass solo, I looked back and realized two of my childhood heroes, Ronnie Montrose *and* Pat Travers, were both playing guitar to *my* bass solo! What a trip!

Life was becoming a series of *pinch-me* moments like this now—moments that I could have only dreamed of as a teenage bass player growing up on a farm in Minnesota. Suddenly, my gratitude meter was at an all-time high, and I quickly took note of where the Good Lord had taken me: from ground zero in 2002, and starting all over, to now having a life full of musical explorations and acknowledgment from my peers.

At the same time, my bills were paid mostly because I was no longer afraid of the other shoe that was going to drop from inside of Megadeth. This was how I had frequently felt over the years, with the drugs and instability inside the band. I myself had been clean for many years by this point, and the feeling of instability from causes beyond my control was no longer acceptable in my life. Being on my own two feet was starting to really pay off.

It was obvious to me that God had moved me out of a big rock band where I was not in control and transferred me to a new position of being able to control my own destiny. It seemed the key to unlocking that door was one magical word, and that was saying yes to life!

2.2 COMING HOME TO MEGADETH

In this you greatly rejoice, though now for a little while you may have had to suffer grief in all kinds of trials.
1 PETER 1:6

A lot happened in those years away from Megadeth. Although it was technically an eight-year span, the group was disbanded for almost three of those, so my time away was only about five years. Still, as I look back on that period of my life, I see that I grew in leaps and bounds as a man, as a professional and as a person with vastly expanded horizons. I am blessed insofar as being resourceful and utilizing my contacts to keep me afloat. This has certainly helped me thrive in the face of fear.

In a way, it was also the beginning of a new renaissance for me. I had learned to step out and play with other musicians and form new bands; I started a church service, went back to college, and ran a marketing division for one of the largest musical equipment and instrument-producing companies in the industry. This was nothing to shake a stick at, for it was all because I had become accustomed to just suiting up and showing up when opportunity knocked. I loved my new life, and I was only going to *add* things to my palette rather than take things off it.

I also learned what it meant to be a servant in a business that is mostly all about expecting everyone to serve you. As I approached the next generation of up-and-coming musicians in my job at Peavey, members of bands like Nickelback, Slipknot, and Kid Rock helped me begin to realize the significant impact my role in Megadeth had had on these artists. We weren't just a metal band—we were a game-changing group that transcended genres and generations. Our music resonated deep within people's hearts and souls and inspired them to grow up to ultimately do great things with their own lives.

These artists trusted my expertise when we talked about Peavey and their careers. I humbly realized how valuable a role model I had been to them. In a way, I was a mentor to them without even knowing it. I started to grasp what it meant to be more than just a musician in a rock band, and my role at Peavey provided an excellent opportunity for me to serve and mentor these artists.

As I went to my kid's sporting events during those years and spoke with the other soccer dads on the sidelines, I realized that most of them had gotten an education and then secured a job. Many of these folks were in banking, real estate, law, accounting, and other similar professions. But their families were the centers of their lives, not themselves or their careers. I realized that the spotlight can be a dangerous attraction to a musician. Sadly, many of us in the entertainment business get lost to our own egos and never grow up. We resort to drugs, sex, and other perilous endeavors to fulfill our dangerous desires with some sort of adrenaline high away from the spotlight of our success.

Ironically, I actually felt a bit *less than* around the soccer dads. I felt like *I* was the one who didn't measure up. It doesn't take a rocket scientist to realize how lucky I was to have had a career with Megadeth, which had helped me buy a home in Scottsdale years before. It had allowed me to be the only breadwinner in my home, and to have a comfortable and somewhat rebuilt career away from the band that brought great success. But as the billionaire J.D. Rockefeller was once asked, 'How much money is enough?' 'Just a little more,' he retorted. Touché.

Although the seeds I planted early on in my life were still bearing fruit in my time away from Megadeth, the music industry is very much a 'what have you done for me lately?' business. I could tell my barrel was starting to run a bit dry. People loved to have 'the guy from Megadeth' around, but when you're not *in* Megadeth anymore, they start to look for the next new guy to walk in the door. I sensed that it was time to get my horse back in the big race again.

I was missing the big stage, the big studios, and the big rock-star life. It is who I am, and I personally think I handled it well, before the breakup of the band.

I felt some residual resentments, too, over no longer being a part of Megadeth. In my mind, back in 1989, I was told the following: 'Get sober or you're out of the band.' I decided I would get clean and remain that way. I kept thinking to myself, *How come I am the one who's not in the band anymore?*

New lessons and a deeper understanding would soon come my way. On one level, I knew what I was in for when we started Megadeth. I could feel that it was going to be a volatile ride, since there was an uncertainty to it. It's what made it unpredictable and enchanting—and also artistically compelling. I decided to buy into the dream from the beginning. In a strange sort of way, then, why should I be surprised now, all these years later, at how the story was playing out?

More than anything, I felt as though my expectations were not being met. It's almost like it had to go this way first, in order for the legacy to continue. Then a true miracle came my way. In late 2007, Dave came through Phoenix and asked if we could meet for dinner. I took the opportunity to clear the air and apologize for my part in our legal dispute from 2005, concerning the dissolving of the band and our shared business interests. As angry as I had been at the time about all those matters, I knew that somehow God had his hand in the matter, and he was taking me on a journey away from Megadeth to have new discoveries in my own life.

Dave stated that he had very much wanted to be in control of Megadeth by 2004, and to get the band back to its roots. By that point, I had new ventures in motion in my life. I wasn't looking to be one hundred percent exclusive to Megadeth—not that Dave & co. were even asking me to. In a way, I had to be the one to let go of the reins of Megadeth and let Dave realize what God wanted to do in his life, but also what He sought to do in mine. I felt it and I knew it, yet the fear of letting it go was why I waged the lawsuit. It was fear of the unknown, and I have since learned that nothing good comes out of acting in fear. In fact, I've found that when we take action on fear, we usually bring about the very thing we feared.

I also knew that, biblically speaking, taking a friend and band member to court was never really going to settle the score. I have since learned that any time we have human issues, they are really spiritual issues. My hang-ups when we parted ways were partly about money, but I was also confused as to what the next step was going to be in life. My identity, income, and life plans had always been framed around Megadeth—plans I'd had since I was eighteen years old. Who would I be if that went away? In some ways, I became enslaved to both money and prestige. I had to let that go in order to grow.

On his way home that evening, Dave sent me a text message thanking me for my honesty over dinner. He offered me his forgiveness, and it felt good to know that after our time away from each other there was now healing taking place.

We spoke several more times after that. A few weeks later, Dave offered an olive branch for me to re-join the band for a recording session, and then as full-time bassist in late 2009.

We were so close, yet my return seemed to get delayed by discussions about my financial participation in the band. I have always understood and appreciated Dave's role as the leader, visionary, and impetus of Megadeth. I was in the room when the band started, and when the vision was cast; I understood the bigger picture, and I therefore accepted my role as the second-in-command to Dave since 1983. All these years later, though, I knew that I also brought 'brand loyalty' and stability to the band. Fans had gotten used to a revolving door of guitarists and drummers, yet one thing they always counted on was Dave and me being together. We were the Jagger and Richards of Megadeth. Some bands have their iconic figures who are the face of the band. In Megadeth, those figures are Dave and me.

In a way, I think the most challenging part of being in any band for a long time is that we create roles when we form the groups, and then, somehow, we have to live inside those roles forever. But people are not static beings; we long to change and grow during our lives. I guess it's like that in any job or career, which is why healthy people move on when a job no longer suits them. The odd thing with bands is that, for some of us, we've been fortunate enough to build these huge legacies and fan bases, and, as a result, the phone keeps ringing for us to return to the studio and the stage to do what we do best. And yet, for some, unless they have invested their money wisely or have taken up some type of side business along the way, being a musician is all they can be in this lifetime. That can be a sad and lonely outcome, when you have to work *for* music, rather than letting your music work for you.

It was refreshing for me to step away from my role in Megadeth and create new paths in life. That was a true test of faith—to trust that God, the Universe, or whatever you want to call it, has a plan, and that our job is to just show up and do the plan. It's also one of the reasons I've discovered prayer and meditation. Time to quiet the mind is important: to listen to that guiding voice inside. That voice is the compass internally wired to guide us. And that voice was prompting me to keep an open mind.

Reconciliation with Dave was happening, and someday we would be back onstage together again. My job was to focus on the opportunity, not my rights. That's the problem when you ask an attorney to settle a score: attorneys will focus on your rights and how someone has violated them. I have found that when those matters come up, I get ungrateful, demanding, and sidetracked from the bigger scope of the opportunity: in this case, a plan God may have set in motion for Dave and me to have our season away from each other, to grow as individuals, before He brought us back together to be stronger and better than ever. I've found prayer to be useful when trying to build something up for the greater good of all.

In February 2010, a fortuitous situation arrived whereby there was going to be another change of bass player in Megadeth. By way of an arranged call with drummer Shawn Drover and guitar tech Willie Gee, Dave and I got on the phone, and, in literally two minutes, any remaining hardships melted away. We agreed to give it a try, and we were both ecstatic at the new opportunity. We decided to give it a go, one more time.

The next day, I put a couple of basses in my car and drove eight hours from Phoenix to San Diego, got in the studio, and jammed with Dave and the band. It was instant magic all over again—like we'd never parted ways.

2.3 HEAVY METAL PARKING LOT

When I came back to Megadeth in February 2010, the band were supporting the newly released *Endgame* album on Roadrunner Records. It was a remarkably strong album, and plausibly the closest to a 'return to form' the band had accomplished since the early 1990s.

Megadeth were scheduled to do a full North American tour with our friends in Slayer called the *American Carnage* tour. Unfortunately, Slayer bassist and vocalist Tom Araya had to undergo neck surgery, and the tour was postponed. As a fill-in for time and income, Megadeth's management presented something that was becoming popular with other bands: the idea of celebrating a landmark album with a tour performing the songs off the record. In this case, the celebration would be framed around the anniversary of the seminal *Rust In Peace* album, which hit the twenty-year mark in 2010.

This was not the only reunion happening in our genre. Metallica had presented to Megadeth, Slayer, and Anthrax the idea of doing several stadium shows together across Europe that summer. These monumental, historic, landmark concerts would be known as the *Big Four*—a title given to the aggregate of the four bands by journalist Malcolm Dome back in the 1980s. Together, the collective represented the most successful forerunners and inventors of the thrash-metal genre. This was absolutely the shot heard around the world in the metal music industry.

As surprising and unexpected as my return to Megadeth was, the other bands in the Big Four camp were also announcing reunions with former members. Drummer Dave Lombardo had come back to Slayer, and Anthrax vocalist Joey Belladonna had announced his return after some years away, too. Could this get any better for our fans?

It's ironic that Araya's neck surgery provided a perfect moment in the timeline of Megadeth for me to return to the band. As bassist James LoMenzo was departing the band, the *Rust In Peace* live show would be intense, the setlist also featuring several cuts from the current *Endgame* album. We would then launch straight into the *RIP* album, played from top to bottom, before wrapping up with a few more classic songs from the band's back catalogue, including such staples as 'Symphony Of Destruction' and 'Peace Sells.'

I had kept up my Megadeth chops during my time away from the band, the *RIP* album in particular. I loved these songs—they were fun to play, and they really represented the uniqueness of my bass skills. My bass lines were recorded exclusively with a plectrum on that album, which had since become an all-time fan favorite among our (then) twelve studio albums. Other records might have sold more copies, but *RIP* defined who Megadeth were on nearly every level of technical proficiency, lyrical content, and overall metal feel.

Fortunately, I was familiar with a few of the riffs on the *Endgame* album, too, as many of the songs were comprised of unused riffs from past studio albums I'd participated in. In fact, it seemed that the three albums Megadeth made when I was away from the group were largely driven by Dave's mission to not be influenced by the past managers and producers who had removed some of those riffs in favor of a more mainstream and melodic approach. In turn, these riffs were all designed to create hit songs for MTV and radio.

The three albums I was not a part of (*The System Has Failed*, *United Abominations*, and *Endgame*) seemed to demonstrate Dave's keenness to re-establish the band's original thrash identity. In fact, during the last business phone call I had with Dave in 2004, he had stated, 'We're going to get things back to when I was in control.'

Learning the *Endgame* songs for the tour that year was not so difficult, for I had actually been in the room when many of those ideas were first composed, back in the 1990s. One song of particular interest to me was 'The Right To Go Insane,' which was to be the next single from the album—we even shot a video before the twentieth-anniversary *Rust In Peace* tour kicked off in March 2010. I knew the song because we had written and recorded a demo of it for the *Cryptic Writings* album back in 1996. It's funny how the bass licks intuitively came back to me, even though I had not heard the song in almost fifteen years!

The *RIP* tour was such a massive hit for Megadeth that we continued to get offers to perform the entire album all around the world for the next year. After the initial North American leg wrapped up in March, we went to South America and then over to Europe, which led directly into the Big Four festival shows that summer.

2.4 THE BIG FOUR BEGINS

The first Big Four show would play to over a hundred thousand people in Warsaw, Poland, in June 2010. It was so monumental that I even saw it advertised in the airline magazine when we flew in from Ireland to play the show!

Once we were on the ground, Metallica invited us to a private dinner for the four bands, to break bread at a local Italian restaurant.

The rules were simple: no managers, no handlers, no security. Band members only! Upon our arrival in a quiet city street, our private cars stopped at the address we'd been given. Metallica bassist Robert Trujillo was waiting for us at the restaurant's secret entrance.

Robert had likely opened for all of our bands as the bassist for legendary punk-thrashers Suicidal Tendencies and their funkier alter ego, Infectious Grooves. He'd then continued to work his way up the ranks, playing with the likes of Ozzy Osbourne and Black Label Society (fronted by Ozzy guitarist Zakk Wylde). He had paid his dues, and now he had landed the bass position in one of the biggest heavy metal bands in the world. We were all proud of him, and he retained his humble roots.

Once inside the restaurant, Lars, James, and Kirk welcomed each of us with grand metal hugs and laughter all around. As we ate, the stories flowed out, and we all got caught up on bands, kids, families, and the like. Of course, the unknown here was how things would go between Dave Mustaine and the Metallica camp, following Dave's sudden departure as the group's lead guitarist in 1983. For the next twenty-seven years, fans had wondered whether Dave and the other members of Metallica had put their past behind them. The next few concerts would provide the answer.

•

As we pulled into the backstage area in Warsaw, the mood was light and the anxieties ran high. The venue was a massive open-air field adjacent to a regional airport. Metallica's dressing room and production compound were set up closest to the stage, with another dressing room area for the rest of us across a small roadway in the middle.

After nervously greeting each other by our dressing rooms, we gathered in the common area for a group photo. Metallica had a vision that this was not just *their* show but a collective performance. This was quite a generous sentiment, but as the world's most successful heavy metal band—and one of the most iconic bands ever, next to the likes of The Rolling Stones, U2, and Queen—it was also an incredibly wise move on their part, to restore some metal credibility. For the other three bands, it was like the hand of God reaching down to lift us up to the status of metal royalty.

For band shuttles, the groups used golf carts, which were positioned by the dressing-room area to transport the respective artists to the stage. James Hetfield made a point of being outside the dressing room to cheer us on as we made our way to the massive festival stage. At the beginning of our careers, we were all striving to outdo one another, but the Big Four events had a very different feel to them. It was like we were brothers coming home to celebrate after the war; we had all been to our own battles over the years, all tasted the victories and defeats. Now it was time for us all to celebrate as friends, and the fans shared this opinion, too.

The show order was Anthrax first, Megadeth second, Slayer third, and then Metallica to close. There was a sense of tension and excitement when Anthrax took the stage, singer Joey Belladonna having been away from the band for quite some time. He'd come back for a stint, then departed again, but the timing of his return before this Warsaw show couldn't have been more appropriate. I recall being backstage in our dressing room, listening to him wail through the songs like it was 1986 all over again. He hadn't lost a thing in his voice, and the fans were ecstatic. The big moment was seeing how he would deliver on the songs Anthrax had recorded with other vocalists like John Bush while he was away from the band. Joey ended up nailing those tunes! There was enthusiasm everywhere in what was a triumphant moment for Anthrax.

Megadeth were up next. Again, James and Metallica were there to cheer us on. There were neither judgments nor arguments, strictly a pure heavy-metal battle cry from the gods themselves. The thing I recall most from the show is how massive the crowd was. Gazing out over one hundred thousand people (I heard they quit counting and just continued to let people in anyway!), it's almost like you can see the curve of the earth—that's how big it is! You literally couldn't see the back of the crowd.

If you've ever wondered what it's like to perform in front of that many people, you will appreciate just how remarkable it is to look out over that sea of bodies. It's quite an adrenaline boost. It took me a few songs to settle in and remember that it was just the four of us on that stage, surrounded by the big huge racket of sound that rocks the fans. It was truly a moment for the ages. To this day, it is something that I continually have such immense gratitude for in—to be able to go and play with my friends in the band.

Dave and I were well on our way to rekindling our friendship by this point, and we spent a lot of time in prayer together backstage. I was happy that Dave looked to me as a solid friend. We could openly discuss our views on religion, family, and the band. When all else fails, pray!

I started to see the significance of my return and the role that I had always played in the band. I also realized that maybe I had misunderstood my role in the past—just how important it was for me to suit up, show up, play bass, and be onstage alongside Dave in Megadeth. I was more than just the bass player; I was a foundational member of the group, and that is key role for me to undertake in Megadeth. My a-ha moment had arrived!

It seemed to work. Dave and I had a lot of laughs, and we got on well. I went out of my way to assure him that as cool as the Big Four was, I was on *Team Megadeth*. In my mind, I was now fully on board with

Megadeth until the band decided to take its final bow in the history books of metal. I had to let go of how our business used to be; I had a bigger role now, and it was one that was bigger than money. I had to trust that God would make sure I had enough and that my bills would be paid. My role in this new season wasn't just show up and be glad to be there, but also to be Dave's cheerleader.

FRANK BELLO (BASSIST, ANTHRAX) ❝I've known David Ellefson for over thirty years, and if I could come up with a word that best describes him, it has to be 'consistent.' Consistent as a great bass player, as a great family man, and as a great friend. We've spent most of our lives on the road, touring with our bands, so we've always had a lot in common, besides being the bass players in Megadeth and Anthrax. I've always trusted Dave's word on bass gear, because he was on the road as much as I was, and the gear we use has to have the right sound for the music we play, and be durable enough to not break down.

I remember when we were touring with the Big Four, I would go onstage behind Dave's bass cabinets at soundcheck—I always like to check out new gear I haven't heard before—and it sounded killer! After that day, Dave knew I was really into the sound of the Hartke gear he was using, so he thoroughly explained everything the amp and cabinets had to offer in detail, which led to him hooking me up with Hartke to start using their gear, and so much more.❞

After two more Big Four shows, Scott Ian sent Dave a text message while we were on the bus to Sofia, Bulgaria, where we knew in advance that the show would be filmed for a live DVD and simulcast to more than fifteen hundred movie theaters across the globe in real time. We were driving across Serbia, down a badly worn, bumpy highway, when the message arrived. It said that Metallica were inviting all the bands onstage for their encore, to perform a cover of 'Am I Evil?' by Diamond Head—a song made famous by Metallica after it was included on the original *Garage Days* EP, and then as a bonus track on the Elektra version of the *Kill 'Em All* album.

For Dave, this was the moment he had been waiting for, for the last twenty-seven years: to be back onstage, performing with Metallica. I was happy for him. I had just re-joined *my* band, so I knew the excitement Dave must have to re-join *his* former bandmates.

We quickly learned the song in our backstage jam room upon arriving at the festival grounds the next day. The excitement backstage that day was a buzz like none I've ever experienced. Anthrax were coming over to us to run through the song together, and we were like giddy little kids about the opportunity that awaited us that evening.

Oddly, the only Slayer member who participated in the jam was drummer Dave Lombardo, who was grateful and thrilled to do it. I didn't understand why the others didn't, other than that maybe they were nervous about doing the song. But it was weird, because Slayer guitarist Kerry King is known to get up to jam and do guest appearances with other artists—he played guitar for Megadeth in 1984, and played a guest solo on The Beastie Boys' song '(You Gotta) Fight For Your Right (To Party!),' so I know *he* could pull it off!

Before Slayer's set that evening, we were invited back to Metallica's backstage room for a pre-show run through the song. James, Lars, Kirk, and Robert were already preparing their warm-ups. Upon entering the room, Robert Trujillo looked up and cheerfully welcomed me as *Junior*, which has been my nickname since 1983. He unplugged his bass, indicating he wanted *me* to be the one to hold down the backstage jam.

I had finally gotten to know James on this tour. We had some things in common—our lifestyles, our families, our music—but unfortunately the one thing we had never done was jam together. And while I was always friendly with Lars, Kirk, and Robert, I had never jammed with any of them, either. In a weird way, I was now kind of feeling what it would be like to play in a band with them all. Lars is always fun, James is one of the most powerhouse rhythm guitar players and singers on the planet, and Kirk is about as chill as they come.

It was an incredible moment as me, Dave Mustaine, Scott Ian, Dave Lombardo, Charlie Benante, Frank Bello, and the whole gang jumped in on the warm-up jam session, going over parts, determining who would play which solo and so on. There was a great feeling of camaraderie and brotherly love in the room, especially to see Dave and James playing guitar together for the first time since 1983. It became a beautiful moment in life, and in metal history itself—one I had never witnessed myself—to see them together as musicians. (Keep in mind, I met Dave two months after he left Metallica, so this was a historical moment even for *me* to be a part of—and even more so having lived only inches from the drama and chaos of the falling out for the previous twenty-seven years.)

As the roaming cameras followed us around the stadium that day to gather B-roll content for the live DVD, I naturally slipped into a sort of 'host' mode. Since re-joining the band, I had been shooting short video vignettes on my Flip camera during the previous few months and posting them to YouTube almost daily. My aim was to take the fans on tour with us via these videos—to show them what an incredible life they have given us.

As we opened our set that day in Sofia, an incredible thunderstorm dumped a massive amount of rain on the crowd. As the audience put on their colored raincoats, which were handed out at the entrance gate, it was the most colorful rainbow of head-bangers I had ever seen—an irony for an audience usually known for its unspoken uniform of black T-shirts.

As the night went on, the moment came for us all to take the stage with Metallica for the encore. As their crew rolled out a second set of amplifiers and snare drums for us to use, James made the introductory announcement and invited all the other bands onstage. The crowd went nuts! We all gave each other big hugs as we entered the stage, the camera money shot being on Dave Mustaine and James Hetfield, which bore witness to how years of brooding resentment could melt away over music and some time away to reflect.

I think Metallica probably figured that if Megadeth sold thirty million albums, that, for Dave, would be like being a quarter member of Metallica. So what does he have to complain about? But for Dave, and even for me, the work and the budgets we worked within to achieve our successes would have been exponentially easier with 120 million records sold, like Metallica had accomplished. If it takes a million dollars to sell a million albums, it only takes another million dollars to sell ten million more albums—and there's a hell of a lot of money to be made from those next nine million albums, which is the type of success Metallica had won in their career. They worked hard, and they were blessed. That band is truly a phenomenon, and it was so cool to be in the middle of it all during the Big Four shows.

•

After the night was over, we left the stage to more hugs and celebration. I recall Lars coming over to me for a last-minute hug as I walked off, which I think is actually captured on the DVD. I wasn't aware he was coming toward me, though, so I left the stage.

Lars and I had had a lot of fun over the years. We partied together all night back in the 1980s, when he'd come to see Megadeth perform in the Bay Area, as well as when I'd see him in Hollywood. We were friends, and it was great to play music together on the same stage.

In the end, Lars was, and is, just a good ol' fan of metal. It was Metal Blade Records owner Brian Slagel who told Lars to start a band, because he was so knowledgeable about metal. Thank God he did! From there, Lars put an ad in the *Recycler*, the local paper that aided in the formation of many legendary LA bands, and met James Hetfield. Shortly thereafter, Dave Mustaine was recruited on lead guitar, and the rest is history.

In a way, Lars inadvertently started the family tree to which I belong, by way of playing with Dave in Megadeth. Now that would be a fun tree to see after all these years. Kerry King would be on there, too, by way of playing in Megadeth in 1984, and Anthrax would be in it as well, by way of harboring Metallica as young fugitives when they landed on the East Coast for their Megaforce Records audition in April 1983 ...

BRIAN SLAGEL (FOUNDER, METAL BLADE RECORDS) "*When David came back into Megadeth—and I've seen Megadeth a bunch of times, obviously with David, before, and then after he left—I think the first time I saw them was the Hollywood Palladium, and they were doing that Rust In Peace anniversary thing. And having not seen him in Megadeth for a while, I didn't realize how much of an integral part of that band he really was. When you see him come back, and see him—especially playing that album—it really blew me away. It was a great night. One of my favorite metal records of all time is Rust In Peace, and seeing that was like ... wow, this is pretty amazing.*"

BACK IN THE GAME

3.1 TH1RT3EN

As the dust settled from the Sofia show, we continued on with several more Big Four shows across Europe during the summer of 2010. Megadeth would then go to Japan before finally wrapping up our year with an arena tour of Australia, the *No Sleep Til ...* tour. It was an odd fit of mostly punk bands and a few emo acts (NOFX, Parkway Drive, Dropkick Murphys), and the idea was that the shows would be called *No Sleep Til Perth*, *No Sleep Til Melbourne*, and so on. The tour was met with decent attendance, but it was a tough time to be asking fans for ticket dollars, just before the Christmas holidays. Big-name festivals like Soundwave and Big Day Out were also coming up the following February, and they had the main attractions and fan loyalty. Still, I was excited to get back Down Under, as I hadn't been there since my last Megadeth tour in 2001, for *The World Needs A Hero*.

We took some time off over the holidays, with the idea being that we would soon begin writing the next Megadeth album. There was a lot of anticipation about the next record, with me back in the fold, and we had only about ten weeks to get it written and recorded before the next round of touring would begin. I suggested we try to get in a room and write as a band for a change, like we did all the years before. The three most recent Megadeth albums were written almost exclusively by Dave, but I figured it wouldn't hurt to at least try to revisit the old method of how we used to work. It did create multi-platinum success for us, so why not give it a try?

After the NAMM show in January 2011, Dave and I gathered with drummer Shawn Drover and guitarist Chris Broderick at the band's studio, 'Vic's Garage,' in northern San Diego. Our usual approach when writing over the years is one that I believe Lars had instilled in Metallica, and something Dave brought into Megadeth. Dave had everyone gather their ideas on tape, mp3, or however they felt best presenting a riff, melody, or lyric to him.

Presenting full songs to Dave tends not to work as well, as he generally looks instead for riffs and ideas that might work in other songs—most often songs he is already developing or conceptualizing. As the chief composer in the band, he usually starts the main riffs to a composition, and then, where applicable, the rest of us make our contributions.

Since the was a new chapter, and none of us were exactly clear on the method of working on this next album, I brought in quite a few demos of things I had compiled in recent years on my own. And, having worked on quite a few collaborations in my years away from the group, I felt inclined to offer ideas as we jammed over some of Dave's riffs, too. Things got tense between us rather quickly when I offered a suggestion, however, so I backed off. Although we had collaborated a lot during our 90s heyday, in recent years the group had been restructured around Dave being pretty much the sole writer, with the other three musicians as his backing sidemen. I acquiesced to keep the peace, once again trying to look at the bigger picture for the greater good of all.

It became clear that my contributions to this album were not going to be in the music department. I was patient, and I let things take their course. In the end, I guess it's like any other job: Dave was the leader, and we were going to follow his lead. The same as it had always been, really. I had been there from the start, so I knew the game plan.

A few days later, I went back home to Arizona, and the *Th1rt3en* album was set into motion.

3.2 THE SUMMER OF MAYHEM

When the *Th1rt3en* sessions started, I suggested we bring in producer Johnny K. of Disturbed and Staind fame. Johnny makes great-sounding records, and I am definitely a fan of his work. I was aware of nu-metal—for lack of a better term—and the late-90s wave of FM-radio hard rock. The leaders were bands like KoRn, Godsmack, Limp Bizkit, Tool, and Disturbed. I knew this wave was coming, and I could see it at the radio festivals we played in 1998–99, on the *Cryptic Writings* cycle, but we weren't clear how Megadeth would successfully traverse these waters.

One night when I was wrapping my session with Dale Steele's band NUMM in Minneapolis in 2002, I got in my car and turned on the radio. The local rock station 93X was on, and this amazing sound came roaring across the airwaves. I would later discover that it was Disturbed. They had the most amazing tone: sharp, heavy, commanding, militant, and modern, yet total metal. This was clearly the next wave in metal music. In fact, its distinct production reminded me of the *Countdown* album.

Ironically, Disturbed was a band that I introduced to F5's executive producer Steve Smith a year or so later, when we met at this house to produce *A Drug For All Seasons*. Steve was well versed in pop radio, but this was a new sound even to him—and he loved it. So much so that, for him, it became the model for F5's sound in the studio, which was fine with me. It was fun to be a fan of a new band—something I found it difficult to do when I was in the capsule of Megadeth for all those years, mostly because we were so focused on our own sound, but being away from the group for a season allowed me to stretch my ears and broaden my horizons.

With Peavey, I worked diligently with many sponsors who were dipping their toes (and wallets!) into the music and touring game. One of those was Sydney Frank, who owned the Jagermeister brand of liquor, among other things, and who had developed the Jagermeister Music Program. It was fortunate for me, because the good people of Jagermeister offered my band, Temple Of Brutality, a string of shows, one of them being an opening slot with Disturbed at Janus Landing in Tampa, Florida, on their *10,000 Fists* album cycle. I was excited to meet the guys and to see them firsthand, because I was definitely a fan.

DAN DONEGAN (GUITARIST, DISTURBED) ❝*The first time I met Ellefson was years ago, as a fan, before Disturbed, just seeing Megadeth at a concert, but it was very brief. He wouldn't have known, 'cause I was just a local kid at a concert. But the first official time we crossed paths out on the road or whatever, I don't know if it was the Uproar tour—I think it was before that.*

Dave's just one of the coolest guys out there. He's just so easy to talk to, he's just so respectful; he talks to you like you've known him for years, just very comfortable. I've had my fan-boy moments of meeting some of my idols like this—David being one of them—and it brought me back to being a kid in the crowd, watching him onstage with Megadeth. It's a surreal moment for us. We grew up big fans of the band, and here we are being friends and touring together at times. It was cool to just meet him backstage and feel that comfortable with him—just hanging out and chatting a bit, or seeing him in catering, or whatever the case may be.

When you meet some of your idols like that, you're a bit hesitant. You're fearful that they may ruin the image that you have of them, of being this cool rock star. Are they gonna have a big ego? Are they gonna brush you off? But David is just such a great guy—there was none of that. He acted like we were friends since the first time I met him—he was just engaged in conversation, just the regular small-talk thing you do with any friend.

When he was in F5, we had done a show in Florida, at Janus Landing, and I knew Dave was in the band—I had heard about it through a mutual friend at our label, Reprise. I knew at that point he had that short break from Megadeth, and I knew he was going out with one of his other bands, Temple Of Brutality. So I knew they were on that bill, and it was cool to see him on that show and kind of cross paths again, for that brief moment. It's just always cool to share a stage with somebody that I've always looked up to.

When we came out, there were so many other great bands, and we've been very fortunate. Our label, Giant, was such a great supporter of Disturbed, and I've always had to credit Berko and Larry, who were our A&R guys. Their passion for us—we just felt like that was the right home for us. These are guys that we knew every day, they were gonna wake up saying, 'What can we do to help this band get further?' And we felt that passion with them. It was an obvious choice to us.

I know there was the label of 'nu-metal' and all that—it is what it is. I'm not shying away from that, but that was just a label that was put on any band that came out at that time. You'd have one band that might have a DJ, with turntables, and they're 'nu-metal,' and then you have a band like us, and we grew up with classic metal, and we were influenced by those bands, but we're lumped into that because it's the same time. Then you have bands like System Of A Down and KoRn and everything else—we're all different from each other, but we're all lumped into that same category.

Our influences were so across the board with all of us, but the main roots of the band are the classic metal bands: Iron Maiden, Judas Priest, Metallica, Megadeth, Queensrÿche. At the point where I really picked up the guitar and started playing, I was even influenced by some of the other 80s bands who had great guitar players—George Lynch from Dokken is one of my favorites, and one of the main reasons I picked up the guitar, 'cause he was such a tasteful, melodic player.

A lot of those bands get a bad rap, with the 'hair metal' stuff, but if you look at a lot of those bands, they all had great guitar players, and that was the time I really wanted to be a musician. But then we went onto things like I said—I was a big Queensrÿche fan, then into the grunge phase of Alice In Chains, Soundgarden— every decade has, I guess, rubbed off on me, as a player. I try to take what I can from each era, and what can I do to better myself as a musician—what can we do as a band—that's gonna take those things and influence us. But the main core of it has always been those classic metal bands—Megadeth, Maiden, Metallica, Black Sabbath, even Pantera. Big, heavy bands that could still be melodic. I'm not dissing any of the screaming bands, but I want to hear the message—I want to know what it is. I want to go deeper, and when it's something like 'Peace Sells' or 'War Pigs' or 'Fade To Black,' there's still messages behind it, and that's what sucked me in, on top of great musicianship. I love the attitude behind the music— no rules, no formula. It sounded like a band that got into a room and wrote what felt right to them.

I remember one show, it must have been [at the time of] So Far, So Good ... So What! Megadeth was opening for Iron Maiden at what is now called the Allstate Arena, but it's a very historic arena in the Chicago area. Their set either ran over, or was behind on time, and I remember the house lights coming on while they were playing, and they just refused to get offstage. And Dave Mustaine, it was just so classic, so rebellious, just that attitude of, 'I don't give a fuck. Keep the house lights on.' They kept playing and finished it out for another two songs. It was just such a cool moment, as a young kid, to see somebody say, 'I don't need the lights. I don't need a lightshow. We're playing our fucking songs, and we're not getting off.' It always stuck in my head, just how much it was more about the music. 🎶

Back in the studio with Megadeth, I recorded bass on a track called 'Sudden Death,' which was featured on the final round of the *Guitar Hero* games. It was mixed by Andy Sneap, who's now the guitarist for Judas Priest. I was excited to work with Andy as I'd loved his production work on the previous two Megadeth albums I was not a part of, *United Abominations* and *Endgame*. However, because of scheduling issues, we had to find an alternative producer for *Th1rt3en*. That's where my recommendation of Johnny K. came in. He'd blown me away with his work on that Disturbed song I heard on 93X a few years earlier. To me, he was a good, modern fit for Megadeth, and also someone who was seasoned with success in the current metal climate.

Meanwhile, Dave started sending me completed arrangements of the new songs via email, and I would then write up my bass charts in order to be prepared to walk in and record. In many ways, it was the same method I'd used when recording with other artists in my time away from Megadeth.

As it turned out, and despite some of my initial concerns about not contributing any compositions to it, *Th1rt3en* was probably the easiest, most relaxed Megadeth album for me to record. Johnny K. had me play through each song three times from top to bottom, the idea being that since there weren't really any vocal melodies laid down yet, he would have be able to cut and paste my bass parts (creating what is called a *comp*) to better match the vocals later on, if need be. On each take I made small tweaks to my performances: on one version I'd play the chorus in the lower octave, and on the next take I'd perform it an octave higher. In pop music, moving the chorus up an octave gives the song a lift and helps set it as the hook. I used that same approach on this record, as I had on previous recordings, too.

For the most part, Dave let Johnny and me work in our own manner while we recorded the bass for the record. He would come in at the end of each song to give it his final approval, which he does on every record, as the primary composer of the songs. This is standard issue, and a course I'm used to following on Megadeth records.

The recording was fun and creative, and I recorded all the bass parts in their entirety in less than five days. While I wasn't credited as a composer of any of the songs, the path of least resistance—to let Dave compose, and for me to play bass on his songs—seemed the best course of action. We had a winner of an album on our hands and a big tour to follow. I was glad to be part of it.

One day while we were recording, I brought up to Dave the idea that we had never used a number for an album title, and that this was going to be album number thirteen. The number itself conjures up macabre notions due to its haunting and superstitious history—things like Friday the 13th and so forth. Plus, Dave loves the number thirteen because his birthday is September 13. So it seemed fitting to name the album *Th1rt3en*, be it as a Roman numeral, a standard number, or just written out. I'm glad the title stuck.

We finished the record and sent it off to be mixed. We then set out on a month-long concert tour of Europe, which included a stop in Tel Aviv, Israel, during Passover weekend. I remember being frustrated that weekend as I'd brought whole-bean coffee with me, but because of the Levitical law of not running any machinery on the Sabbath, I had to crush the beans with my boot on the balcony of my hotel room. Then, on Sunday, after the Sabbath had passed, I went to the kitchen of our hotel and asked them to now grind my beans. They told me that the beans weren't kosher, so they couldn't be in their kitchen. Really? Sometimes traveling the world presents these little annoyances.

I find it ironic that there is this massive pilgrimage to Israel for Passover—which is, of course, a time of mourning from the Old Testament—but then, once the sun sets twenty-four hours later, on the Sunday, the rockers came back out to party. I guess even the major religions of the world can't hold down a good rock'n'roll party!

Following the show in Tel Aviv, we flew back to the USA for the next Big Four show in Indio, California—which, ironically, was on Easter weekend. We were hitting all the religious holidays on this tour! By now, Jeff Hanneman was no longer performing with Slayer due to his failing health, but he did make an appearance in Indio for a photo op to celebrate the Big Four DVD achieving platinum status in America. I never saw him again after that moment. He passed a few months later, from complications of liver failure.

The next day, Easter Sunday, I saw Dave and his sister eating breakfast together at the hotel. I stopped over to say hello, and he told me that Metallica had offered us another Big Four show in New York, at Yankee Stadium, on September 13, on what would be Dave's fiftieth birthday. I said this could be viewed as the ultimate fiftieth birthday celebration for him—in front of fifty thousand of his fans, who would be beyond thrilled to see the show *and* celebrate his birthday!

Shortly thereafter, the show was confirmed. Our American fans were beyond thrilled, because with each Big Four show, we never knew if there would be another one. As long as everyone behaved and played well with each other, though, it seemed the opportunities could continue, with more shows popping up around the world.

The *Th1rt3en* album was released in July 2011, just as we were wrapping up another round of massive Big Four shows across Europe. We then flew home to northern California to embark on the massive Mayhem Festival tour, a six-week trek playing to amphitheaters across the country every night, wrapping up in Florida in mid-August.

I was thrilled to discover that Disturbed would be headlining the tour, with Godsmack as direct support and Megadeth third from the top. Many of our fans might have wanted to see Megadeth as the headliner, but the USA is a whole different ballgame than our bigger tour markets—places like Latin America, Asia, and even parts of Europe, where we receive top billing on festivals and headline our own arena-level shows. All these years later, that sense I had in the late 1990s of the

MORE LIFE WITH DETH

changing tide in metal music was now very much present. Godsmack used to open for Megadeth in the late 90s, but now they were a slot above us. I wasn't bothered by it; I had become of fan of theirs, and I'd watched them develop a ferocious live show as far back as 1999, when they played directly before Megadeth at the Woodstock Festival.

Then, after a short break, it would be time for more Big Four.

3.3 BASS MASTERS

The next big Megadeth event was the Big Four show at Yankee Stadium on September 13, 2011. I was especially excited for Anthrax, as this was their New York hometown play, and to grace the deck of that stadium is the stuff of childhood dreams for any New Yorker.

The night before the show, my friend Mark Menghi put on a monumental Metal Masters event at the Best Buy Theater in Times Square, with many of the Big Four band members—including me, Kerry King, Dave Lombardo, and the guys from Anthrax—in attendance. Mark was the man responsible for creating the Frank Bello/David Ellefson dual-bass clinics that had begun earlier in 2011, which is where the idea for Metal Masters came from.

Putting these events together was an easy reach for Mark. He was able to invite several of his high-profile Samson and Hartke clients (me included) to participate in a fifteen-minute clinic, followed by an all-star concert. The fans loved it, and it was a format that we could easily replicate elsewhere.

MARK MENGHI ❝*I met Dave through our mutual friend, Tim 'Ripper' Owens, at the Winter NAMM show in January 2008 or '09, I believe. At the time, I was the art director and artist-relations manager for Hartke Amps, Samson, and Zoom. It was at the Anaheim Hilton Hotel in the evening, and I remember vividly that Ripper and I were about to head out to an artist dinner I was hosting across the street at JW's Restaurant in the Marriott.*

We ran into Dave in the lobby, and Ripper introduced us. Of course I knew of Dave through Megadeth, being a bassist and loving his tunes, and then as a peer, as he was then working in artist relations for my competitor, Peavey. I remember setting up at NAMM shows years prior to that and seeing Dave across the way, as our booths were right next to each other. I would plug into an amp and play 'Peace Sells' (wrong, of course), obnoxiously loud, just to bust some balls. I was busting his balls before he even knew me.

That night at JW's, Dave and I sat next to each other at a table of ten or twelve artists, and we talked all night. From that moment on, we've been like brothers. I proceeded to sign Dave up as a Zoom artist and sent him a bunch of gear to try out. I purposely did not mention anything Hartke to him, as I respected his position with Peavey. You've got to remember, we were in the heyday of endorsement deals, and there were AR vultures out there. I always respected what people played, because as a player myself, tone and being comfortable with what you are playing—and endorsing—is the most important part of one's individual identity as a player.

I remember telling Dave I could give a flying fuck if he was in Megadeth or not (at this point in time he was not). I just told him, 'You are a good dude, and I love talking and working with you.' We immediately clicked—we both played bass, both did AR, both loved the same music—and Dave, being a forefather of thrash, that of course helped. So Dave and I began a working relationship with Zoom, until I got a phone call one evening in March, where he told me he wanted to try the new Hartke HyDrive gear. I asked why, and he said he was re-joining Megadeth and wanted to go back to his original Hartke/Jackson tone. I said, 'No problem,' dialed Dave in, and the rest is history. ❞

FRANK BELLO ❝A bunch of musicians from different bands would get together for a show and play metal songs. We had a blast because all the musicians were friends and had toured together through the years, so there was a great vibe throughout the whole show. It was great for the fans also, because they got a chance to see musicians from different bands that you wouldn't ordinarily see jamming together.❞

MARK MENGHI ❝Metal Masters stemmed from the Bello/Ellefson clinics I was doing around the country. I remember planning a Bello/Ellefson clinic in southern California, and, as I was on the phone with Dave, giving him this initial idea of doing one right before that monstrous Big Four gig, the other line rang, and it was Anthrax drummer Charlie Benante.

I told Dave I would call him right back as I needed to speak to Charlie about something. After a few minutes of New York bullshitting, I told him about what I was planning with Dave and Frank. He loved the idea and asked if we needed a drummer. I said, 'You know what? What good is bass without drums? Lets do it.' And right as I said that, I received an email from Mike Portnoy—as I was on the phone with Charlie—with a video clip of a recent Bello/Ellefson clinic, saying he would love to do something like this in the future.

Think about this for a minute. I was on the phone with Dave, giving him my idea, Charlie interrupted that call and inserted himself in—thank God—and Portnoy emailed, asking the same, as I was on the phone with Dave. This was one hundred percent coincidence, as none of them knew what was happening in that span of five minutes. I replied back to Mike and said, and I quote—I still have that email—'Booking an Ellefson/Bello clinic in SoCal the night before the Indio Big Four show. On the phone with Charlie now and he is joining us. Two bassists and a drummer sounds like a bad joke. How about two bassists and two drummers? Are you in?'

Thirty seconds later, he replied back: 'Fuck Yeah.' From that point on, Metal Masters was born.❞

The first Metal Masters event included me, Frank, Charlie Benante, and Mike Portnoy and took place a Sam Ash music store in Cerritos, California, the day after the *Revolver* Music Awards in Los Angeles, and the just before the Big Four show in Indio.

Metal Masters would become a *huge* hit across the USA during 2011–13. Our roster grew to include about twenty or so of the biggest names in metal and hard rock, including Kerry King, Steve Vai, Billy Sheehan, Geezer Butler, and Phil Anselmo, and of course many of the members of the Big Four.

MARK MENGHI 66*Metal Masters 1 was still relatively small, held in a music store in Cerritos, California. I swear there had to be about a thousand kids trying to get in, helicopters circling the store, cops keeping the peace outside the place—it was madness. That small town in SoCal has never seen anything like this before. Now I am thinking to myself, Okay dude, if people are lining up like this to see two drummers and two bassists, what else can we do? How much further can we take this? Hence Metal Masters 2, held in my hometown of New York City before the Big Four show at Yankee Stadium. At this point in time, it went from a music store to the Best Buy Theater in Times Square—the first clinic to ever be held in a venue of that size. Of course we had Frank, Dave, Mike, and Charlie, but we added a few guitar players, and a vocalist, by the names of Kerry Fucking King, Scott Ian, and Mr. Philip H. Anselmo.*

Over the course of a three-year period, we did Metal Masters clinics at the Key Club in Hollywood, the Gramercy Theatre in New York City, and the Anaheim House of Blues. We had everyone from Geezer Butler of Black Sabbath to Steve Vai join us. Sometimes we had two drummers, other times we had three drummers set up onstage, all at once. Sometimes we had one bassist, others time we had four going at once! It's crazy, what the initial idea of a clinic with two bassists led to. And, all during this, Dave was the glue that kept all this together. 99

HEAVY METAL FAITH

4.1 HEAVY METAL SEMINARIAN

I began my year of Lutheran seminary training for the SMP (Specific Ministry Pastor) online course in August 2011, just weeks before the final Big Four show at Yankee Stadium. The course is designed for adults in the church who had a desire for higher religious education, with the intent that they may move into a pastoral position in the church. The reason I decided to take it is because I had learned from my past that I had no idea how long Megadeth would continue, and when the opportunity presented itself, I knew that the Good Lord was bringing it into my life for a reason.

I had no real plan to become a minister or work full-time in the church, but when the offer came along to attend seminary as a *potential* career transition one day, I knew not to have contempt prior to investigation. I learned when Megadeth disbanded in 2002 that it's better to be proactive regarding new ventures when times are good than trying to grasp at anything when the chips are down. So, I said yes—as had become my mantra—and enrolled in the program.

The introduction to the course required me to attend a week of orientation at the ground campus of the Concordia Seminary in St. Louis, Missouri, which I did in August of that year. Day one was the usual pleasantries and hellos, but on the second day we went straight into some heavy stuff about sex and how the devil can use temptation of the flesh to corrupt a pastor through human desires. I was intrigued to learn that if a pastor falls to pornography, or an affair, then human judgment would set in and lead to the usual, 'See, I told you those Christians were hypocrites!' From there, it would only be a matter of time before a congregation lost faith and the church began to fail.

Whoa, I thought, *this is pretty hardcore.* As I would learn in my further training that year, the Good Word of God contained in the Bible returns to three main topics over and over: eternal salvation, money, and sex. *Hmmm*, I thought, *sounds like the kind of book I'd like to read!* And read it I did.

One day, I received an email about an interviewer from the St. Louis Post who wanted to interview me about being a student of the course. I agreed to the interview, did it, and then forgot all about it. Then, as we rounded the corner into 2012, Megadeth had a major tour on sale, Gigantour, which was set to run from late January to March. Gigantour was the tour brand Dave had created in 2005. In the years since, the tour had its greatest success in the winter/spring season, when it was not up against the major summer tours. The 2012 lineup would include Lacuna Coil, Volbeat, and Motörhead, with Megadeth as the headliner.

Just before the tour kicked off, I was at the NAMM show in Anaheim once again, making a round of celebrity appearances for the musical equipment companies who had sponsored, endorsed, and supported the previous year on tour. While sitting at the autograph line for Samson/Hartke, fans began congratulating me, telling me that they'd read the *St. Louis Post* story about me being a seminary student. The story had popped up on the newswires that afternoon. I received such positive reaction and was met with some great compliments— 'You are a good fit for that!' and 'Couldn't think of a better man in rock'n'roll to fill those shoes.'

I was thrilled. I called my pastor in Scottsdale and told him about the overwhelming positive response from the fans that afternoon, only for him to tell me that some of the elder generation at headquarters were upset that a heavy-metal rock star had somehow gotten into the SMP program, as if it were some kind of blasphemy.

I was like, *You have to be kidding?* It seemed to me that becoming a seminarian in the world of heavy metal would provide the perfect platform to carry a gospel message directly to an audience who may be a bit prejudiced or put off by it. But I did find it ironically amusing that the supposed 'sinners' of rock'n'roll supported me, but the 'officials' back at seminary didn't.

Apparently, the elders had been combing through the lyrics of Megadeth and Motörhead songs, and had deduced that just being *around* that music would automatically make me a sinner. Guilty by association, I guess. But I wasn't there to cause any trouble for anyone—I was just doing my theology studies.

'If it's better for me to withdraw from Concordia to avoid any issues, I will,' I told my pastor. 'I'm just here to study the Word and get an education. I mean no ill will.'

Fortunately, my pastor had my back, and he fought the good fight for me at seminary. So, for the time being, I remained enrolled.

We began the 2012 Gigantour on January 26 to massive success, playing twenty-five cities across in a six-week run. The tour had gone from clubs and a few arenas in 2008 to now mostly all arenas. Megadeth were definitely seeing a big upswing in sales and popularity, while the newcomers to the bill, Volbeat, were a huge hit. They were absolutely amazing, and you could tell there were big things in store for them.

Motörhead, however, were beginning to struggle by this point. We had all grown up on the band, and we hoped for the best with them, but Lemmy was nearing seventy years old, and at that age the natural human condition begins to work against you—especially when you've lived the ultimate rock'n'roll lifestyle, as he had. Regardless, we all hailed him, and we were honored to have his band on the bill with us.

I continued to do my seminary studies on the bus and in hotel rooms each day, and, in many ways, it helped me transcend the tour boredom that can set in, when the concerts are on a sort of autopilot. I enjoyed learning and having my mind opened to new ideas. The real deciding moment came later that year, when the seminary wanted an answer as to my future direction. The question was pointed and clear: 'When is the rock band thing going to end, so you can commit to becoming a pastor?'

To me, it was a no brainer: I'm a rock'n'roll man first, and playing in Megadeth was my true calling, not being a full-time pastor in the church. At least not at this point in my life. I love the Lord, and I spend time in the Word every day. It's my heart's desire to grow closer to God in this life. But it had also become clear to me, through the fans' response during NAMM, that *they* supported my efforts too. So, to me, it felt perfectly fine to rock the world *and* walk hand in hand with God at the same time. After all, music is a talent *He* gave to me in this life. To not use it, I feel, would be to shortchange God out of his gift.

It is my experience that there is more than one way to be a light in this dark world, and after consulting with my pastor and my supporters at my home church in Scottsdale, it was expressed to me that I didn't have to have a seminary degree to live a Gospel life and help people in spiritual need. The vehicle of Megadeth could be a sort of magic carpet that allows me to do the Lord's work in many other ways, listening to fans and friends in need, and being ready to help them when asked.

So, after a year of schooling, I applied for a leave of absence, and eventually I withdrew from the seminary in good standing, on the understanding that one day there might prove a new season in my life to re-enroll.

•

As Megadeth's touring continued, we decided to do another album-anniversary celebration. We were at the point in our career where many of our albums were reaching these ten-, twenty-, and even twenty-five-year milestones. So, that fall, we decided to embark on a tour to mark the twentieth anniversary of *Countdown To Extinction*. It would be similar to the *RIP* tour we did a couple years earlier: we would open the show with a few fan favorites from the catalogue, then launch into the performing the *CTE* album from top to bottom.

Since *CTE* is one of my personal favorites in the Megadeth catalogue, I really enjoyed performing it each night. We toured South America and finished up in North America, and filmed a live DVD in southern California to capture the experience.

Overall, it had been a productive and successful album/tour cycle. Much like when the *Cryptic Writings* tour wrapped up in 1998, I was ready for a break—to refresh, regroup, and prepare for the next album in early 2014 or so. But I would quickly learn that there would be no break or time to rest.

I had seen this movie before, and I already knew the ending.

4.2 METAL ALLEGIANCE

The *Super Collider* album/tour cycle of 2013–14 almost identically mirrored the *Risk* era of 1999–2000. Both albums saw the band rushing into the studio to record highly anticipated follow-ups to the records and tours that preceded them (*Cryptic Writings* and *Th1rt3en*, respectively).

In both cases, however, there wasn't enough time off to rest, refocus, and gain the proper perspective to write a quality of songs to take the next step upward. In the case of the *Super Collider* album, tour dates had already been booked through 2014, and the album was on a schedule that had to be adhered to.

It has become the industry standard when marketing the launch of a metal album to lead with a hard-hitting track. The idea is that, in hearing this first, an audience can form a sense of anticipation as to what the rest of the album will sound like. The theory is that once you have your audience locked in with a heavy track, you can be a bit more daring on melodic radio offerings later on in the cycle.

It seemed clear to me that the opening track on *Super Collider*, 'Kingmaker,' would be the perfect metal track to lead with. Instead, the powers that be elected to go straight to a melodic single as the first look from the album: the title track, 'Super Collider,' which also came with a music video starring the band and others in a sort of sophomoric takeoff of the 70s TV show *Love, American Style*. As they say, first impressions are lasting impressions, and this was not the impression our core thrash-metal audience was hoping for. I could see it happening—it was going to be the same story as *Risk* all over again. And, as a result, the *Super Collider* cycle faced struggling ticket sales and an urgent need to rebuild the band within our core fan base.

It's in these moments, of course, that the blame game starts, and in this case the management was sacked. One of the band's former managers—Ron Laffitte, who had managed us through the *Rust In Peace, Countdown To Extinction*, and *Youthanasia* albums—was brought in. But while this idea had merit based on past performance, Ron was now at the top of the management heap in Hollywood, looking after such huge pop acts as Pharrell Williams and One Republic, and also working closely with major legacy acts like U2 and Madonna. As big as Megadeth had become in our genre, heavy-metal money was *tiny* in comparison to what Ron was earning in commissions from these top pop artists. I remember talking with Chris Broderick on the tour bus in early 2014, soon after the management change, and while I was optimistic about the changing horses, he was not. It turns out he was right. He ended up leaving the band over it a year later.

During all of this, my only brother, Eliot, was dying from stage-four colon cancer, which had been diagnosed fifteen months earlier. Our participation in the Australian mega-tour Soundwave in February was canceled, and following the passing of my brother in May, our European summer tour was also canceled, allowing Dave to focus on writing a new album.

With the band members only getting paid when there were tour dates, secondary career moves were now in motion. Chris Broderick and Shawn Drover began to plot a new band, Act Of Defiance, during the Japanese leg of the tour in the summer of 2014. They asked me to participate too, but I knew my place was in Megadeth, so I declined.

A few other pivotal things happened in the months that followed—things that would again open up new creative opportunities for me. One July afternoon, Mark Menghi, my former artist-relations rep from Hartke, called me. He had recently been let go by Hartke's owner, Samson, following a corporate downsizing, and was currently enjoying the summer with his family.

I urged Menghi to continue his Metal Masters concept, because he had the most difficult piece in place—getting the famous guys on board. We hung up, but then, literally twenty minutes later, he called me back with a new name, Metal Allegiance, which he had already called his lawyer to secure a trademark for. I love that kind of urgency—it's what gets my blood churning!

We made plans to launch Metal Allegiance at the 2015 Winter

NAMM convention in Anaheim, California. It would be the perfect all-star concert for NAMM attendees.

Then Megadeth—now under new management—abruptly canceled their headlining spot on the upcoming maiden voyage of the Motörhead Motorboat Cruise, which was to take place just a few weeks later, in October 2014, as a result of the back problems Mustaine was suffering from (caused by complications from a previous spinal surgery). My good friend Danny Hill, the organizer of the Motorboat events, had been angling to secure Megadeth for one his music cruises for a few years. Now his headliner was dropping off the bill, and he called me in a panic, asking me to explore options for a replacement.

DANNY HILL (ORGANIZER, SHIPROCKED CRUISE) "*A David Ellefson biography is about the stories: the stories of how we randomly met on a Linkin Park tour in 2003, and me pretending not to be star-struck as he pitched Peavey products to me; how he selflessly gave his time to help us raise money for Chi Cheng of the Deftones in 2010; or how he helped us salvage Motörhead's Motorboat with Metal Allegiance in 2014, when Megadeth had to cancel.*

David is a rare breed. One of the few that I know I can count on for honesty, integrity, and to be there no matter what the situation may be. I can say that I'm lucky to call him a true friend."

As we spoke, an idea suddenly hit me. 'How about Metal Allegiance step in as a replacement?' I said. I told Danny that Chris Broderick and I were already planning to be on the boat with Megadeth, and Chris had already participated in Metal Masters, so he knew the drill. Anthrax and Testament were performing on the boat, too, so no doubt they'd pitch in, and rock-star drummers Mike Portnoy and John Tempesta would be on board as well. It seemed like an easy fit—and a no-brainer at that.

Danny loved the idea, and after thirty minutes with the booking agents, the deal was done. Metal Allegiance was now the replacement all-star band for Megadeth.

MARK MENGHI ❝I had decided in April of 2014 that it was time to focus on my two children, and I used that entire spring and summer to figure out what I was gonna do next in life, while spending much-needed time with my children. I still kept in touch with a few artists and music industry friends—not a lot, but Dave was one of them. Remember, Dave and I had an instant bromance dating back from our first NAMM introduction. He called me on a summer morning—August 26, 2014, to be exact—as I was packing up to head to the beach with my kids. I was standing in my kitchen, making sandwiches, and when I picked up the phone, he didn't say, 'Hey man, how are you?' or 'How are you doing?' He said, 'Dude, Megadeth just canceled Motörhead's Motorboat, we're up to bat.'

I initially thought he'd gone back to drinking and drugs as I said, 'Are you crazy? What are we gonna do—jerk each other off on a boat?' Dave wanted to reform the band … the band of misfits that made up Metal Masters. I told him there was no way I could or would even entertain that idea. However … I have something new I am toying with, and it's called Metal Allegiance. I explained to him how I literally just trademarked the name and was saving it for a later date, as at that point in time I wanted out of music and the business altogether.

I was mentally done with the music business. But Dave being Dave, he convinced me the time was now. And, you know what, he was one hundred percent right. August 26, 2014, is the day my life changed forever. Once I agreed to do this with the Metal Allegiance name, Dave put me in touch with the promoter of Motorboat, a few back and forth conversations that day, and Metal Allegiance was booked on Motörhead's Motorboat Cruise.

Later that evening, I called Charlie, Frank, Scott, Philip, Chuck—they were all booked on the boat already, with their respective bands—to tell them that I am coming aboard with a thing called Metal Allegiance, and we're starting over. Every single one of them agreed to participate without hesitation. ❞

I felt good that I could help save the day, and that the community pitched in to help for the greater good. Again, I think that is often my role in life … to help make lemonade out of lemons! I love these impromptu 'leave your ego at the door' kinds of events, where everyone rallies together to support and create unity for the fans and our genre. To me, that's the heart of rock'n'roll, and that has always been the heart of Metal Allegiance—bringing the community together as friends, to make some great music, just like we did as kids.

In Metal Allegiance, all the members have full-time jobs in other major-league bands. As odd it may seem, it can be easy to lose the plot and lose the joy of just playing music for fun, because this is our career. The schedules, budgets, agendas, and career plans are important, but they can steer you off the course of just enjoying music. For me, Metal Allegiance had become just that—an outlet for good friends to have fun making great music together.

A great example of that is how we were in the backstage band catering area, after the first show, and Alex Skolnick was grabbing a quick dinner before his set with Testament. We got talking, and it seemed we all knew some Van Halen songs, and a few others were discussed as well. We discovered we'd all shared essentially the same record collection as kids! A true bond was formed, and Portnoy, Menghi, and I quickly invited Alex to join us for our second Metal Allegiance show. Literally minutes before our second and final show on the boat, we sat with Alex and ran over what would become our debut performance of side one of Van Halen's first album, the setlist created as we marched up the stairs to the outdoor deck where we would play our set on that night.

MARK MENGHI ❝*Two very important things happened on that boat to shape the course of Metal Allegiance. Number one: Alex Skolnick. Number two: deciding to write a record. This all happened within a twenty-four-hour span. We had a day off* *in Cozumel, Mexico, where the boat docked for the day. I went out and ventured around Cozumel with a good buddy of mine, Darren 'Bubbers' Sanders. He's the brother of Troy Sanders of Mastodon, and he was teching for us.*

Darren and I got into some light cocktail mischief while enjoying some Mexican fun. As we were walking back to the boat he split off, and I ventured into the artist catering area on the boat with a broken straw hat on, a local drink in hand, and shorts and sandals, and I saw Dave, the Anthrax fellas, Portnoy, and Alex Skolnick all having dinner together. I stumbled over to them and pointed at Alex and said, obnoxiously loud, 'Dude, you are jamming with us tomorrow—Dave, can you work it out?' and proceeded to stumble back to my cabin on the boat. Low and behold, they worked out a Van Halen portion for our second show the following day. Alex completely shredded, and he was now part of Metal Allegiance. 🎵

There was magic in the air that night—the fans and the band became one under the flag of heavy metal on a boat in the middle of the Caribbean. We all knew the songs because they were the backdrop to all of our teenage years—the songs that formed us into the metal stars we've become in our own right.

MARK MENGHI *At this point in time, there was a serious storm going down in the Caribbean. The boat couldn't dock at one of the locations, which was Key West, Florida. Dave, Mike, and I were just hanging on a balcony on the side of the ship, talking, and I remember asking Dave, 'What is that giant Island we keep circling?'*

'Dude, that's Cuba!' he replied.

Right then and there, the idea came from, I believe, Mike, who said we should get together and write a record of original material.

We were wondering who we could get to play guitar. Who would venture into something like this? Is this even possible? We'd done the cover thing long enough, and as much as we loved doing it, we all agreed the next step was to write some original music and bring what we started with Metal Masters to a whole new level with Metal Allegiance. Has an all-star cover band ever attempted to get together to write original music? Can we get all genres of metal to join us? There were so many unknowns, but we just decided to do it and not give a shit what anyone thinks.

The main question that kept coming up in our talks was who we could we get to play guitar, and I mentioned Alex. I thought he would be the perfect fit. 🗲🗲

Portnoy suggested Skolnick, Menghi, and I go to his house in early December to begin writing some songs. We didn't know what we would create, but the buzz about Metal Allegiance on the Motorboat was huge, and we were excited to see what this eclectic batch of metal merry men would compose together.

We met at *Casa de Portnoy* in eastern Pennsylvania during the first week of December 2014. Alex, Mike, and I began throwing some riffs at each other, under the musical direction of Mark, to create what would become an epic thrash record. That first night we wrote the tracks 'Scars' and 'Destination Nowhere,' *plus* we had the makings of two more. And so it was, the magic of Metal Allegiance continued!

The next day, Mark came out to Mike's house from Long Island, New York. Listening to what we had created, Mark picked up a bass and began chugging out some really cool riffs that had a sort of Black Sabbath darkness, but with a Pantera swagger. We quickly set to work on his ideas, and suddenly two more songs, 'Gift Of Pain' and 'Let Darkness Fall,' were birthed that afternoon.

Later that evening, I picked up a guitar and wrote 'Wait Until Tomorrow,' which was titled as such from a demo vocal Mike laid down a few days later. The music for 'Pledge Of Allegiance' and 'Can't Kill The Devil' was laid down next, and our spirits were as high as high can be! The session was a true success, and like all great bands with momentum, we wanted more. It was agreed that we would reconvene a month later to write a final batch of songs to complete a full-length LP.

MARK MENGHI 66*After a lot of back and forth via text and email, Mike, Alex, Dave, and myself were at Mike Portnoy's house to begin writing for the first Metal Allegiance album not even two months later.*

At this point in time, I was still a behind-the-scenes dude, but then Dave and Mike asked me to be a part of the creative process and be a part of the writing team. I was in shock that they wanted this unknown musician to be a part of this all-star writing team.

Dave put it best. 'You're one of us. The public might not know you, but we certainly know what you can do.' And from that point on, the 'core four' writing team of Metal Allegiance was born. We spent a few days in December at Mike's, came home to enjoy the holidays with our families, and resumed writing in January back in Pennsylvania. 99

We paid for all the travel out of our own pockets, and by working at *Casa de Portnoy*, we had few recording or lodging expenses. I chose to stay at home for the second writing session, but via Skype I brought in the instrumental 'Triangulum' and tweaked a few parts of 'Wait Until Tomorrow.' Mike tracked drums for the songs at his home studio, and we were on our way.

With the music written, the drums recorded, and singers and guest musicians selected to participate with us on the LP, we moved on to record the overdubs at the famed Sabelius Studios on Long Island. Menghi, Skolnick, and I gathered in February and March to finish recording and produce the album, at which point Portnoy got the attention of metal A&R god Monte Conner, who came out to the studio from New York City to hear some cuts.

Monte seemed genuinely blown away by what he heard, and he offered us a generous recording contract with Nuclear Blast—with an option on a second album. We secured a publishing advance, a manager, and a booking agent, and now things were in full swing.

MARK MENGHI ❝*We wrote nine songs in a span of eight days between December of 2014 and January of 2015. We started recording in February, in Roslyn, New York. We recorded the entire album before we even had a record deal. We spent our own money, our own time, and our own resources. It was simply four dudes in a room, making music for the love of making music. We called all of our friends to participate, and again, without hesitation, they all agreed to take part in this monstrous task.*

Now think about this. Over the course of nine months, from December 2014 to September 2015, we wrote, recorded, mixed, and mastered a full-length album, featuring over twenty-five musicians, signed a global record deal with Nuclear Blast Entertainment, and released the record on September 18—while holding a massive record-release show back at the site of Metal Masters 2 in New York City, at the Best Buy Theater. Talking about coming full circle.

I am completely grateful and humbled that Dave and I had that brief encounter many years ago at NAMM. Look where we are now: he is back on top of the world with Megadeth, a co-founder in Metal Allegiance, and is rocking with EMP. I am proud to be working with Dave, but even prouder to be his friend. We have had many, many great moments together over the years, from dual-bass-playing together onstage and writing many tunes together. ❞

We did it. We were really in the game now with Metal Allegiance, and with all of my Megadeth work going away the previous year, this was a godsend, both creatively and financially. And as much as my true *allegiance* is to Megadeth, it has been a blessing to find different personal and creative outlets away from it in these other seasons. Somehow, the Good Lord finds a way when there seems to be no other way. It's all part of the continuing renaissance of life!

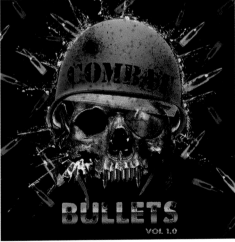

ABOVE Rockin' the stage on the *Dystopia* world tour, 2016. Photo by Rick Triana. **LEFT** *Combat Bullets Vol 1.0,* the debut release from our revived label.

ABOVE Onstage with Metal Allegiance, September 2015. Photo by Ignacio Orellana. **RIGHT** A day off in Nashville while recording the *Dystopia* LP in 2015. **BELOW RIGHT** At the 2014 Houston Comic-Con with Marvel creator Stan Lee.

LEFT The debut album by Metal Allegiance, the all-star band featuring Mark Menghi, Alex Skolnick, Mike Portnoy, and me. BELOW Onstage with Metal Allegiance at the Best Buy Theater, New York City, September 2015. Photo by Rick Triana.

RIGHT The Grammy-winning Megadeth album *Dystopia*.
BELOW Onstage in Phoenix in 2016, playing the opening bass part to 'Peace Sells … But Who's Buying?' Photo by Rick Triana.

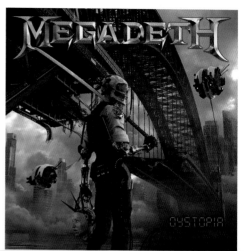

LEFT Julie and me relaxing at the Grammys following our win in 2017. **BELOW LEFT** With my childhood friend Greg Handevdit in 2016. We have remained best mates since grade school.

ABOVE Dinner with the Coopers in Scottsdale. *Left to right*: Dash Cooper, Thom Hazaert, Alice Cooper, Roman Ellefson, and me. Photo by Melody Myers.
RIGHT Backstage with Post Malone in Stockholm, Sweden. He has a super-sweet Megadeth 'So Far, So Good … So What!' tattoo. It's fun to see artists of all genres being influenced by our music.

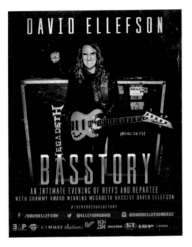

ABOVE The admat we used to launch and advertise our Basstory events around the world. **TOP RIGHT** With Mary Jane's grave at the Jackson County Historical Museum in Lakefield, Minnesota. **CENTER RIGHT** Promoting my love of Ellefson Coffee Co. from my home kitchen in Scottsdale. **BELOW RIGHT** Hosting the book tour for Alice Cooper bassist Dennis Dunaway in Phoenix, Arizona.

ABOVE Onstage with my dear friend, Anthrax bassist Frank Bello, during an Altitudes & Attitude show. Photo by Boris Danielsen.

LEFT Frank and me on the cover of *Bass Player* magazine, January 2019. Photo courtesy of Future plc.

4.3 WATCHING THE WARHEADS RUST

In a surprising twist of fate, I was asked to be part of the Metal All Stars tour of Europe in November 2014. The tour's organizer is now notorious for putting the names and faces of famous heavy-metal musicians on posters and websites to trick fans into thinking there would be this second-coming-of-Christ level all-star tour. It was all bullshit. The promoters would apparently offer a ton of money, fans would buy the tickets, and then, lo and behold, there was no tour. He was finally caught by the FBI and indicted on fraud charges ... but not before I was called on to participate in the final round, all of this unbeknown to me at the time.

As was typical with Metal All Stars, the month-long tour of Europe was suddenly rescheduled to include only one date in La Paz, Bolivia, and another in São Paulo, Brazil. I opted to keep my commitment and go, but many didn't. As it turns out, the support act for the two shows would be Brazilian prog-metal act Angra, featuring guitarist Kiko Louriero.

Ozzy Osbourne's guitarist, Gus G., had been advertised to be on the shows too, but he opted out due to the wishy-washy nature of the organizer. As a result, vocalist Geoff Tate (formerly of Queensrÿche) was now in need of a guitarist to perform his two songs in the show, as well as a few other select songs for which Gus G. had been scheduled to cover guitar duties. Kiko was asked to fill in. After running over the songs for an hour or so at the hotel in La Paz with Geoff, Kiko had his parts dialed and ready for action.

KIKO LOUREIRO (GUITARIST, MEGADETH) ❝❝*I first met Ellefson at the NAMM show—I think we did some signings together for Hartke and Samson. Then I was with my band, Angra, in South America—Bolivia and São Paulo—and it happened that they needed a guitar player to play some songs, so I said, 'Okay, I can learn the songs and help you guys out.' I played a few songs with Geoff Tate, Vinnie Appice, and David, and it was awesome. We played a Sabbath song, and a Queensrÿche song, and then in São Paulo they asked me again to go and play with them. That night, David asked me for my phone number, just in case …*❞❞

The next day, we were all at soundcheck in La Paz, running through the set. I played through the Tate songs with Kiko, and I noticed what an absolute gem of a player he was. He had a super-light touch on the guitar, and he was a virtual acrobat onstage—he could pretty much play anything you threw at him with the greatest of ease. I took note of this and asked for his phone and email information. I felt a change was coming again in Mega-land, and Kiko might just be the light at the end of the tunnel.

You see, just a week or so prior, I had caught wind that Broderick and Drover might exit Megadeth, probably by the end of November. Ironically, Dave had called me the night I was in La Paz and asked me what I thought about getting Nick Menza and Marty Friedman back in the band, adding that the management was pressuring him to do it. Assuming Marty might not even be into the idea, I expressed my concern that the first thing we needed to do was get in a rehearsal room with Nick and see if he could even play drums.

Nick had had quite a down spell in his years away from Megadeth, and although I'd always liked him, this was the big leagues, and the drumming of his I'd seen on YouTube in recent months was not going to cut it in the band in this day and age. In a lot of ways, I think drummers have it the worst with aging—and even more so with guys like Nick, who faced the challenges of age, physical conditioning, and his own bar, which he set so high when he was at his physical peak back in his twenties.

Dave and I made a plan to get together at his house in December, just before Christmas. It was clear on Nick's arrival that day that he was not going to be physically ready for the demands of a world tour. I ran through a few songs with him, and though he was surprisingly able to play things like 'Killing Is My Business,' he was less impressive on the songs he'd recorded with the band, like 'Symphony Of Destruction.'

As a sober guy for almost twenty-four years at that point, I couldn't put my finger on what was happening with Nick, but I knew he was not in possession of his full mental faculties. As always, I tried to be the cheerleader and diplomat for the effort, but just like in 1998, I had to agree with Dave that Nick was not going to make the cut.

A month later, during the winter NAMM show, I called a band dinner meeting in Anaheim, so that Dave, Nick, Marty, Ron Laffitte, and I could discuss the reality of whether this *Rust In Peace* lineup was going to go ahead. Because I had been forced to fend for myself so many times over the years with Megadeth, when it came to common sense, I was the one pretty much calling the shots with the management at this point.

Ron seemed detached. I sensed that with his prior history of managing the band in the 1990s, he probably had some lingering reservations about fully engaging with all of this again. We already knew that Nick was unlikely to be physically able to do the gig, and Marty, though he was going along with the charade for now, was happily enjoying his own career as a solo artist in Japan. To me, it seemed clear that the stars were not aligning.

Dave and I rode over to the restaurant together in a chauffeured black Chevrolet Suburban, to show our loyalty as Team Megadeth. Upon our arrival, Dave quickly went upstairs to be seated at our table, hoping to avoid any real face-to-face time with Ron, who was barely even at the helm at this point. Nick showed up next, sulking and feeling like an outsider. Finally, Marty arrived with a full TV camera crew in tow, there to film footage for some sort of reality TV show he was part of.

Dave agreed to let the cameras film the dinner, partly as a way to have the meeting documented. Honestly, the conversations about the old days were sort of fun, and there was a sense of camaraderie around our accomplishments all those years ago. Then, after our meal, the conversation quickly turned to the reunion, the impending new album, and the tour. While Nick sulked in the corner, Ron stated, 'Rock is dead,' to which Marty replied, 'If you think rock is dead, you don't know what you're talking about!' The mood at the table grew tense—it was like we were all different islands, trying to come together with a common vision.

I brought up the idea that we should do what KISS did with their reunion in 1996—push back the idea of a new album and just do a summer tour. The 2015 Mayhem Festival tour had been announced, and we already knew it was going to have Slayer on it. Ron liked the idea, and it seemed a plausible course of action to pursue—one that would take some of the pressure off of us having to immediately go in and cut a new record with this lineup. I thought it would allow us to see how we actually got along onstage and on the road, and perhaps help us find our footing before embarking on a new album together.

At the very least, the tour idea would provide a means to explore the highly anticipated fan-favorite reunion tour. And if the reunion only lasted the summer, then so be it. We would have at least *tried* it, and we could let it truly rest (or rust) in peace after that. Dave and I could move on finding new members for the band, and we could all get on with our lives.

I called Ron the following day, and we shared our disappointment about how the dinner meeting had gone, and how it was quite clear that we were all far away from the reunion happening. One of the big issues was money. Nick's manager had the grand idea of asking for $7,500 per week, which was far beyond the salary cap in the band anyway, let alone what a returning member who had been let go so many years before might deserve. In addition to that, he wanted to use his own drums and cymbals, and call his own shots, when in fact Dave had arranged through his endorsement deal with Dean to have their drum brand, DDrum, provide a kit.

After speaking to Ron, I called Nick and told him straight: 'Just accept Dave's salary and endorsement offers. My experience is, just get on board and things will work out. You've been out of the spotlight for years so just get on board and let's go.' Even as I was telling him this, however, there was the bigger issue of his current state of health, and whether he could actually play the songs in his current capacity. (This isn't meant out of any posthumous disrespect to Nick—it was simply a fact.)

Within a few days, Marty put forth *his* salary request, which was double what Nick was asking for, and now the entire deal was dead in the water. Honestly, I think Dave and I were relieved. As much as it meant we were back to the drawing board when it came to rebuilding the band, at least we could hold our heads high, knowing that we had explored every possible option to reunite the famed *Rust In Peace* lineup, and that it was not our fault that it didn't work.

•

Since I successfully re-joined Megadeth in 2010, not only had Dave and I had a chance to start a new friendship and brotherhood but we'd also navigated some tricky business and career transitions. And, at the end of the day, we came out the other side stronger for it. No, the reunion everyone wanted didn't happen. But no one can say we didn't try.

BOBBY GUSTAFSON (FORMER GUITARIST, OVERKILL) ❝❝*Back in the early days of Overkill, I went out to California with my friend Metal Maria [Ferraro], who worked at Megaforce. She became friends with Dave—Metallica was here when Dave was still in the band, and worked with Jonny Z. and whatnot, and we became friends as well.*

This was obviously after Dave was out of the band, and Maria wanted to take a trip to California, and I was like, 'Yeah, I'll go with you.' So we drove out to California, and my brother was out there; she stayed with the band, and I think I stayed with my family. I have some pictures from the Country Club—I think they might have done a show in LA first, before they went up to San Francisco. And it was a great show—Hirax, Laaz Rockit, and Dark Angel. All those bands took off, too.

We drove up to see that second show in the Bay Area—I know it was with Exodus, and I think it might have been with Slayer. One night, we went by their practice spot, which was in some huge warehouse type of place in Rosemead, where there was just a ton of bands. We went there, then we drove up to San Francisco and saw them there, and then on one of the days when we had off we said, 'Lets do something,' and we went to Knott's Berry Farm. We just took off and had a day and hung out— we were hanging out at the apartment that they both shared.

I remember one day, going up on the roof with Dave, and this is before the album was even out. And we were sitting up on this rooftop, in lounge chairs, talking about what we wanted to do for the future. We were both young kids, and we were like, 'We're gonna be rock stars' and 'We're gonna do this and do that' … we had just gotten signed to Megaforce, and I'm like, 'Yeah, I'm gonna do my first album.' This was before our first album—this was, like, '85, before either of us had anything out yet—and we're talking about becoming big rock stars and stuff.

Obviously, Megadeth got a lot bigger than we did at that time, but we stayed friends. After Peace Sells I saw them at L'Amour, and I saw them at another place called Manhattans that was in New Jersey, or just over the border in New York. We had our second album out, and we'd opened up for Helloween for two months in Europe, then we were home for two days, and then we started the Peace Sells tour, down in Tampa. That tour was just great. With that album, with them kind of made up on the back, there were tons of girls at every show. After playing with Slayer and Helloween, and there's no girls, the Megadeth tour was awesome.

We just had a great time. The only sore spot was a show in Philadelphia, where I think Dave was having it out one night with Gar [Samuleson]. Gar had thrown a stick out into the audience, but it end up hitting Dave in the back, and it stuck between his guitar strap and his back, and he just turned around, like, 'What the fuck?' He went over to the side of the stage, and one of the roadies had pulled the stick out and showed it to him, and he just stood there for, like, two minutes with his back to the audience, just staring at Gar. We were kind of thinking, Wow, they are gonna kill each other. Stuff was breaking backstage. Dave wanted to call the whole tour off. So I was in the back of their bus, I was like, 'Let me go talk to them.' It was me, Dave, and Mike Schnapp. Dave was like, 'I can't take this anymore. I can't stand those guys. I don't want to play with them.' He was like, 'Do you want to join the band?'

I'm like, Oh, man … at that point, I didn't know my drummer was gonna quit at the end of the tour, so I'm thinking, Man, our album just came out, it's doing pretty well … I dunno if I can do that. It turned out that the end of that tour is when Rat [Skates] left, and that was weird for us. But we kind of stayed in touch, and I'd see them here and there. I don't know if I ever really regretted not playing with them, 'cause I don't know if we would've stayed together. We may have only done one album—who knows with what was going on at that point? But at that point, I felt like I was secure with Overkill—we really started to grab momentum after that tour, and the Slayer tour, and Helloween. And I'd put so much time and effort into Overkill.

Later in the year, after Overkill opened on the Peace Sells tour, we had sort of a temporary drummer, 'cause we did the Christmas On Speed show with them—

95

that was in Leeds, England, in December, and we met up again. Obviously they headlined, and we opened, and we got a chance to hang out again. And Dave was trying to push Nick Menza on us—he was their roadie at that point. Chuck [Treece] was Gar's roadie, and then after Gar was gone, Chuck was playing drums, and Nick Menza was his roadie.

So Chuck had played the show, but Nick was his roadie, and he was like, 'Nick's a good drummer, why don't you try him out for your band?' I had heard Nick was doing a book, too, and he said he never forgot this day either, but when we first met with him, and we told him about that, the first thing out of his mouth was, 'How much are you gonna pay me?' We were like, 'Oh, that's the first thing you're worried about?' So that didn't work out. He didn't come with us, but he ended up being in Megadeth, which I think was a good thing anyway—they did some of their best material with him. But that was kind of funny. 🗝

RYAN GREENE ❝*I had a great time with Megadeth, recording the demos for Countdown To Extinction. I got off the elevator and the hallways were lined with road case after road case, and I just remember thinking, Holy shit, this is a lot of gear to do a preproduction recording.*

Menza was funny—he was the first one I met—and right away we were joking about his massive kit taking up half the tracking room, then Ellefson walked in, and right when you thought the jokes would stop, they kept on going. I remember it like it was yesterday, and I wish everyone could experience a session like that.

The band knew exactly what they wanted and were very sure of how they wanted the recording to sound, and they were one hundred percent confident on the direction. They walked in prepared—there was no fucking around. It didn't hurt that they were all killer players. I remember when it was time to get Mustaine's guitar sound, he wanted to hear every speaker on every cabinet, so I mic'd up five Marshall stacks and we went through every speaker until he said, 'That's the cab.' When we started tracking guitars, Mustaine got into a stance and looked at me and said, 'I'm ready.' I pressed record and he ripped though the song. I was thinking he has to make a mistake at some point, but he played the song top to bottom flawlessly.

When we were tracking, Marty asked if he could write the song title names on the spines of the tape boxes, and at the end of the session I went to put the two-inch tape reels in the boxes and noticed he'd written all the names of the songs in Japanese. Years later, Mustaine called, asking if I knew where the two-inch tapes were from the session, because EMI couldn't find them. I suggested to have them search for anything written in Japanese. They found them. 🎵

•

On May 22, we were in Albany, New York, with Megadeth, ready to perform at the Rock & Derby festival, when Dave rang me in my room at 4am, hysterical.

'Nick's dead!' he exclaimed through the tears.

I was trying to get my bearings at such an early hour of the day when Dave explained that his son, Justis, had called him and told him the news—that Nick had died onstage at the Baked Potato in Studio City, California, while playing drums for Megadeth alumnus Chris Poland's jazz band, OHM.

I was shocked and in disbelief. It turns out he had suffered a *massive* heart attack just before the group's third song of the night and was pronounced dead on arrival at the hospital, although paramedics tried to revive him.

The next day, at breakfast, Dave's mind was racing with ways we could help Nick's two young boys. He wanted to host a concert featuring all former members of Megadeth to raise money for the Menza family. He even mentioned it in interviews later that day at the venue, before our show, which got people excited about the prospect of such a monumental show. Unfortunately, as big as Dave's heart was to think of such a cool idea, we were about to begin a huge campaign for our new album, *Dystopia*, and the schedule of tours in motion simply didn't allow for it.

As sad as it is that Nick is gone, I was told that he was at real peace with his life in the weeks before his death. And, in hindsight, I'm really glad we made the attempt for the *Rust In Peace* reunion. Although it didn't pan out, we all made the effort. And, in the end, Nick got to leave the planet doing what he loved best—playing his drums onstage, for his fans. In a way, it brought a poetic and peaceful ending to a larger-than-life character who gave so much with his life, his music, and his charm. May he rest in peace.

4.4 GET IT OUT

One evening in London, on the Big Four tour of Europe, Frank Bello and I were performing a dual-bass clinic for Hartke, who proudly endorsed both of us. I suggested to Frank that we write some songs together, even if just for use as backing tracks for our bass clinics. I hate getting up in front of a music-store audience and just playing along to a CD of previously recorded music. I'd rather have something new and fresh for the event.

'Let's do what Steve Bailey and Victor Wooten did with their *Bass Extremes*,' I said.

After some discussion, Frank suggested we enlist Anthrax producer Jay Ruston as our third wheel. Jay is a bassist, a terrific producer, and someone Frank trusts, which is important.

FRANK BELLO ❝*Dave and I were backstage waiting to go on, and he said, 'We're doing all this jamming at these clinics … why don't we write some songs to play at them?' That was the moment Altitudes & Attitude was born. Dave and I started to write some songs together, and then got our friend Jay Ruston on board to produce. Jay really got what we wanted to from the start because he also plays bass, and it's been a great musical experience ever since. We were really psyched to hear people's very positive reaction to the idea of the two bass players from thrash-metal bands Megadeth and Anthrax doing a 'hard rock' project.* ❞

A couple of months later, Frank introduced me to Jay at the *Bass Player* LIVE! event at the Key Club in Los Angeles. He was right—Jay was super-chill guy, and he was really excited to be approached about such a unique endeavor: two well-known bassists making a record together. Quickly thereafter, Frank and I began emailing song and riff ideas to each other. Frank sent me some mostly completed ideas that he had masterfully created for guitar and vocal.

As it turns out, Frank is a very charismatic singer who composes some super-catchy and fun little three-minute songs. I was blown away, and within a few email exchanges between Jay, Frank, and me, it was decided we could go to Jay's studio in Sherman Oaks, California, to cut some tracks.

Frank came through my hometown of Phoenix with Anthrax in the fall of 2013. I picked him up, and once we were at my house we sat down with acoustic guitars and did a simple little preproduction on two of his songs, 'Booze & Cigarettes' and 'Tell The World,' which were already mostly done.

I threw some riffs and song ideas at him that were largely arranged but just needed some vocal melodies and lyrics. Frank is great at being able to hum a simple melody to my songs, which helps me start phrasing lyrics. That's how the song 'Here Again' came into being. I had the riffs, and once Frank helped me get a vocal melody, the lyrics easily fell into place.

Bass parts for Frank's songs came to me immediately. Suddenly, a whole new world of bass playing opened up for me—stuff I hadn't explored since I was a teenager, when skinny-tie new-wave bands like Joe Jackson and The Cars came onto the scene. Suddenly, I was out of my metal zone and just being in the moment with the music, having no expectations or preexisting models to conform to. This was so liberating!

As Frank and I volleyed ideas to each other in Jay's studio, the three of us were like young music fans all over again. While Frank and I have our roles in our other bands, it was so invigorating to be creating something brand new, from the ground up. I had so much fun breaking out my alt-rock bass licks, and playing bass for another respected bass player like Frank was really exciting.

When Frank writes songs, he isn't thinking about bass. I guess the same is true for me and my songs, too. So, to present bass ideas without resistance was really a refreshing approach.

Jay recommended we bring in Jeff Friedl—known for his work with Eagles Of Death Metal and A Perfect Circle—to cut the drum tracks. We only had three songs to begin with, so after a day of preproduction at Jay's studio, we rented a larger drum room over in Burbank to cut the tracks. Jeff is incredible. He's super-fast, he plays great parts, and he's a lovely human being.

We then took the tracks back to Jay's studio and began the final overdubs. It was in that moment that the name Altitudes & Attitude came to me, so I suggested it as a band name. It seemed to fit the music, the vibe, the intent, and now the outcome of the songs. We were creating something that was uplifting (*altitude*) yet it still had our metal teeth (*attitude*). In some ways, Frank's songs created the altitude, and mine had the attitude. It was a perfect match!

We discussed our options for releasing the three songs and decided that Missi Callazzo at Megaforce Records (also home to Anthrax) would be the best choice. She had grown up with Frank and his uncle, Anthrax drummer and founder Charlie Benante, and she understood our desire to have a voice away from our regular bands. Missi loved the songs and agreed to release them as an EP in January 2014. She pushed out 'Booze & Cigarettes' to our friends at Sirius radio, and before long we had a little hit on our hands. We then debuted the act live during the winter NAMM show with Metal Masters at the House of Blues in Anaheim.

A week later, we did a press junket in New York City with the then-new LoudWire news site, and we were invited by Eddie Trunk to appear on VH1's *That Metal Show*. Earlier that day, we enlisted videographer Matt Hanrahan to shoot a video for our second single, 'Tell The World.' It was below zero outside, so when you see us freezing on a park bench in Chelsea, we are not faking it. We really were freezing.

Fans and media alike seemed to like and appreciate A&A. They know our history, and the history of our bands, and because we aren't leaving our bands to go solo, they appreciate our efforts to put ourselves out there in a different genre, away from thrash metal. In a nutshell, that's what A&A is: two musicians stepping into each other's shoes to do something neither of us would do on our own. We lift each other up and help each other to explore new avenues and be comfortable stepping out of our comfort zones. Frank playing guitar and singing, me playing guitar and writing lyrics, both of us playing the eight-string bass guitar, and so forth.

Almost four years later, in January 2019, our full-length LP, *Get It Out*, was released, again via Megaforce in North America and Europe and via EMP/Universal in Japan. It's a continuation of the process we've enjoyed since 2013. It's so great when music can remain fun, which is exactly what A&A is.

FRANK BELLO ❝*The EP really resonated with people, and that led to a full-length Altitudes & Attitude record being released in 2019. Altitudes & Attitude is a whole different vibe for Dave and me. As I mentioned before, the idea of it came from Dave suggesting to me during a bass clinic that we should write some songs, so we could play something different at these clinics. That thought spawned a creative outlet for us that we genuinely enjoy and have a great time with. We just bounce ideas off of each other until it feels right. It works because we have a lot of fun just writing hard rock songs. Dave and Jay were really behind me stepping up to the microphone for the vocals, which I will always be thankful to them for.*❞

As of the time of this writing, the *Get It Out* LP has successfully hit the the Top 40 at rock radio, and even the Top 10 on the Classic Rock Radio chart. Our fans and colleagues have given it rave reviews, which gives a real validation to Frank and me as artists in a new setting. Additionally, my dear friend Slash was kind enough to let us open some of his shows across Europe as a way to support our new venture. This is once again a real testimony to musical friendships.

In many big bands, there is a method to how things operate, and defined roles for each member—even more so as success builds. But often creative outlets away from those groups are needed to help musicians get a sense of exploration and validation of their ideas. As much as Frank and I are in two of the world's biggest thrash metal acts, we create other music that would never fit inside Anthrax or Megadeth. Rather than create conflicts inside our bands, A&A has provided a cool outlet for us to take our exploratory compositions and make sure they have a vehicle to be heard. And, it turns out, our fans really like to hear this side of us, too!

5

A NEW MUSICAL JOURNEY

5.1 DYSTOPIA

Throughout 2014, Dave was writing new songs. We jammed a few of them backstage on tour earlier in the year, and one of them became 'Dystopia.' I even spent some time with Dave at his home studio in Fallbrook, California, in June, laying down bass parts to his ideas and presenting a few new riffs of my own.

One thing that was clear with this next album is that we needed to get back to our thrash roots. We weren't quite there yet, mostly because we had gotten stuck in a rut in the mindset of the 90s, when managers urged us to write 'radio hits.' As a result, we'd spent the last fifteen years trying to get back to our roots of just being a kickass thrash band. But this next album *had* to be the album to put us back on top. To his credit, Ron Laffitte said as much, too, and as much as it sucked to have so many weeks of touring taken off the calendar, given the resulting loss of income, writing the best album possible was our top priority.

Ironically, during the *RIP* reunion discussions, Marty Friedman had brought along some new musical paradigms to share with Dave and me, mostly to do with drummers and energetic riffs. Whether he was in Megadeth or not, he wanted to see the band energized and enlightened with a freshness that he felt we hadn't enjoyed for many years. I firmly believe that his 'forest from the trees' insights helped turn the corner as Dave began to write the thrash frenzy of *Dystopia*.

One of the reasons Marty left Megadeth in 1999 was that he wanted to explore new musical horizons. He was intrigued by the younger generations of musicians. Now, all these years later, he was sharing with Dave and me his discovery of hotshot young drummers and how their youthfulness might very well provide a much-needed energy burst to Megadeth's music.

Still more ironic was the fact that, just before Dave and I headed over to the ill-fated *RIP* reunion band dinner at NAMM, we had gotten word that hotshot thrash drummer Chris Adler from Lamb Of God might be interested in cutting the drum tracks to the next Megadeth album, if we were still looking for someone by the time we entered the studio. We all knew Chris, and it was a stated fact that he was a massive Megadeth fan, *So Far, So Good … So What!* having been the album that got him in the music game as a teenager. With that knowledge, we knew that as the *RIP* meetings were going south by the minute, we would soon land on our feet with a lineup that could come in and kick ass and get down to business.

A few months later, in February 2015, I was tracking the Metal Allegiance album in Long Island when I received a call one evening from Dave, who told me he was going to change managers once again. This time he was doing so at the urging of Chris, who had just commissioned the very credible heavy-metal management firm 5B to manage Lamb Of God. I knew the 5B guys and fully trusted their instincts, so I was happy to hear of Dave's decision.

Dave and I were speaking almost daily during this period. Once again it was back to just 'Dave & Dave.' We discussed a shortlist of new potential guitar players, and one thing he assured me is that no matter who came into the band next, I would always be the highest-paid second member of the group. This was comforting, and I thanked him for it.

Although Dave and I had been through hell and back a gazillion times by this point, I think he knew I could have walked out of the door at any point, given the recent debacles, but instead I stayed to soldier on with him. I was on his team. Through thick and thin, we remained the heart and soul of this thing called Megadeth.

•

I was happy the ill-fated *Rust In Peace* reunion attempt was behind us. It was now time to move forward, whatever our fate may be. I felt comfortable with 5B managing the band. They had the right instincts to lead us where we needed to go, with bigger moves and bigger looks for the band at this stage of our career. It was time to work smarter, not just harder. The next steps would be to find a new guitarist and a new producer, and to make an album.

One morning in late February, Dave called me and told me he found our new guitar player.

'Yeah? Who?' I calmly replied.

'Kiko Loureiro!' he said. He had watched videos of Kiko and could see that he could play all the electric stuff, but he also liked his Brazilian nylon-string jazz-guitar chops. Dave clearly wanted a real guitar team again, like the old days, with Chris Poland or Marty.

'That's great!' I said. I told him I had just played with Kiko back in November, at the Metal All Stars shows. I offered to reach out to him, which I did via email.

'Your number came up!' I told Kiko. 'Do you want an audition with Megadeth?'

Kiko had relocated from São Paulo to Los Angeles about a year earlier for just this sort of opportunity. He told me he had just gotten home from a tour with his band, Angra, but would get right on with creating the three-song audition videos we'd asked him to film.

The truth is, Dave had already made up his mind that Kiko was the right fit for the band. He's like that. When he's ready to go, he's

106

committed—he doesn't really want to hear *no*, or *let's take a moment to think about it*. He wants to go, now!

KIKO LOUREIRO ❝In February 2015, just a few months after playing with him in South America with Metal All Stars, I got an email from Ellefson: 'Can I call you?' I was like, 'Of course.' So he called me the same day and told me about Megadeth. There was a list of guitar players, and I was on that list, which was cool, and of course I was very excited. Mustaine I think called me the same day. It all happened very fast. I got the email from Ellefson, then he called, and we talked a little bit about songs, and Megadeth, and then Mustaine called me. I remember I was sick—I had a little flu—and I was coming back from a tour. I had to learn four songs in that weekend, and then I flew to Nashville to talk to Mustaine on Monday.

The whole thing was, like, three days, something like that. I remember I was really sick, but I'm like, 'Man. The guys are calling me to join Megadeth—I need to be ready for this audition. I need to learn the songs.' So I was on YouTube, just watching everything on Megadeth. Listening to the songs, watching interviews, whatever, everything, for, like, twenty-four hours.

Then when I was better, maybe a day or two after, I just grabbed my guitar and I learned four songs—'Hangar 18,' 'Symphony,' 'Trust,' and 'Holy Wars'—in two days, and filmed a video to send to Ellefson and Mustaine and the management. Then I flew the next day to Nashville. In the end, it was more conversation—I had a lot of conversations with Mustaine, some more conversations with Ellefson on the phone—and then, maybe fifteen days later, I was in Nashville to record Dystopia. ❞

In March 2015, Kiko and Chris Adler headed to Nashville to join Dave for preproduction on the new album. Because of all the time off the road the past year, I was still busy with other events and endeavors away from Megadeth—I went on my first ever *My Life With Deth* spoken-word tour of Australia that month, and did my first ever solo bass concert in Mexico City—so I wouldn't get to Nashville until a little later.

I headed to Nashville in early April, and once I got there, I was the first one up to bat to record. While there were some rough demo tracks of drums and guitar I could reference, the recording was going to be me by myself, playing bass to a click track, with Dave at my side, going over the parts as I recorded them.

Recording bass before drums is unusual, but the truth is, I can intuitively navigate the musical waters with Dave, without the band around us. When I'm onstage, I groove to the drums, but I know my parts, and I could easily play an entire show without hearing anyone else in my mix. You have to know your parts inside and out, and recording bass by myself was no different.

KIKO LOUREIRO ❝It was all so fast. It was like in a one-month period, a three-week period, from the first email from Ellefson to being there in Nashville, at the studio. And then it was announced, and I was in the studio already, just to hang with Mustaine and Chris Adler, and then David came to the studio to record his bass parts, and we hung out more, and it was cool.❞

The songs were intense. They were like math problems with complex nuances in the fingerings, but Kiko seemed to pick them up with no problem. I think it was a bit of an eye-opener for Adler that this was not going to be four guys in a room, jamming for a month to write a record. Those days are long gone in Megadeth. These days, Dave writes the songs, we all come in and record them, and then we go home when they're completed.

While I will always present new material to Dave when he asks, I've also learned to keep my expectations realistic, as to it being used for final tracks. When I came back to the band in 2010, I refocused my vision on that matter. More than most, I've always respected that Megadeth is Dave's creative vision. While I love to collaborate, each album is different. Still, there is a lot of fun in it all, and I look to guys like Ian Hill of Judas Priest and Cliff Williams of AC/DC—great bassists who hold down the low end for their bands. They may not be the front stars of the group, but they have their place, and you'd certainly know if they *weren't* there.

I guess, in the end, the same is true for me and Megadeth. We all have our place, and mine is being the glue that holds the fabric together. Being the servant rather than the served.

After ten days of intensive recording in Nashville that month, I returned home to Arizona to rest and regroup. A big wave was coming, and I needed to be ready for it.

5.2 MY MEGADETH

When we went into the studio to record *Dystopia*, Chris Adler had a witty yet accurate benchmark for what should be allowable in the 2015 version of the band. As we recorded our musical parts, discussed the live show, and talked about past incarnations of the band, Chris would say, '*My* Megadeth would (or wouldn't) do that!'

'What is *my Megadeth* supposed to mean?' I asked him.

In turned out that Chris tied everything cool about Megadeth back to the album and era when he first heard and first became a fan of the band. That album for him was *Peace Sells … But Who's Buying?* So many of today's major artists have told me that they discovered Megadeth in the period from *Peace Sells* through *Rust In Peace*, all with their own distinct stories of what the band meant to them. Everyone from Creed to Lamb Of God were inspired by that early era of Megadeth, mostly because of the age they were when they started listening to metal.

I get it. 'My KISS' is the *Destroyer* album, which was new on the record-store shelves when I was eleven years old in the summer of 1976. From there, I went back and bought all of their previous albums and became totally immersed in the group and it's earliest history. But *Destroyer* was the album that I went back to, as the benchmark of all things cool for KISS. In fact, I still do today! So, when Adler began to wax philosophic on the things he liked and didn't like about the mid-to-late-90s era of Megadeth, he got our attention.

Kiko Loureiro had his own version of 'My Megadeth,' too, having first seen us perform live at Rock In Rio 1991. As we played several times across South America during the *Dystopia* world tour, he emphasized the importance of the band from *Rust In Peace* onward until today. As Kiko pointed out, because Megadeth's continent-wide penetration of South America didn't really begin until the 1994 release of *Youthanasia*—when the ensuing tour included stops in Chile, Argentina, and Brazil—the band's 80s records aren't as widely recognized by mainstream rock fans there. Aside from show staples like 'Peace Sells,' 'Wake Up Dead,' and 'In My Darkest Hour,' many of the songs from those records were not as popular in Latin America. And he was right!

Having new guys several years younger than Dave and me helped to get Megadeth back on point for *Dystopia* and the three-year tour that followed.

THOM HAZAERT ❝As David and I went around the country on the *Basstory* tour, more and more the Chris Adler 'My Megadeth' story went around and around. David would tell it onstage, talk about his KISS and the fact that my Megadeth was So Far, So Good … So What! After that, fans started telling us about their Megadeth. It truly took on a life of its own.

I got into Megadeth at the tail end of Peace Sells, but the first album I waited for and went to the store to buy on the release date was So Far, So Good … So What! From the opening notes of 'Into The Lungs Of Hell,' the defiant, angry, piss-and-vinegar thrash-punk crossover of that record changed my life—and metal as we all knew it. Megadeth innovated probably more so than any other metal artist, moving forward in leaps and bounds with every new record, and their ascension to greatness truly began, for me, on So Far, So Good … So What!

While I think Peace Sells is a top-to-bottom masterpiece, Rust In Peace is arguably the most important thrash-metal record ever made, and Countdown To Extinction is Megadeth at a whole other level—the point where the band truly hit their stride as world-class songwriters. With the unbridled power and sloppy punk-rock abandon of '502,' 'Liar,' and 'Hook In Mouth,' the haunting atmospherics of 'Mary Jane' and 'In My Darkest Hour'—and not to mention the mind-blowing performance closing out Decline Of Western Civilization Pt. 2—SFSGSW is like a frozen moment in time, forever stamped on my teenage psyche, when Megadeth were literally the coolest fucking band in the world, and no one could ever touch them. I hear often about how they weren't happy with certain aspects of the recording, the mix, the cover, but to me, it is true sonic devastation in its rawest form—and, personally, I wouldn't change a fucking thing. 🙶

MARK TREMONTI (GUITARIST, TREMONTI, ALTER BRIDGE, CREED) 🙶My Megadeth is definitely So Far, So Good … So What! That was my first Megadeth record. I remember the guy's name, John Itchon—this Asian kid I went to school with who gave me a tape—he would photocopy the covers of records and give them out to kids at school. I bought it from him for like five bucks, and I loved it. I went out and bought Peace Sells and Killing Is My Business after that.

I actually went to meet Megadeth at a local record store in Detroit. I went to this meet-and-greet in-store signing, and I didn't really bring anything—I thought they'd have something and they didn't, so I just bought a guitar magazine in the shop. Ellefson actually didn't sign it, he just handed it to Dave Mustaine, because he was on the cover of this magazine and the rest of the guys weren't, so I didn't get his autograph that day. But it was great—that was the first time, those were the first big time celebrities that I had ever met.

I definitely grew up on metal. When I was in grade school, I think The Beastie Boys were probably the biggest band that we all listened to, and then, all of a sudden, I couldn't fall asleep one night, I borrowed a tape from my brother—it was Metallica, Master Of Puppets, and I absolutely fell in love with it and became a metalhead. And from there on out, I just chased down the heaviest, hardest, darkest stuff I could find. Along the way, I found Megadeth, Slayer, Exodus, Testament, Death Angel. Speed metal is my favorite.

I grew up in Detroit, and then we moved to Chicago for a few years, then back to Detroit. Then, when I was fifteen, we moved to Orlando, and I hated it. Those were some of the darkest years of my life. I didn't have many friends; I spent all my time by myself. But if I didn't have those years, I wouldn't have become a songwriter like I am now. You know, when you're fifteen years old, you just hate the world because you have no friends, and you're stripped from your band—I had a great band in Detroit before I moved. And then, when I moved down to Florida, nobody played instruments. I had my four-track, I had all the time in the world to just sit in my room and write angry songs and record them, and I think that's what made me a songwriter—all those years of just being angry with whatever circumstance I was put in, and writing about it.

When I was a kid, I was riding in the back of Mom and Dad's car, listening to 70s soft rock—Rod Stewart, Jerry Rafferty, Seals & Crofts, even Journey. I loved the big melodies of all those old tunes. When I ran into metal and became a songwriter, I tried to combine those worlds, so I tried to write the heaviest thing that was the most fun to play, that still had that melody, because I think melody is the most important part of the song.

And I think a lot of metal bands, they just try to be as heavy as they can possibly be, and the melody just fits in where it can. The way I write is melody first, everything else next. Like I said, I try to cram those two worlds—the speed-metal world and the melodic, 70s soft-rock world—together, to see if I can make them share the same space.

With writing any of the Creed stuff, I kind of had to write outside my own box. When I got together with the guys from Creed, they'd look at me crazy when I had my speed-metal riffs cranking out. I just couldn't do what I did normally—I had to write different stuff. A lot of the years with those guys, I pulled more from that 70s soft-rock part of who I was, and not the metal guy. Even when Alter Bridge happened, I couldn't use that stuff, 'cause I was using the same rhythm section with my band, so I had to wait until my solo project to pull out the fast, speed-metal gallops and the tremolo picking—you know, the speed-metal stuff. It was something that I couldn't use for, how many years? Fifteen? After fifteen or twenty years of being a professional musician, I was so happy to be able to finally do it.

Imagine if you grew up listening to Slayer, Mercyful Fate, Megadeth, and all that stuff, and then you get into a commercial rock band that gets popular, and everybody's asking if you're a Christian band, and all that nonsense. In my mind, I'm like, If you only knew what I grew up playing. It was just circumstance. I just ended up with a certain group of guys that I was writing music for, that didn't dig what I grew up obsessing about. But I worked it out, twenty years later.

Music is such a powerful thing, Megadeth was such a big part of my childhood, and my development as a musician, even if I couldn't play their stuff—it was way beyond me. For many years I couldn't play it, but in my room I had a Megadeth Peace Sells poster, I had the Iron Maiden Somewhere In Time silk flag on my dresser, and I might have had a King Diamond hat, and that was it. Megadeth was such a big part of that. When you're a kid, you can only afford so many things, so I had, like, my favorite twenty bands, and Megadeth were, like, four of those tapes.

I remember going to NAMM a few years ago and seeing David there and speaking with him, and since then we've done a lot of festivals with Megadeth. I first shared a stage with them in '99, at Woodstock, and since then I've shared the stage many times either with my solo band, Tremonti, or with Alter Bridge. We played with Megadeth recently in Barcelona or something—KISS was on the bill, too. Never really in Creed, but we've played with them a lot with my other projects. But I'm still that kid at heart. I got to go play like a seven-week tour with Iron Maiden this year. That was the first band I'd ever seen, and my solo band got to go open for them, and every night I got to say, 'Next up is Iron Maiden.' And that was probably the most badass thing I've gotten to do in my life. **"**

KRISTIAN NAIRN (DJ, MUSICIAN, ACTOR) "I first heard Megadeth around thirteen or fourteen years old. Until then I had studied classical music. I was at my friend's place, and he had the So Far, So Good ... So What! album, and I believe he was playing 'Set The World Afire,' and I had never heard anything like it at the time. I had never heard such aggression before in music—it was all new to me then. I mean, you can go pretty hard on a violin, but ...

After that, a few weeks later, it was a Friday night, there used to be a TV show here called Raw Power, and it was on at, like, three o'clock in the morning, and it was, like, all the current heavy-metal songs of the moment. They played 'Holy Wars,' and I was like, 'Motherfuck. Is that the same band my friend was listening to?' And it was written about my homeland, too ... **"**

When we were on the *So Far, So Good ... So What!* tour, we played up in Northern Ireland, and it was very hostile. It was everything that U2 sang about on 'Sunday Bloody Sunday': machine guns at the border, passport control—the whole thing. And we were onstage and we were trying to just find out what this whole thing was about.

We'd heard about the Protestants and the Catholics, and the North and the South, the British and the Irish. We were asking a question about our merchandising, where was our merchandise, were we getting paid on the merch, and they just said, 'You don't ask about that. That just goes to *The Cause*.' Well, The Cause was a military cause. Onstage,

Dave made an unknowing comment to the effect of, *This one is for The Cause ... anarchy in Ireland!*

As we then ripped into the tune, all hell broke loose—there was some misunderstanding and some very upset local concert organizers. Immediately after the show, we were quickly escorted out of the venue in a bulletproof bus, and they were like, 'You guys need to get out of here, now.'

KRISTIAN NAIRN ❝*I actually had a friend who was at the gig, at a venue called the Antrim Forum. Northern Ireland is a very complicated country. It's very beautiful, and the people are wonderful, but back then, it was slightly more incendiary. And everyone has a different point of view. I believe Dave had spoken to someone backstage and got a point of view. So he plays 'Anarchy In The UK' onstage, makes a comment, and the place went ape-shit and started to riot. The concert had to be cut short. They have these crazy Land Rovers here that are like armored, massive tank-style vehicles, and the band had to be 'rescued.' They avoided Belfast on tour for a while after that, which I don't blame them for. That had to have been an unpleasant experience.*

When I first saw the video for 'Holy Wars,' I thought, Oh, yeah, this is about the Middle East and Iraq. And then I sort of read the lyrics, and I thought, Hang on a minute, is he talking about the gig in Antrim? And then I saw an interview a couple of weeks later, and he talked about it, and it totally was.

'Holy Wars' was actually the first song I learned how to play on guitar, and it's a fucking hard song. Honestly, the day I met them at Hellfest, it meant so much to me to play that song with the band. My whole journey started with that song, and here I am in France, with Dave Mustaine and David Ellefson, Kiko and Dirk, playing that song with them. I got to introduce them onstage that day. It was really an amazing moment.

I love a band that plays in synergy together, really in synergy. I know Megadeth has had a lot of lineup changes over the years, but that is something they somehow always managed to keep together, regardless of who the drummer and guitar player were.

My love of Megadeth has kind of frozen around Youthanasia. My life these days is sort of filled with dance music, like a lot of metalheads around my age group. I busted my ass to be a guitar player for years, but by the time I got to, like, twenty-one, twenty-two, heavy metal was dead. I was trying to join a band, no one wanted to play the kind of stuff I did. So I stopped playing guitar for a long time, and I got into DJ-ing, which I absolutely loved. In dance music, I can find the same emotions in hypnotic bass lines—the same adrenaline—that I can find in metal.

I got to play at Blizzcon—the convention for Blizzard, the company that makes World Of Warcraft. I created a version of the Game Of Thrones theme, as an experiment, with, in the middle I play a guitar solo sort of based on the Game Of Thrones theme, and people fucking go nuts for it. At Blizzcon, at the end of the GOT theme, I decided to do a version of 'Symphony Of Destruction,' and everyone just lost their shit.

It was Blizzard who sent me to Hellfest and got me to interview Megadeth. I get to meet big, famous actors all the time, and, literally, I couldn't give a shit. But that day at Hellfest, I was freaking the whole fucking day. That's what really means something to me, because that's what everything is built on for me. I was a very shy teenager, and I sort of channeled what I was feeling into the music, and that's why it's so emotional for me. I think a lot of us were troubled teenagers, and that's where the angst comes from. That's why it's so fucking personal. That's why it's so emotional. And when you're sat in a room with those guys, whose music helped you get through so much shit, and you want to tell them, but you don't want them to think, This guy's a fucking psycho. **"**

CHRIS ADLER (DRUMMER, LAMB OF GOD, MEGADETH) "It was difficult really at the time—I'm talking to my idols, and I've got kind of the dream gig of everything I've ever wanted to do, in the band that turned me on. It was hard to say that, knowing that, even in my own career, everybody really wants you to put out the album that you've put out before—to just repeat yourself. And there's a special time in everybody's life where an album kind of hits them for a reason, and that's what makes career-long fans, but it also makes career-long critics, when you don't repeat yourself the exact same way.

However, in that I had a successful band going at the time, I wasn't afraid to tell my truth about that exact thing, in that I am still and always will be a huge fan. I was hoping that the band could reach backward a little bit. That's the worst thing—when I hear that, it drives me nuts, because everybody wants to move forward. But there was a special moment in my life where I caught on to Megadeth, and it was important for me to at least try and bring some of that back. So, when I was in the room with Dave, I said to him—I was in Australia at the time on tour, and he had sent me some demos—that I was ecstatic about playing, and there's a million other people that you guys could get to play with you, so it was still intimidating, but I had something else going on, so I was able to say, 'I don't know about this one, man. That's not my Megadeth. That's not the Megadeth that I want to be in.'

And he caught onto that real quick, and kept bringing it up. 'Tell me more about your Megadeth.' And so it was a conversation at his house: 'Tell me about that, tell me about why that is, explain this to me.' It's not a matter of the music—it's more a time in life that can't ever be replicated. It's not like the quality of music went down at all—it didn't. But there was a moment, where it gave, for me, a huge boner. It's like … I know what I want to do in life now. Things changed from there—it wasn't worse, necessarily, it was just really me changing in my life.

Point being, that was the spark, and then it was re-fired and assured and made a lifestyle. So when I came in and heard Dave's demos and I was in Australia, that was a scary conversation, but one that I felt like I needed to have. It was kind of trying to explain to him, and everybody, where I'm coming from in this whole thing—what I love about the band and what the band has done. And it's not that there's anything that I hate, but here are the things that I love, and here's why.

The conversation was more about where I was at the time, feeling that kind of teenage angst, frustration, push, 'I don't want to work at a bank'—that kind of normal, 'testosterone' vibe. I was interested in pushing that little bit. 'Here's this demo. This song's really great, can we speed it up by about 50bpm?'

I still have that angst—about the world and politics and all that stuff, you know? I'm a lot more educated now, but that was a special thing to me about Megadeth to begin with, in that it was kind of always on the verge of super-intelligent, compared to all the other stuff. It wasn't about girls and stuff like that—there was talk about world events, and politics, and I loved that aspect of it, and I think maybe that was just kind of me being interested in not being a bum, and learning about the world. So I just kind of wanted to push that a little bit. And that was 'My Megadeth.'

My mother, by herself, took a Thrasher magazine, went through the back of it, because I was skateboarding at the time, found the plans to make a half-pipe, and built it by herself in the backyard of her house. It was fucking awesome. I would have all my friends over, and we'd be skating and doing our thing. And at the time, there was this great, kind of tape-trading thing going on, where you'd pass off this, like, 'I gotta check this out, check this mix out'—it's a bunch of different bands, you know, from Circle Jerks to Cro-Mags. And then, all of a sudden, Megadeth.

And I'm on the ramp—I'm into punk rock before this. You know, my first album was Thriller, I think—Michael Jackson—and then it was the first Aerosmith record, and then I get this tape. I'm listening to The Accused, Circle Jerks, blah-blah-blah, then a song from Peace Sells comes on, it's 'Devil's Island,' and I'm on the ramp, I'm actually skating, I got my helmet on, I remember I'm trying to get some air, and this song comes on, and I'm like, 'Holy shit!' The World just absolutely changed right there, as I'm probably falling on my ass trying to get some air on the ramp. And that may have been it, getting the wind knocked out of me, and having 'Devil's Island' in my ears, but that was it, man. It was a very, very specific moment, where this is not only fucking awesome, this is what I want to be—this is what I want to do.

It was Peace Sells, and then, of course, I followed into everything else. When Rust In Peace came out, that was a superior product to everything else out there. This is the only band I need to listen to, ever. 🗨

5.3 JUST SAY YES

'Dad, can you be the celebrity judge at my high school talent show tonight?'

Saying yes to that one question from my son, Roman, pretty much changed the arc of my life as I now know it. It was Friday afternoon, February, 28, 2014, when he came home and asked if I'd be a celebrity judge at the Rock Revolution talent show at his school.

'Sure,' I said. 'When is it?'

'Tonight!' he said.

I said yes, of course, even if it was just to have some fun hangout time with my boy. Sometimes that's how life happens. You just do it with no time to question it. But my findings from that night would lay an interesting path for me the next few years. New career moves and things that had always intrigued me about the music business were presented that evening, just by my saying yes.

I settled into the 1,500-seat high-school theater auditorium as the event began. Eight or nine of the school's finest performed, and then the final act was introduced to the audience.

'Ladies and gentlemen, please welcome tonight's final act: Doll Skin!'

A young, all-female rock band took to the stage and just blew me away with their unified look of rock'n'roll thigh-length skirts, Dr. Marten boots, Les Paul guitars, and Marshall amplifiers. What hit me most wasn't any one thing in particular but all of it combined. They stormed the stage like a great rock outfit ready for the business of rocking the house. They came on as a group; they melted faces and left as a group. I was thrilled to see this talent in front of me. They had a *sound* to them that was undeniable. This singer was a star, and she got the entire audience on their feet singing along to some not-even-so familiar covers. That takes balls!

I believe all of us judges—five in total—gave them a resounding ten out of ten, thus crowning them the winners of the evening's program. I met the band after the show and starting asking them questions.

It turned out this was their very first show ever. The drummer, Meghan, attended the school and had wanted to put something together to participate in the talent show. She had met the other girls at the local School Of Rock chapter in town.

The singer, Sydney, was a freshman in middle school, and the guitarist, Alex, had been in a guitar band camp with my daughter, Athena, just a few years earlier, where they scratched their way through Nirvana and Joan Jett covers. Now here she was, clearly having stepped up her game. There was a real zeal and charge to her playing. She was captivating to listen to—as were the other girls in the band—and as she laid down some kickass guitar work, I knew she was just scratching the surface of what was going to be a real career for her.

I was motivated to help. I stayed in touch with the band over the next couple of years, and then my dear friend Randy Spencer recommended I take them in the studio to cut some demos. He was familiar with them too as he worked for Alice and Sheryl Cooper's Solid Rock foundation, which hosted similar talent-show experiences for young rockers in the area.

What I discovered in the studio were five really compelling original songs of theirs, as well as a great cover tune. With six songs in total, I started making calls to friends at record labels to gauge interest on the band, and to hopefully secure a deal to push out an EP. I had been down this road before with Dale Steele's band, NUMM, a decade earlier, and I found the rules of the game hadn't changed.

'Give them a few years to develop and keep me posted,' I was told. The usual blow off. I also got, 'We don't want to deal with teenagers and their parents. Call me when they are all over age eighteen.' The problem was, this band had something *now*, and if it wasn't cultivated at that very moment, the moment could pass.

In short, I quickly came back to the same realization I'd had before: that without a cheerleader in this business, you get nowhere. You can have the songs and the talent but no one to get you through the door. In other words, you're still left outside in the cold. Suddenly, I became that cheerleader. I got very possessive and protective over the band because I had seen them rock the house, and I understood the fundamental raw talent and connection they could make with an audience. I knew their strengths and I wasn't afraid to put my name on the line for them. I knew their potential because, in a weird way, I saw a bit of me in them, from when I was young and coming up the ranks. Breaking this band became my mission.

RYAN GREENE ❝*I got a call from David back in 2016. He mentioned he was producing a demo for a band called Doll Skin, an all-girl punk-rock band, and asked if I'd be interested in mixing the project. It was typical David—do what you do, don't give any limitations—he was interested more in the vibe than anything else, which I find refreshing. I remember him saying, 'Listen to the tracks and you'll totally get it.'*

The tracks were super-raw, super-punk-rock, 'Fuck you, I don't care.' David did something record companies did years ago but don't do anymore: find a band and develop and guide them. When I saw them play live, I totally understood why he signed them. The singer was fearless, the guitar player is a star; all together they had a thing that just worked. Over the past few years they have really grown as players, and stylistically are a much more mature band. ❞

A year earlier, Missi Calazzo at Megaforce had put out the *Altitudes & Attitude* EP via the label's MRI subsidiary. She indicated that part of that process was to open up imprint label options for Frank and me to sign more bands. So I called Missi about putting out the Doll Skin EP, which we did via my new imprint, EMP—an acronym for Ellefson Music Productions, the umbrella company under which I was now running my producing endeavors.

This was late October 2015, just as Megadeth's *Dystopia* world tour was getting under way. Needless to say, I was busy! Touring full-time in Megadeth, managing Doll Skin, and now managing a startup record company—it kept me at full capacity. But I loved it! In fact, I thrived on it. So many years I spent on the road, just traveling, and, as I got on in my years, I relished having new endeavors outside of Megadeth—things that were actually adding to and building *my* legacy. But I needed an assistant, or at least some professional friendship—someone who was on *Team Ellefson*.

Well, I found that in my current record label and business partner, Thom Hazaert. He understood where I had been during my years in Megadeth—my commitments to building that band only to have it taken away from me for the greater good. Thom became a real friend and professional confidante, and we both committed to building the Ellefson brands together.

I felt like I finally had the cheerleader I spoke of earlier. Thom became someone who would be my pit bull when needed, a trusted advisor in times of question, yet someone who would shoot straight with me when I needed to hear the truth. These were not easy shoes to fill, but Thom did it.

In a past life, Thom was a major-label marketing and A&R man during the nu-metal era of KoRn, Limp Bizkit, and others who were tearing up the charts in the late 90s and early 2000s. He also managed the band Chimaira for Roadrunner Records, who I worked with during my stint at Peavey back in the mid-2000s.

Thom and I had reconnected a few months earlier in 2015, when he approached me to do interview segments for a film/music project he was commissioned to oversee for the soon to be re-released *Shocker* movie. Megadeth had performed a cover of Alice Cooper's 'No More Mr. Nice Guy' for the soundtrack back in 1989, so Thom felt it fitting that I be a spokesperson for the participation.

Thom and I began to speak almost daily while I was on tour with Megadeth. The Doll Skin record was being released under MRI, and Thom and I began discussing strategies for the record. He also coached and guided me in marketing, and we soon realized the band needed a new home where we could really ramp up the necessary elements for their career.

It was at this point that Thom said to me, 'Dude, I've run record labels. We can start our own label, with our own distribution, and do this ourselves.' We then set out to do just that by creating EMP Label Group. I like the name 'Label Group' because I wanted this endeavor to be open to anything I produced—to be more than just a metal label. Yet I saw the credibility of metal labels like Roadrunner and Victory, who specialized in certain genres. So this was our task: build a multifaceted record label with credibility.

Thom secured us North American distribution via eOne—probably the largest major independent distributor at the time. In turn, eOne brought us our European distribution via the world-class SPV label in Germany. Thom had radio and publicity people in place, and interns working diligently for our cause, and suddenly we had a real international label!

We had a few snags here and there, but for the most part, signing bands was easy, because we set the bar high for quality, and stuck to our stated mission to make the deals artist-friendly and always keep their needs in mind. It's been my experience in life that if you serve others with your gifts and talents, you can't help but create a win–win scenario for everyone.

As of the time of this writing, we have released well over fifty titles through EMP, and as the record business continues to change rapidly, we have found a real niche to serve both newcomers and legacy artists in getting their music out to their audiences. To me, that is a summarization of my life today: using my life and career experiences to help others continue theirs, too.

5.4 NEVER SAY NEVER

There are two things I always said I would never do: manage a band and start a record company. Somehow, in the span of only one year, I had ended up doing both.

THOM HAZAERT ❝*I originally met David Ellefson in the 2000s as a manager, when he was working as an artist rep at Peavey and handled some of my bands. Not gonna lie: I fan-boy'd a little every time I talked to him. Fact is, I grew up a huge Megadeth fan. And like people have their favorite Beatle, or Stone, or guy in KISS, Megadeth was my favorite band, and Ellefson was my guy in Megadeth. He was a kid from the Midwest, not even that much older than me, who up and moved to LA and became a rock star—the exact escape plan teenage me had been hatching in Green Bay since the first time I watched Mötley Crüe Uncensored in 1986 and* saw Nikki Sixx and Tommy Lee walking around the strip, Vince Neil rolling around Hollywood in a hot tub in the back of a stretch limo with a bunch of strippers. Eventually, I moved to Hollywood to do a bunch of stuff of my own, but that's another book.

Our paths would cross again in 2015, when he had returned to Megadeth and I was working on special features for Scream Factory's special-edition Blu-ray release of Wes Craven's Shocker. Although I'd worked in the music business my entire adult life, film—especially horror films—is another of my undying passions, and I'd had some dalliances there from time to time. Through a random twist of fate, IMDB, and the grace of Heather Buckley of Red Shirt Films, I became acquainted with Michael Felsher, the undisputed master of special features, and helped them produce a few things for People Under The Stairs, Army Of Darkness, and so on—and then they told me they had been commissioned to do an upcoming edition of Shocker.

That film and its soundtrack—which prominently features Megadeth, with their life-changing rendition of the Alice Cooper classic 'No More Mr. Nice Guy'—was a pivotal moment for me. And, as for so many others, they both profoundly impacted my life. I began a relentless campaign to contribute. Obviously, a special edition of Shocker would be absolutely void without a serious nod to the soundtrack, and who better to put it together than a hardcore fan-boy nerd such as myself. I also was acquainted with—or had a line to—several of the artists on the soundtrack.

That was my pitch, and I guess it worked. Finally, I think through sheer annoyance, I got the call from Felsher, giving me the green light to put together the mini-documentary that ended up being No More Mr. Nice Guy: The Music Of Shocker. It went something like, 'You have two weeks to finish, and no budget.' Of course, all I heard was 'yes.' So I got to work.

I reached out to my dear friend Jason McMaster of Dangerous Toys, who obviously said yes; to Alice Cooper, who didn't end up in it, unfortunately, but don't worry, we'll cross paths later; to Desmond Child, Kane Roberts, and Bruce Kulick; and of course Megadeth's management, who never got back to me at all. But being an asshole who doesn't give up, and knowing this thing does not fly without Megadeth in it, I reached out to David directly via social media, and miraculously he saw it—almost as if it were divine destiny—and almost immediately got an answer. I think we all know how that one turned out.

So I ended up co-producing and directing a killer thirty-minute documentary on the Shocker soundtrack—literally, one of the proudest moments of my life—and through that medium, got reacquainted with David, who apparently had recently started managing and producing artists. He told me about this band Doll Skin from Phoenix he was managing, and said to keep him in mind for any projects.

Within ten minutes, I called Arise In Chaos—a band from Denver I was managing who were in the middle of making a record—and said, 'Hey, how would you guys like to have some stuff on the record produced by David Ellefson from Megadeth?' Obviously, they were thrilled with the prospect, but as the record was mostly tracked except for the vocals, we arranged for a few of the guys to go down and track some with David in Phoenix.

Not five minutes into the session, I got a text from David: 'I fucking love this band. Let's do something with it.' I guess you can say we did. There was talk of co-managing them, and then David mentioned that Megaforce—the label that released Kill 'Em All—had offered him an imprint label, and he was considering starting one to put out a record for Doll Skin. Well, why didn't we put Arise In Chaos on it as well? So that's what we did.

Within a few weeks, the contracts were signed, and the ball was in motion. The band I managed was signed to EMP Label Group, David Ellefson's new record imprint through Megaforce. Over those weeks, David and I got friendlier, and I also offered to help run the label and oversee the marketing and promotion, which I had done for years, not only with major labels but with several of my own independent labels as well. Eventually, as it developed, I became a bigger part of it, and a few months in it came time to make a decision about distribution overseas—whether we just do it digitally, through Megaforce, or try to make a bigger play.

I said, 'David, give me forty-eight hours.' Within twenty-four I had a few different offers on the table for legitimate European licensing; we went with Cargo, who distributed our initial releases for us in Europe.

A few months later, things weren't really working with Megaforce—probably because their original plan was just a small imprint label with a few releases and minimal marketing, and I was already seeing this as something way bigger. Megaforce is a great label, and they do great things with Anthrax, Mushroomhead, and even with David and Frank Bello's Altitudes & Attitude, and I actually ended up working with them closely on that. But I thought EMP deserved a little more than it was getting, and we needed a little more control.

So, once again, David let the dog off the leash, and via our mutual friend Scott Givens—who I had met years before, through the Ozzy camp—I secured a multi-year manufacturing and distribution deal with eOne Entertainment, who had previously distributed my label, Corporate Punishment. That was the real beginning of what became the EMP everybody knows.

While it started out modestly enough with Doll Skin, Arise In Chaos, and Green Death—who we had also just signed after an introduction from our mutual friend Corey Taylor—that first year we released, like, twenty-five records, and it became something way bigger than I think either of us really imagined. I'd love to say I totally didn't see it coming, but as far as I was concerned, it couldn't be any other way. 🙶

MARK SLAUGHTER (VOCALIST, SLAUGHTER; SOLO ARTIST) 🙶Thom, who reached out to me, was talking to me about what the label represents. He knew the Slaughter music well and was a big fan, very passionate about it. I was talking to other labels—my first solo CD I put out on my own label—but I just felt like it comes down to when people really give a shit. Those are the people you want to work with.

Thom was somebody who was very passionate about the music, and Dave was on board—he knew me more on the human being side than what I was doing musically, but he obviously trusted Thom. But as he heard the record, he thought, 'Wow, this is pretty fucking cool! This will work for my label,' because even though I still write songs, it was a little heavier. So I would say it was a two-punch thing. It was talking to Thom, and then David probably seeing what the label was representing in his mind and seeing that this could work. It had an edge, and he got it.

It's an independent record label—it's an independent artist, really—and it was really writing songs that I think the Slaughter fans would understand but would also appeal to people that like stuff a little heavier. Even though Slaughter had a harder edge in some of our records that no one ever really heard, the stuff on Halfway There was really a different direction for me, and people noticed. I think some of the stuff that was a little harder came out first, and people were pleasantly surprised. First, they were like, 'Wow, this guy's a guitar player?!' And second, I don't think it was really what people expected from Mark Slaughter.

I think the important aspect was redefining me as an artist but doing it with friends, and people that were really passionate, instead of a bunch of label heads, or people who were in it for the wrong reasons. And we did that. **"**

JASON MCMASTER (VOCALIST, DANGEROUS TOYS/WATCHTOWER/BROKEN TEETH) **"**_Along my travels I had met a character named Thom Hazaert, and this character was, basically—I feel weird saying this now, but he was a big fan of my stuff. He has a Dangerous Toys tattoo on his fucking leg. He's a fan-boy, I'm a fan-boy, you get two fan-boys together and you know what happens. So we started plotting to take over the world via rock'n'roll, somehow, someway, in the near future. We did a few things with his earlier label, Corporate Punishment, and we always stayed in touch, so when he hooked up with Ellefson, we ended up working together again. Now EMP has now released a handful of my projects, it's fucking awesome: reissues of Dangerous Toys records, Broken Teeth, Ignitor, Evil United, and we're looking to hopefully release a new Dangerous Toys album before I fucking die._ **"**

6

RENAISSANCE MAN

6.1 WITHOUT A LEG TO STAND ON

THOM HAZAERT *"I remember getting the text from David to say that he had fallen backstage in Hungary and seriously injured himself. Shortly thereafter, I got the update that he had actually broken his foot. And, somehow, I think Mustaine was live streaming through the entire thing. Thirty minutes later, it was everywhere. I remember thinking, Well, this should be interesting ..."*

I heard the bone go *SNAP* as I fell to the ground backstage in Hungary. The grass was cool, the night air was damp, and before I could even stand up and put pressure on my foot, I knew it was probably broken. I had never broken a bone in my life, but somehow this didn't seem like it was going to be good. As I tried to stand up I was cussing like a sailor. As the headliners, we had our closing show set to start in literally two hours, and I knew this was now going to be an interesting night ahead.

Dave came running over from the catering area, about twenty feet away. He was on the scene like white on rice, asking, 'What's wrong? What happened? Are you okay?' As I lay on the ground, not so much in pain at this point, but rather in frustration, I said through clenched teeth, 'I think I broke my foot.'

Dave called out to the two paramedics sitting close by in the backstage hospitality area to hurry over to look at the injury. They rushed over to me and went through a quick series of medial checks, asking *does this hurt* and *does that hurt* in their broken English, and it was quickly decided that, yes, my foot was indeed broken. Our tour manager, Mike

McGee, quickly began to consider the options of how best to deal with the issue before showtime.

It was suggested by the paramedics that I go to an emergency hospital only five minutes away. We were literally in a field by a lake—how in the heck would there be a hospital in these parts? But, there was one, and I was relieved. I wasn't so much in shock at this point, just stunned, and the thought crossed my mind that a hospital anywhere in these parts might be a bit scary. But I had to take my chances and get an X-ray and proper treatment.

After the X-ray, the doctor came in and confirmed the break and put on what is known as a fly cast, which is a quick plaster cast with a gauze wrap over it that allows the cast to breath for expansion in altitude on an airplane. The cost was only $60 US, and because we had no local currency, they let us slide without paying. You've got to love socialized health care!

Less than an hour later, we were back on the festival site, where Dave had determined we would be canceling the show, as well as the final two shows due to follow that weekend, so that I could go home and get proper medical treatment. We were scheduled to embark on a robust six-week tour of Latin America ten days later, and while I hated to cancel on the fans who had waited to see these shows in Europe, I knew it was the right thing to do for my health and longevity.

Additionally, two months earlier, in May, just before we started the European tour, I had been informed by the medical staff overseeing my dear sweet mother, Frances, at the nursing home where she'd resided for the past six years in Jackson, that after suffering a massive stroke, she was now suffering from congestive heart failure and would be put on end-of-life care. I tried to put thoughts of this out of my mind during the European tour through June and July, hoping that she would be able to hang on until I got back to the USA.

After seeing the podiatrist in Scottsdale, I was given a new X-ray, a new boot cast, crutches, and a scooter to assist my travel. Within two days I also began getting calls from the Good Samaritan home in Jackson, Minnesota, telling me to book a flight and get back to see my mom as soon as possible. She was near the end. So, with my broken foot, crutches, scooter and boot cast, I hopped—no pun intended—a plane to Minnesota, where I was able to spend two days with my mom before she passed.

6.2 THE RETURN TO MY ROOTS

Flying home to be with my mom as she drew her last breath was not only the greatest gift I could have given her, but also the best gift she could have given me. To be with someone as they depart this earthly plane is an experience I had longed to have, if for no other reason than selfishly wondering what it's like when the spirit leaves the body. In this case, my mother, who gave me my first breath, gave me the gift of assisting her as she drew her last.

I had begun preparing for this moment when her doctor called a family meeting with my wife Julie and me about her end-of-life care a few months earlier, but I still wondered if I would be ready for it. Mom was a devout Christian woman, a nurse, and certainly one of the most dedicated servants the Lord could ever know. In a way, I knew she would be fine in the transition from Earth to Heaven.

As I learned, one moment you're here, and the next you're not. It's really that simple—it's almost uneventful. I think that moment of being with Mom at her passing instilled in me the faith that if death is not something to be feared then neither is life. As much as she brought me to this Earth, in her death she reminded me to not be afraid to live it until it's finished here.

Julie and the kids were actually on vacation with her side of the family in Duck, North Carolina, and they flew to Jackson to be with me as Julie planned the funeral. Fortunately, my family had been steadfast in their financial planning over the years, and with funeral costs already covered by insurance, the memorial went rather smoothly.

My mom was one of the most loved people ever to walk this earth, and it was comforting to see so many family and friends be there to say their goodbyes. I remember reading a Wayne Dyer book years back, which started out with the quote, 'Live your life preparing for your funeral. What kind of life do you want to be remembered for?' Mom's life and memorial is one that I can only hope to emulate with all the love and people she helped and cared for during her time her with us.

Julie mentioned that some of the people at Mom's funeral had asked if I would return now that she was gone. For the past two years, since my brother's passing, I had held sole power of attorney, and I looked after Mom's healthcare and financial affairs. Her house was now in my name, and would be something I would have to tend to, but as far as making trips back to see family, those desires and obligations were now complete.

As Julie, the kids, and I headed east on Interstate 90 from Jackson to Minneapolis to catch our plane home, I had a realization that my life in Jackson was pretty much over. I was born and raised there, before leaving to pursue my dreams. Then I was brought back to look after my mother, but now that she was gone—as were so many of those childhood friends of hers—would there be any need to return often, if at all?

My father had been gone since 1994, and my brother Eliot was gone from cancer in May 2014. Now, with Mom's passing in July 2016, I had a haunting and lonely feeling. In the weeks that followed, while I was back out touring the world with Megadeth, I thought a lot about my mother. I had a few teary moments where she felt near to me. She was my biggest fan and a great supporter of my making music my business. She had musical talent, too, and was a fan of Elvis. She was thrilled every time I told her of yet another hill we conquered. The celebrities I met and the grand gala of showbiz was her tickle. In many ways, this brought a grin to my face and helped me soldier on with my career as a musician. I knew Mom approved, and that was a bright spot in my life.

After the funeral, my family and I flew home to Arizona to reconnect after a seven-week tour and now the passing of my mother. In less than a week, I would be off to South America to embark on a massive concert tour. The next challenge was to see if I could still play bass with a broken foot.

6.3 DYSTOPIA CONTINUED

"I make the hard stuff look easy, while the posers make the easy stuff look hard. **"**
GAR SAMUELSON

As we prepared for the release of *Dystopia*, I was also starting to get some traction for Doll Skin. The girls were invited to perform on the

2016 ShipRocked Cruise in January. I joined them on the trip as a sort of manager-cum-chaperone, as well as to be part of the cruise's all-star band, The Stowaways, which featured artists like Lzzy Hale, John Tempesta, members of Papa Roach, and more.

This year's cruise was on a massive Norwegian cruise liner, and we sailed from Miami to Mexico. Doll Skin held their own alongside notable heavyweights such as Five Finger Death Punch and Halestorm. It was fun to watch the girls grow into the big time. I felt proud to be their mentor.

After docking in Miami on the morning of Friday, January 22, we flew directly to Anaheim to meet Thom and the EMP crew for the NAMM show and a Schecter Guitars event the band would perform at that night. This grueling schedule reminded me of the *Peace Sells* tour and many more that followed. Like I tell all bands I work with, 'If I'm willing to still make records and tour, I certainly expect you to as well.'

The *Dystopia* LP was released that very same Friday. I picked up a copy of that day's *USA Today* newspaper, which had a major story on the album's release. It would be our highest charting album since 1992's *Countdown To Extinction*, coming in at #3 in the USA and #2 in Canada, and climbing to the top of the charts around the world.

Megadeth's North American tour kicked off in February, with Chris Adler able to join us as our drummer for this leg. We knew the long-term drum position in the band would have to be addressed at some point, but for now we had a blast touring with Chris, and the fans were thrilled.

Our drum tech, well-known deathcore drummer Tony Laureano (Dimmu Borgir *et al*) filled in from time to time, when Chris had commitments elsewhere with Lamb Of God. The matter came to a head as we began preparing a summer of festival shows, with a full swing of dates in South America to follow shortly after that.

Adler had always spoken highly of Dirk Verbeuren, drummer

in Swedish metal powerhouse Soilwork. This led to us approach Dirk, initially to fill for Chris for a few weeks in Europe. Dirk flew in to Columbus, Ohio, to rehearse. We counted off 'Symphony Of Destruction,' and we knew by the time we got to the first chorus that he was just what the doctor ordered.

DIRK VERBEUREN (DRUMMER, MEGADETH) ❝I grew up in Belgium, but then my dad got a job in Paris, France, so we moved there when I was, like, eleven or twelve years old. Once I got there, I had some friends in school, and we would do tape trading and skateboarding and stuff. That was like the big thing back then, and I was totally into it. One day I was out skateboarding and there were these few stalls in this little town that we lived in, just people selling stuff on the street. And I was like, 'Oh, there's some vinyl there,' so I go look through it, and that's when I first discovered Megadeth's Peace Sells. I'd never heard of the band—I'd known Metallica a little bit, but I hadn't heard Megadeth yet—but I loved the cover art. So I bought it for probably, like, three bucks, brought it home, and from there on, it was obviously a legendary album, and I got hooked on it. From there on out, I was a fan.

A couple of years later, I started being old enough to go to shows in Paris by myself, and one of the very first shows I've ever went to happened to be Clash Of The Titans in Europe—it was Slayer, Megadeth, Testament, and Suicidal Tendencies. So that was, coincidentally, one of the first shows I happened to get tickets to. At the time, it wasn't as easy as it is now—it was a word-of-mouth kind of thing. There wasn't, like, Facebook, internet, to see what was going on. That was when I saw Megadeth live for the first time, which was amazing. I mean, all the bands killed it that night, but Megadeth obviously was one of the best ones. After that, I always kind of kept in touch with the band's music.

Fast-forward fifteen years later, I'm playing in Soilwork—I joined them in 2004, and in 2005 we were playing the Ozzfest, when it was still a tour, a two-month tour throughout the summer. The way Ozzfest worked, there were a lot of days off between the shows, so we played a lot of off-day shows as well. At some point we were in Arizona, and we pulled into the festival, and there's David Ellefson, who at the time was working for Peavey. He just showed up on the bus—I think Peter Wichers, who was our guitar player at the time, was working with him. So, all of a sudden, there was David, and I got to say hi to him, and, like, 'Oh my God, I'm a huge fan.'

It was just a brief little meeting, but that was kind of like my first encounter with somebody in the band, and my only one—until, fast-forward another ten years, and I'm actually in the band. It's been two years now, and it still feels completely surreal for me to be playing with David and Dave, you know—it's so far removed from anything you could even imagine, even if you're a dreamer and you want to try to make a living as a musician.

In France, metal is not very big. It's not like the US—certainly back then. There was a tight underground scene, but it was very small. Nothing on the radio, or very, very little. So for me to come from that, and then end up here, I don't think I'll ever get used to it. To be playing with these guys who invented the genre, along with some other people—they are certainly the forefathers of it, and they're amazing musicians. And the coolest thing is, there is still a lot of inspiration and passion in the band to this day.

When you listen to Peace Sells and Killing is My Business, the early work, one of the things that's striking to me is that David has such a creative way of approaching the songs, and such a creative way of composing, and, when it's not stuff he's writing, contributing to Dave's stuff—it really stands out, and I think there's a reason why the bass is so audible on those records. There's a lot of metal bands, back in the day, where the bass player was really just in the background, holding down the low end, not really being creative. David always stood out to me in that regard. He's a guy who is not just playing the simple version of a guitar riff—he's really adding tension to the songs, stepping back when he needs to, but also being at the forefront when he needs to.

To be able to lock in with that, obviously his stellar musicianship, thirty-something years of experience—he has his own style, he has his own sound, so for me it's really been a pleasure to kind of find my place in that. It took some time, 'cause when you learn to play with somebody new—which I've done a number of times over the years—there's always a bit of searching at first. You kind of see where they fit in the grooves. It's a lot of listening at first, and paying attention, and, in this case, obviously studying the material we play, how it was done on the record. And I'm still working on that. I'm currently working on a bunch of the older stuff. It's a long-term thing, but at the end of the day, it's amazing to play with them.

Like I said, David is really a creative force in the band, and I think anyone who is a Megadeth fan can recognize that. Anyone who really knows the band knows that David isn't just a guy who shows up and plays some low end, he's a creative force, and he brings a lot to the band. He's just a magnificent bassist. Being the other half of that rhythm section, it's not only an honor, it makes every show a blast for me to play. I can always count on him to be right there. Plus, he has such a cool attitude onstage, and he has so much enthusiasm night after night, even though he's been doing this for so many years. 🎵🎵

Dirk definitely fit the bill—so much so that after only a few shows, we knew it was time to invite him to join the band permanently. His first show was a trial by fire a few days later in front of a giant festival crowd at Rock On The Range, and he absolutely killed it. Once we settled in with Dirk and saw what he could do, there was no looking back.

DIRK VERBEUREN ❝❝I was touring with Soilwork at the time—we were in the middle of a tour when I got the call. I got home, and I think the gigs started about ten days after that. So I had about ten days. That wasn't too bad—I've had to learn stuff in short amounts of time before—but it was a lot of songs. I think it was maybe eighteen songs they wanted me to learn.

So, obviously, I spent those ten days pretty much just doing that, really focusing on it, because I knew that the first show was Rock On The Range, in Columbus, which is a pretty big festival—I think it's like a forty-thousand crowd or something.

So I knew we only had like one rehearsal the day before, so basically I just had to show up and know my stuff.

I did the best I could to assimilate eighteen songs in ten days. Even though I knew some of those songs pretty well, being a fan, and having heard them a million times before, still, it was a task. I'm pretty good at taking notes and writing stuff out, so I made all my scores. And I remember going into that first rehearsal, meeting the guys—I had met David and Kiko before, but that was the first time I met Mustaine. So obviously a little bit of tension, 'cause you want to perform when you come into a situation like that, you want to convince the band that things are good.

Before we even played, I was just getting my stuff setup. I took out all my scores, which I'd brought with me, and I put them next to my drums, and David was like, 'Dude, you did your homework. That's awesome, man, you came prepared.' He was complimenting me before we even played, and he knew I was serious. I like to pride myself—if I take a gig, I don't do it half-assed. I show up and I know my stuff, even if it means I don't sleep for a few days.

So, yeah, that was it, the trial by fire, Rock On The Range. It went great. People were excited—it was a fun show. And I think, considering the time I had and the nerves and stuff, it went really well. It was pretty relaxed. I honestly thought there would be way more issues with what I brought to the songs, but they were all respectful that I had a limited time to learn the songs, and maybe not all of the smaller details. Thankfully no one, even Dave, overloaded me with notes or info, which would've added to my stress for the show. We did get more into the smaller details as we moved on, as I became a member of the band, and we started touring more.

Dave was like, 'Look, I know you can play this stuff exactly as it is on the albums, with every single detail.' So I went back to my scores, and instead of them being outlines, I started analyzing every single note, which again gave me a newfound appreciation for Dave's work, for David's work, obviously all the drummers that played on all those records, Marty, the older guitar players. It really gave me a newfound appreciation, because when you really dig into it, even records you've listened to for such a long time, you really rediscover all the genius that goes into it. It's a high level. I would say, for me, some of the trickiest stuff has been the Gar Samuelson stuff, because he really had a swagger that was, you know, pretty much impossible to replicate. I do the best to get close to it, and kind of get into that feel by studying all the parts and stuff. I really understand where he was coming from, how he approached the stuff, how he locks in with David.

That's another important part of that whole process: as a rhythm section, you don't just think about the drum parts, you think about how it works with the bass. And some of those small accents can be really important. Maybe it's not accenting something that the guitar is doing, but maybe it accents something the bass is doing, and it's an important note in that section, you know. Those things that can be challenging. But I get to practice and play all that shit at home, in my home studio, and when I show up and it all locks in, it's a blast. 🎵

Dirk is a sweet and laid-back guy, but he is also known for inventing the 'grindcore' drum style. Plus he was born in Belgium and raised in France. Now, with Dirk and Kiko, Megadeth had become a band with fifty percent non-American members, which added a certain international cool factor. Between us, we now have the English, Portuguese, Spanish, French, Flemish, and Finnish (Kiko's wife is from Finland) spoken fluently in our band. I love that!

•

While we were enjoying the fruits of our thirty-five-year overnight success, I was becoming aware of little physical things hurting on my body. At twenty-five, I'd get injured, and after some time the injuries healed. But at fifty, when the pain came, it stayed.

While I go to great lengths to stay physically fit and am happy with aging gracefully, this was beginning to leave its mark on me. While we were in Edmonton, Canada, we went out and drove some tanks with the army, and I cracked a rib on the bottom left side of my rib cage. It caused me great pain when I lifted my bass for my signature stage move. At the same time, the big toe joint on my right foot was flaring up and giving me a chronic pain—something that had been brewing since our stop in Perth back in October, just a few months prior. And then the broken foot from Hungary really was a doozy. Mom dying and the broken foot was like, *Okay, how much can I take this year?* That was when I started to have fun with it all.

My first decision was whether to perform standing or sitting. I know how the adrenaline hits me, and autopilot just takes over onstage. Plus, sitting down to play Megadeth songs is physically challenging on the back and arm muscles. So, at the first show of the summer tour, in Ecuador, I decided to go for it and stand for the show. Fortunately, even with my boot, I found I had a pair of stage jeans with a super-wide flare on them, and the pants fit over top of the boot perfectly. You really couldn't tell I had anything wrong!

There were moments of pain, but I was able to artfully hobble around them. I remember our first drummer, Gar Samuelson, had this saying, 'I make the hard stuff look easy, while the posers make the easy stuff look hard.' When we got offstage, Dirk and Kiko were raving about how well I'd done. It was much-needed support, and put wind in my sails to carry on to the next.

Making my way around South America with my boot, scooter, and crutches was challenging, but between the band and crew we learned to have fun with it. In South America, we travel by air, not bus. For our road crew, helping me on the plane became a bit of a competition. They quickly discovered that if they could assist me on the airplane, they'd get preferential seating—maybe even upgrades to the front of the plane. We had a lot of fun with that, and in the end we made lemonade out of lemons.

The final tour of the year was a North American arena tour with Butcher Babies, Metal Church, and Amon Amarth, with Megadeth as the headliner. The US and Canada now have these small- to medium-sized hockey arenas that are a perfect fit for Megadeth. We can take out a full arena production, yet not *too* big, and it gives a good feel for the audience, too.

We wrapped the year with a week of really fun events in New York. *Revolver* magazine, the unspoken representative of all things metal, were honoring Dave Mustaine with a 'Lifetime Achievement' award at their big event in NYC, where we would also play a short set of classic songs.

As a warm-up date, we played a show at the infamous St. Vitus bar in Brooklyn, under the pseudonym Vic & The Rattleheads. It was a kickass small club show and we banged through a short set of tunes, leaving the fans thrilled and exhausted. Mission accomplished!

Another highlight of the *Dystopia* tour was an appearance on NBC's *Late Night With Seth Meyers*, where we played the newly Grammy-nominated 'Dystopia.' Those types of late-night network shows offer huge exposure to mainstream audiences. It was good timing, too, that former Slayer drummer Dave Lombardo was sitting in with the house band that night. And it was fun meeting Seth, as my family have watched him anchor the legendary *Saturday Night Live* 'Weekend Update' segment for years, and we watch his show many nights of the week as well. It was a super-fun day, and we even got to go watch a rehearsal of *Saturday Night Live*, as the *SNL* studio is on the same floor inside Rockefeller Center in Manhattan. The now-popular Chance The Rapper was the musical guest. (Performing on *SNL* is still a bucket list item for me with Megadeth … hopefully, one day!)

Back at the hotel after the Seth Myers TV performance, I got a text message, followed by a phone call, from my longtime Phoenix friend, concert promoter Danny Zelisko. He was asking if we might be available to support Scorpions on a major arena tour in the fall. He had just met with Scorpions' agent, and when he threw our name in the hat, they'd said we'd be a good fit. I agreed!

We already had a tour lined up with Meshuggah for the summer of 2017, but we agreed to the Scorpions tour as well, which would start in September. The opportunities coming to Megadeth seemed to be getting bigger and better with each day.

6.4 MUSICIANS IN CARS SELLING COFFEE

My love for coffee has accompanied me around the world for my entire musical career. Just like the spirit of a culture or the melody of a song, the enjoyment of coffee brings people together and creates harmony among us. The beans in this bag are traceable to their global origin and exemplify the spirit and culture of the people who grew them. It is my aim to bring this roast to our tables and awake our taste buds, fire up your rock'n'roll spirits, and continue the global fellowship of music, art, and coffee. **"**

DAVID ELLEFSON

I was on an island somewhere in the Atlantic during the 2016 ShipRocked Cruise when a former Megadeth production assistant called me over to her spot on the beach to tell me about her friend, Paul Waggoner, who as well as being the guitarist for Between The Buried & Me also had his own boutique coffee roasterie, Parliament Coffee Roasters. She felt Paul and I would hit it off well, given our shared love of coffee, and said I should contact him upon my arrival back at shore. She got me his info, and I looked him up when I returned home from the cruise.

From our first phone conversation, Paul and I hit it off like we were old friends in a band together, and in a way we were. We waxed nostalgic about our love of coffee and what coffee culture meant to each of us. We agreed that he would send me some samples of his coffee to try, and I would conjure up some names for the roasts. Together, we would create my own line of coffee. How hard could it be?

I quickly rang Thom and told him of my call with Paul. He was thrilled, and, as Thom does, he started spinning his creative marketing wheels, and in that moment the Ellefson Coffee Co. was born. Our first roast would be Roast In Peace, a fun play on the Megadeth album title *Rust In Peace*. The idea was that we would offer our coffee online via our EMP Label Group portal, which meant each bag would produce a small profit. No brick-and-mortar retail outlets, no sales force, just a simple passive income that Paul and Thom could easily manage.

As with most good ideas around here, this would one would germinate and grow, bringing with it enthusiasm and a labor of love. I asked Paul if he had a bean from Kenya, which he did, and thus our medium roast, Kenya Thrash, was born. Then came She Wolf, our light roast, which rounded out the 'big three' of the ECC roasts.

By December of that year, Thom had found an investor with extensive experience in the food and beverage concession industry, in particular inside large entertainment and sporting event venues. Suddenly, an opportunity came our way that would change the course of our coffee company, as well as answer some questions about my return back to my little hometown of Jackson, Minnesota.

During visits back to see my brother and mother in Jackson in recent years, I had often visited what I considered the cool shop of the town: a small boutique coffee shop called Coffee Choices, located on Main Street. I loved the quaint feeling of the shop, where locals met for coffee and conversation, which was so indicative of this warm and lovely farming community. Additionally, they offered one of my favorite desserts, the Scotcharoo, the chocolate-frosted Rice Krispy treat I knew so well from growing up on the farm.

While I was in Jackson, I began to chat with the proprietor, which led to the idea of creating a Jackson hometown brew, which we called Urban Legend. This would make reference to me, as a local hometown hero, but also to the story of Mary Jane Terwilliger, who was buried in the nearby Loon Lake Cemetery.

THOM HAZAERT ❝Around the same time, we hooked up with paranormal investigator Adrian Lee, who was writing a book called Mysterious Midwest about urban legends from the region, for which David (with me as his trust ghostwriter) wrote the introduction. During that process, we had the idea to develop a coffee in homage to both David's hometown of Jackson, his status as a local legend, and the legend of Mary Jane Terwillegar, and release it around Halloween, in conjunction with Adrian's book.

If you are somehow unfamiliar with the legend of Mary Jane Terwillegar— which, if you're reading this book, is unlikely—she is the focus of an urban legend from David's hometown of Jackson, Minnesota, a young girl laid to rest in the decrepit Loon Lake Cemetery who was rumored to have been buried alive for being a witch. The story goes that anyone who violates her grave would meet a tragic end—and what bored Midwest teenager would not take that bait?❞

As daring teenagers without much else to do, my generation of youngsters would often sneak into Loon Lake to taunt these gravesites, knowing that no deed would go unpunished. Creeping around among ominous graves by moonlight, illicit, irrational fear building in your gut, as the chilling Midwest winds blew. The threat of being caught by the local authorities loomed, a distant second to the supernatural wrath we feared we were about to unleash.

THOM HAZAERT ❝Of course, this was all forever immortalized in the classic Megadeth song 'Mary Jane,' and, like so many great stories, it has become an official part of the heavy-metal canon. So we figured, what better way to pay homage to David's hometown and its place in Megadeth history than with its own coffee? (We would later launch a second roast with a nod to Jackson, the Jackson House Blend.) We hired Sam Shearon to do the artwork, and Urban Legend was born. While it was intended to be a limited-time seasonal roast, people liked it so much it stuck around, and it is still available to this day. ❞

Although my family was now gone, suddenly new roots and ties back to Jackson were once again forming. Shortly after we created the Urban Legend roast, Thom presented me with another opportunity: with a small investment to Coffee Choices, we would be able to put the Ellefson Coffee Co. name on the door and have our own legitimate retail store on the main street of my hometown. I was thrilled.

'Yes,' I said, 'let's do it!'

On January 2, 2017, the announcement went out and became a trending news story all around the world. We quickly made plans for an immediate soft opening prior to a grand opening in April 2017. Thom brought in Pamela Trepanier to oversee accounting and some bubbling retail accounts, including the Jackson store account. Things were growing quickly—it was like preparing for a world tour. Game on!

As I headed back to Jackson for the grand opening, a peaceful thought came over me, that this was my first visit to Jackson in almost twenty years without there being a focus of failing health in my family.

My mother had passed, Eliot's cancer had taken him two years earlier, and my father had died in 1994. Sadly, they were all gone. Now I was the last standing Ellefson from that generation, and as much as I wondered how it would affect me emotionally on this trip, I was looking forward to just simply being alone with my thoughts and wonderful memories of past days from Jackson.

At the grand opening I was given what could only be described as a hometown hero's welcome. We were met with major national and regional fanfare. It was on the front page of all the local papers, Rock'n'roll comedian Don Jamieson appeared, as did other notable stars from the EMP Label Group stable, including vocalist Stephen Shareaux of Kik Tracee, who absolutely killed it.

THOM HAZAERT ❝ For the grand opening, Adrian Lee led us all on a paranormal investigation out to Loon Lake. Me and Drew Fortier of Bang Tango/ZFM also roped David into an impromptu acoustic performance of Megadeth songs. I got to sing 'Peace Sells' and a medley of 'Tornado Of Souls' and 'Symphony Of Destruction' that Drew and I had worked out the night before in our hotel room. Bucket list level eleven! ❞

We had sold out of all of our coffee and merchandise by the second day. We were left with such a high from it all that we began talks for the next big event. The local racetrack wanted us to get involved with them, and we ended up sponsoring a racecar with local stock-car racer Luke Sathoff. Other local businesses reached out to have ECC participate in or partner with them. We were suddenly a real force in the community, and one that inspired me to give back to the people who supported me as a youth, and now adult, from the fabric of their town.

But as I'd learned with rock bands, with triumph comes tribulation. As an official sponsor of the Chicago Open Air festival—featuring

KISS, Megadeth, Anthrax, KoRn, and more—that summer, we found ourselves understaffed in the face of all the requests coming our way. And, at the same time, the owner of Coffee Choices was looking for an exit strategy from her store and business. As helpful as our bailout had been, she was burned out and no longer feeling the passion to show up each day and 'make the donuts.' Thom and I looked into the possibility of purchasing the building and running the business ourselves, but to be an offsite owner while on major concert tours seemed like a sure way to lose money, so we passed on that option.

As the walls closed in on ECC Jackson, I ran into another local business owner, an energetic young man named Donnie Schoenrock who had successfully taken over a local BBQ restaurant called Kat's Hog Heaven. As we discussed the imminent closing of Coffee Choices, we decided to move our coffee footprint two blocks down the street to his location, where the local patrons could still enjoy Ellefson Coffee Co. and visit our ever-growing *Museum Of Deth* collection of rock'n'roll memorabilia.

Somehow, the coffee gods were smiling upon us. As we prepared to relaunch at the new location, the media again showed favor, with the Minneapolis CBS affiliate and more swooping in. We were back in business without missing a beat.

More than anything, Thom has made it his mission to properly rebuild my legacy as its own entity, away from the volatility of any one band or setting. Now it was *my* name on the door, and we were all working as a team to build, create, and inspire each other and our fans, customers, and faithful supporters.

It might be my name on the bottom line, but that's what also continues to inspire me. It also drives me to continue to say yes to the endeavors that have been unfolding for me these past years. Just as Dale Steele reminded me when I re-joined Megadeth in 2010, I was successfully rebuilding and making preparations for a life after 'deth, as well as a life full of fun endeavors while the band continues to work.

As retail accounts open with my friends like Nicko McBrain of Iron Maiden and his Rock'n'roll Ribs restaurant in Florida, providing coffee at the USA's largest rock concerts for Danny Wimmer Presents, and even being allowed to serve coffee at the NAMM shows I've mentioned so many times in here, it seems my time has come, in the music business and beyond. My mission statement of letting coffee serve as a vehicle to bring people together, like a good song, was working. And, as we quickly became the largest rock'n'roll coffee company in the world, it was fun to let people in!

THOM HAZAERT ❝*That has been the fun of doing coffee. David and I have been involved every step of the way, from flavor profiling the roasts to developing the names and concepts behind them. We do the branding and marketing, too—we didn't just give someone David's name to put on a bag. We developed a brand, an identity, a lifestyle. A rock'n'roll coffee company, that continues to live and grow.*

In 2016, we were featured in Revolver magazine and on major rock sites like Loudwire. In 2017, ECC started making appearances at major festivals like Chicago Open Air, Rock On The Range, ShipRocked Cruise, and we had a booth at the NAMM Convention. We launched our first Signature Artist Roasts with Autograph, Skid Row, and Michael Wilton of Queensrÿche, and later released artist roasts for Altitudes & Attitude and Eddie Ojeda of Twisted Sister. Our coffee is now available in over thirty retail locations, and that number continues to grow.

I say to David all the time: ECC is like a band. We go out and tour, we release new roasts, we collaborate with other artists. We push the envelope. But at the end of the day, we just try and make really great fucking coffee. ❞

KIKO LOUREIRO ❝*I've told him this already, and everybody who meets Ellefson knows this. He's, like, the most amazing person I've ever met. Because when you're* on tour, even for Megadeth, it's not easy. You're away from home, sometimes you don't sleep well, you're constantly traveling, airport after airport, and it beats you up. Ellefson is a person that, anytime of the day—it can be 5am, after waking up in a hotel at 3am, before the show, or after, it doesn't matter—he's always in a good mood, he's always saying something cool, or it can be funny, or smart, or nice advice. He's just such an amazing person. I don't even really know how describe it, but I think everyone who knows him knows that.

He's, like, this peaceful person, and he makes you comfortable. I don't know how to explain it, but it's just this comfortable feeling to be around him, and it's so great. He has this positive thing, but it's not only being happy, some people just smile all the time, it doesn't mean they are happy. David's just comfortable the way he is. He has an internal peace. He succeeds in music, in the music business, and he succeeds as a person, in his own journey, with religion, with not drinking. And he shares things with people, and you just feel comfortable and welcome. Anytime you need to talk to him, he just welcomes you.

It's not about the smile, it's about being comfortable with what he achieves in live—with family, with the band, with music, with all that. And everybody can feel that. I had a great moment with him in 2014, then he called me, and now I'm here in Megadeth, and I'm so grateful to have him as a friend, bandmate, and partner.

You know, I've been playing with great musicians, doing music, for a long time. And David is a guy who knows what he's doing. He's the best. He decided to be this heavy metal bass player with this unique sound and style. You have different kinds of bass players that can play shred, or slap, or whatever, but he's just like the metal bass player at his best. He's solid, has amazing tone, and there's no mistakes, ever. He's like Geezer Butler from Black Sabbath, or Jimmy Bain. Geddy Lee, Chis Squire—some bassists just have this tone that you can recognize, like a personality, that's so solid. No mistakes, just perfect.

He gives this foundation to the band. He's not a crazy progressive, math metal, whatever—Megadeth's music is really related to the guitars, the guitar work. And David, he's just the perfect bassist for it. When you combine that with David as a person, and his tone, and style, and he's just so consistent, he's the perfect guy to be around as a bass player. And he knows the industry—he knows everybody in the industry. He's very creative with ideas. It can be, like, the stage presence, or the lights, or the sound, or what to answer in an interview. And all the stories, man, he knows how to tell a story, and it's great to be around him to listen to them.

On top of that, he's a business guy who is passionate about coffee. And I'm enthusiastic about his coffee brand and ideas and flavors and all that. I'm always telling him to go for it, because the coffee is amazing—the ideas, the names of the coffee, all the marketing is great. I just think he should go for it. I'm always teasing him, like, 'I'd do this, and this, and this,' and I believe in this coffee thing. It's so good because it's his passion. He loves coffee. He lives the coffee thing. And I love coffee, too. It's a great idea, it's a great business, and it's going to grow. You guys deserve it. Call me when you have an IPO! **"**

THE NEXT FRONTIER

7.1 FULL CIRCLE

"You are not God's gift to music … music is God's gift to you!"
DAVID ELLEFSON

BRIAN 'HEAD' WELCH (GUITARIST, KORN) "When fans approach me in public and I notice they are nervous to some degree, I actually get nervous from detecting their nervousness! To break the ice, I always offer a truth that I've learned throughout the years: all famous musicians are fans of music first—just like they are. It's so true.

Back in 1995, I was that nervous fan when me and my KoRn brothers landed the Megadeth tour. Up until that point we had mostly toured in clubs with bands like House Of Pain, Biohazard, Sick Of It All, Marilyn Manson, Danzig. The Megadeth tour was a whole new level that gave us the opportunity to get in front of some bigger crowds, and we were amazed to see results almost immediately. We jumped from selling 1,000 records a week to over 3,500 by the end of the tour. It was so surreal to get to know the Megadeth guys on that tour, because we had become big fans over the years, and we had much respect for them.

Nowadays, I am a fan of David Ellefson for different reasons. The guy just doesn't quit! He owns his own record label, EMP Label Group; his own coffee company, Ellefson Coffee Co., which KoRn had the pleasure of donating memorabilia to; he manages the band Doll Skin; and he's preparing to launch a new booking agency. It's a good thing Ellefson found some time to write this new book, because I cannot wait to read it to figure out how he does it all!"

THOM HAZAERT ❝ *The first time I saw KoRn was opening for Megadeth, with Fear Factory and Flotsam & Jetsam, right after the release of the first record. It was life-changing. They ended up becoming my favorite band (sorry, Megadeth), and I was lucky enough to get to intern at Immortal Records when Life Is Peachy and Follow The Leader were out, and get a front-row seat to their insane, meteoric rise. I also got to hang out with Happy Walters, Peter Katsis, and a lot of the guys who made it happen, and learned so much I could never properly put it into words.*

This was, at the time, the closest I'd been to a band blowing up, basically from the beginning and, somehow, I was lucky enough to kind of get to hang out and watch. I can honestly say that KoRn, and that experience, are one of the main reasons I pursued the career I did, and one of the biggest reasons I am here. Thankfully, it seems like, for the most part, the universe has always put me in the right place at the right time.

Several more bands I worked with even more directly—Limp Bizkit, Staind, etc.—blew up pretty much solely via their proximity to KoRn, and that was even more exciting to watch. I'll tell you one thing, when other bands can go platinum just by being next to you, you know you're doing something right. And then I managed Switched, and got them signed to Immortal Records, the label KoRn built, in much the same fashion that Megadeth had done with Combat. Really, so much of the formative years of my career revolve around KoRn that I couldn't ever even really express the gratitude, and sheer love I have for that band, and the guys in it.

Thankfully, I got to reciprocate a little by giving KoRn one of their first, if not the first, feature in a major magazine, interviewing them for Circus, when they were on tour supporting Ozzy, with Deftones, who I saw and met for the first time that night. In all honesty, I really don't think that they get enough credit, because KoRn truly was the band that reinvented metal, or at least created the machine that managed to keep it on life support long enough to get healthy again. Those five guys singlehandedly opened the eyes of a whole new generation to the power of heavy music, and led them straight to other bands like Slipknot, who led them right back to Megadeth.

It also goes without saying that Head is one of the coolest guys in rock'n'roll, and I am honored to call him a friend, and have gotten to bond with him over our mutual musical fandom and my love for KoRn. I sat in his hotel room one night, crudely showing him how to play 'Symphony Of Destruction,' so we could jam it together with David and Dirk the next day. Who could make this shit up? It's another one of those spiritual, almost too-good-to-be-true, full-circle threads that have showed up throughout this book. Megadeth inspired KoRn. They both inspired me. And here we all are, three generations, inspiring and inspired by each other, proudly waving the flag of rock'n'roll. 🍾

Maybe the most fun part of this whole gig is remembering why we are here: we all started out as fans! As our professions continue to move us down the stream of life, there is no cooler feeling than standing side by side (professionally and literally) with your idols and heroes.

I got to experience this with Megadeth, pretty much from the beginning, when we opened for Alice Cooper, Iron Maiden, Dio, Judas Priest, and so many more. And when Gene Simmons and Paul Stanley of KISS bestowed us with the honor of 'Best Thrash Band' at the Concrete Foundations Forum in Los Angeles in 1991—that was a true 'call home to Mom' moment. If there was ever a moment where I felt like I had 'arrived,' this was it. That is why, when I'm in the headliner position, it's so important to remember that the guys performing on the stage before me might have grown up on my music, too. How I act and treat them will either grow or reduce my own legacy in their eyes.

This was certainly the case with many of the Megadeth support acts over the years—Pantera, KoRn, Alice In Chains, Stone Temple Pilots, Fear Factory, and so many more who went on to astronomical heights, in their own right, after we ushered them into the arenas much the same way our idols did for us.

The same goes for business. With EMP, Combat, our artists, even the coffee company, everything we do is out of genuine love, respect, and passion for music. And that all comes from being a fan. And, that, truly is the reason we are all here. That's what brings so many of these relationships full circle. Just like Thom and Head have so eloquently stated (and so many others in this book), as musicians and fans, we all share a common thread: music made us who we are, and we helped make music what it is!

7.2 'AND THE GRAMMY GOES TO...'

I'd heard these words before, at the four previous Grammy Awards shows I'd attended. It's a bizarre moment when, in that very second, you realize you might actually win. What will you say if you're called onto the stage? How excited will your friends and family be at this Cinderella moment? These thoughts raced through my mind as I again pondered a win on music's greatest night. Megadeth had been granted twelve Grammy nominations since 1991, our first being for 'Hangar 18' off the *Rust In Peace* album. I knew we wouldn't be able to attend that year because of our heavy touring commitments, but just the nomination brought immediate worldwide credibility and recognition.

In 1993, my soon-to-be-wife Julie and I went to the Grammys with Marty Friedman and his girlfriend. This time we were nominated for 'Sweating Bullets,' the second big single from our recent double-platinum album, *Countdown To Extinction*. It was the first year the heavy-metal category would not be televised, due to the growing number of awards being handed out. There had also been egg on the face of the Grammys a few years earlier, in 1989, when the mighty Metallica lost that year's first 'Best Metal Performance' category to none other than Jethro Tull! It was an embarrassment to everyone, and I think one the Grammys wished they'd done some more due diligence on, if for no other reason than to not put Jethro Tull in the metal category … and certainly not up against Metallica, who were racing up every chart and breaking box-office records every day!

As the limo dropped us off on the red carpet, our industry and media friends congratulated us in advance with comments like, 'You'll definitely win this—it's not even a competition.' Hell, we had sold two million albums, our single had been on MTV every day for months, and tickets to our arena tours were selling like gangbusters. It did seem like a no-brainer that we would win.

We took our seats in the smaller auditorium of the infamous Shrine Auditorium in downtown Los Angeles, where the non-televised awards were being given out that year. Our category came up quickly, as the third one of the program that afternoon. Lyle Lovett and Mary Chapin Carpenter stood at the podium, reading the list of nominees. Here it came, that tense and surreal moment where you actually leave your body for a second, wondering what it's going to be like to actually win a Grammy. You could hear a pin drop in the silence as they read the card:

'And the Grammy for Best Metal Performance goes to … NINE INCH NAILS!'

We were stunned! How could we not win? We were clearly the lead horse in this race! We knew of NIN, of course, and we were even fans of the band, but this was *insane*! They were the newbies and we were the industry titans of metal. This made no sense at all.

Marty stood up. 'Fuck this,' he said. 'Let's go!' He wanted to leave immediately. 'Call the limo, we're outta here … now!'

'Don't you want to at least go see the rest of the show?' Julie asked. 'We have our tickets and we're already here.' She and Marty's girl had bought new gowns and were prepared for this big gala night out on the town.

Julie had been to the Grammy Awards before, as she was working at the time for the iconic McGhee Entertainment management firm, first holding down the office in New York City before relocating to Los Angeles. Their clients—Bon Jovi, Mötley Crüe, Scorpions, Skid Row, The McCauley/Schenker Group—were the biggest in hard rock at the time. They were on MTV every hour, and they made millions of dollars.

Julie encouraged Marty to change his mind, telling him he would enjoy the evening regardless of not winning, but Marty was having none of it. He was done and ready to go.

I called the limo driver from my cell phone and asked that he come back to pick us up, telling him that we didn't win and were leaving to get something to eat up to the San Fernando Valley. Even he was stunned that we wanted to leave.

•

Unbeknown to the fans and industry at the time, there was more brewing under the surface in Megadeth that I'm convinced was contributing to Marty's frustration. While we'd had huge success that year with *Countdown To Extinction*, it wasn't all smooth sailing. There was a major drugs relapse inside the band, which led to the cancelation of a tour with Stone Temple Pilots as support, as well as a major arena-level tour of Japan, which was to include our first ever appearance at the famous Budokan. While Marty and I were at the Grammys, there was convalescing behind the scenes, to try to regroup quickly and recover from our loses. But it was not to be, and that was a shame—one that would instead leave regret inside our camp.

Riding high on our successes just a few weeks earlier, Marty and

I had gone to Japan just before Christmas 1992 to do a full-blown media blitz to set up the tour that was scheduled to begin the following April. We had a blast! We were wined and dined like rock stars by our record label, Toshiba/EMI, and given the golden treatment on *every* level, including photos outside Budokan, which would appear in all the major Japanese rock magazines. It felt big, just like seeing our heroes KISS and Cheap Trick with their famed Budokan live albums and appearances when we were teenagers.

By now, Marty was fluent in the Japanese *Kanji* dialect. He was turning Japanese each and every day. He studied the language, connected with the locals, and dated only Japanese girls. He steeped himself in their culture and their customs. For Marty, the tour of Japan represented one of the pinnacles of his guitar-playing career and gave him a firm foundation in the Japanese culture. Not winning the Grammy, and then the tour's cancelation, was the beginning of the end for Marty's enthusiasm in Megadeth, although we wouldn't totally comprehend it for several years to come.

I remember Marty telling me on the *Cryptic Writings* tour in 1998 that the cancelation of the *Countdown* tours took the wind out of our sails in a way that we never really fully recovered from. Sadly, he was probably right; many more addictions, rehab stints, and other drug-related events would follow in the lead-up to his departure in 1999, and the subsequent breakup of the band in 2002. One can only guess what success we would have had if the *Countdown* cycle had not been interrupted. But I digress …

As for Julie and me, we had met in August 1988, during McGhee's short stint of managing Megadeth. I walked into the company's LA office on Sunset Boulevard to pick up my tickets for the MTV Awards that month, and there was Julie. It was her first day in the office following her relocation from New York, and we hit it off immediately. I knew it was taboo to date the office girl, but my instincts got the better of me, so I asked her out.

Our evening date consisted of going to see an LA Kings game at the Fabulous Forum, where McGhee had box seats. I then took Julie to dinner at a Mexican restaurant on Sunset Boulevard, across from the Guitar Center. We ordered a couple of drinks, finished our meal, and then I stopped by to see my friend to pick up some cocaine—a detour Julie was completely unaware of at the time. (While she was no prude, she also isn't an addict.)

By this time, I was addicted to heroin and cocaine, which would in fact become part of the reason McGhee ended up stopping working with us. And though Julie stood by me through the first of three stints in drug and alcohol rehab over the next year, we split up in early 1989. Like any sane and reasonable woman, she didn't want to deal with my addiction, so she got on with her life while I tried to get sober and figure out mine.

We reconnected in early 1990, when I turned the corner into my sobriety, and since then we have enjoyed a wonderful relationship and now twenty-four years of marriage. At the time of writing, I also have twenty-eight years of continuous sobriety, and it has become the cornerstone of my life as a husband, father, and musician.

In many ways, my sobriety since 1990 is my way of making amends to our fans, and to Dave and the Megadeth organization, for the embarrassment and loss of income caused by my addition so many years ago, not least when we had to cancel three Monsters Of Rock festival shows with Iron Maiden in the fall of 1988.

It's also nice to know my kids have never seen either Julie or me drink. We have raised our family in a sober household, and as a result, by the standards of rock'n'roll households, they have had a terrific and unusually sane upbringing. I always say that decadence seems to have skipped a generation in our house. I couldn't be happier.

Julie retired from management in 1993, which is the year we moved from Los Angeles to our current home of Scottsdale, Arizona. We are so blessed that I have been able to float the boat financially for our family, allowing her to be a stay-at-home mother to our two children, Roman and Athena. In many ways, our life today mirrors my life growing up on the farm: Mom stayed at home to raise my brother and me while Dad worked the farm to ensure we were financially provided for. It's been a good arrangement, and one I wouldn't change for anything. We are truly blessed.

Fast-forward to 2017, and Megadeth have been nominated for a Grammy Award for the twelfth time in our career. I had attended a few more award shows since 1993, including the 2014 Grammys, when I took my daughter Athena along with me. Although we didn't win, that night was a win on a whole other level. Not many teenage daughters get to actually go the Grammy Awards and see their entire Spotify playlist perform right in front of them! Athena was beyond thrilled to have the experience. But while the Grammys are always fun, it is disheartening to get your hopes up, only to hear them say, 'And the Grammy Award goes to … not you!'

But 2017 was different. *Dystopia* was an incredible album and tour campaign. I credit 5B for strategically managing the band to the point where it now felt as if we might actually win this time.

Julie and I flew in to LA for the show, and Dave and his wife Pam were there, too, as was our new drummer, Dirk Verbeuren, and his wife Hannah. Kiko rode down to the Staples Center with Julie and me, and we were all spiffed out in our tuxedos, ready to walk the red carpet together as a band.

We settled inside the Microsoft Theater in Downtown LA, where the non-televised part of the ceremony was held, waiting for our category to be called. Category 69, 'Best Metal Performance.' As the nominees were listed, I remember holding Julie's hand in tense suspension. And then, the moment we had been waiting for since 1991: 'And the Grammy Award goes to … Dystopia, Megadeth!' I get chills even typing it—the memory is so unreal.

The Grammy moment came, and it was ours to have. Head from KoRn, who was also nominated in the 'Best Metal Performance' category, ran up to give us a high-five. As we walked up to the stage with our heads held high, the orchestra struck up Metallica's 'Master Of Puppets' as the song to correspond with the metal category. I don't think we cared; we *floated* to the podium to receive our award.

After a wonderful and witty acceptance speech by Dave, casually referencing the Grammys' unorthodox song choice, we were whisked backstage to make a shout-out to the Grammy.com live broadcast, then to have our photo taken with the committee, and finally escorted to the 'winners' circle' backstage at the Staples Center. We were nothing but smiles ear to ear. We were so unbelievably happy, we honestly didn't even have words to convey our joy.

KIKO LOUREIRO ❝The whole Grammy thing. Isn't it crazy? Like, twelve times the guys are nominated, and then I join the band and record an album, and two years later, a Grammy. I'm from Brazil, so that's not something I ever even thought of. And I have a Grammy here now—it's crazy. I didn't know what to expect.

To be honest, I was very positive. I didn't know anything about the Grammys— how it goes, who votes, what are the possibilities. I think Mustaine and Ellefson, because they were there twelve times, they were probably, like, 'Whatever,' but for me, I was very positive. It's a great album, all the fans like it. It's Megadeth. How could everybody not vote for Megadeth? I was very positive. It has to be the best album. It is. And not even 'cause I was there. It is. If I was not in the band, from the outside, what, thirteen times they've been nominated? You guys deserve it. I was very positive, like, 'Yeah, this has to be.'

But then, when I was watching all the other awards, the other styles of music, and seeing who won, now I understood that it's not easy. Sometimes the winner is a big artist, sometimes it's not. Sometimes it's a new, trendy person in that style, so it's not really related to the legacy. So it could be anything. And then I realized it was gonna be difficult. You had KoRn, Mastodon, Periphery ... I thought, well, maybe not. So I was kind of nervous before they announced the name. It's, like, five artists, so our chances are, like, twenty percent. But before the event, I was thinking we have to win ... we're Megadeth. I think, in a way, you have to be positive. I think it helps. And then it was crazy—suddenly we were onstage in our tuxedos. 🇯🇯

THOM HAZAERT ❝ *It was a pretty awesome moment when you guys won. I remember calling David, literally right as you guys won—it was pretty early in the afternoon, so I figured it was safe to call. And he actually answered and was like, 'Dude, we just won the Grammy.' I was in the car with my kids and just started fucking screaming at the top of my lungs like a lunatic. My kids thought I'd lost it. But it was amazing to get to share that moment, and it really says so much about David, that he actually, in the middle of winning a Grammy, right as you guys were about to go onstage in one of the biggest moments of his career, he actually answered the phone to tell me. And I was so happy.* 🇯🇯

KIKO LOUREIRO ❝ *I was very happy, but I was really happy for Mustaine and Ellefson. I could feel how important it is for them. So many times being nominated, to finally win. To me, it was just so distant, being from Brazil, winning a Grammy is like, 'Do you want to go to the Moon?' It was just so far from my reality. But everything is possible right? But for the guys, I could see their happiness, and how excited they were. It's so important for them, not winning twelve times, and seeing other bands winning, every year. For me, it was amazing, and I was so happy to have the Grammy, but also to see the happiness of Ellefson and Mustaine. After all those nominations, and being invited so many times, after, what, thirty-three years, to finally win. It was amazing.* 🇯🇯

As the night wore on, I received congratulations from so many of our friends and peers—people like Nikki Sixx, members of Disturbed, and so many family and friends around the world. We were truly finally in the winners' circle with the likes of Beyoncé, Bruno Mars, and Elton John, and it felt great.

Following the award show, we party-hopped around town, well into the night. This was our night to enjoy, and we did! The next day, Julie and I flew home, and on the journey we were reminiscing about the time we left the 1993 awards as sore losers. Now, twenty-four years later, we were able to enjoy the moment together. In a way, it was as much a triumph for me and Julie, and all that we had been through in a rocky career with Megadeth.

As the saying goes, behind every great man is an even greater woman, and Julie is the backbone of my life. She allows me to live my dreams while she raises our family. Because of her, I lead a charmed life. We really do have it all!

7.3 GRAMMY-WINNING RECORDING ARTISTS

The Grammy win was certainly the right way to ring in 2017. In fact, I can regularly feel the increased notoriety that came to the band from that one event. Megadeth and Beyoncé on the front of Grammy.com? That's not something you see every day! And, from that moment on, we were officially 'Grammy Award–Winning Recording Artists'! Not something everyone can say.

We continued the *Dystopia* tour into Asia in April and May, with those shows including our debut appearances in Malaysia and Hong Kong, which was really cool. Hong Kong is just one of those truly iconic cities, and being there was another bucket-list item to check off.

Just when you think you've been everywhere, there are more nations to conquer with metal. I love that about Megadeth; we go everywhere to take our music to our fans, and it keeps things fresh for us, too! We continued onward into our second visit to Shanghai and Beijing, and then wrapped the run in Japan, with Anthrax as our support.

In September, we kicked off the Scorpions/Megadeth tour. We've played with Scorpions many times over the years, but this tour would prove legendary for the way it brought several generations of metal fans under one roof. The Crazy World tour, as it would come to be called, took us to some of the largest arenas in North America. We played Madison Square Garden in New York City, as well as several other major basketball arenas around the continent.

Unfortunately, Scorpions had to cancel the last five shows due to vocalist Klaus Meine contracting severe laryngitis. But not before we got to play the Forum in Los Angeles—another first for me. I'd seen so many bands play there when I lived in LA from 1983 to '93, and to me it represented arriving at the absolute top of the heap. I'd seen bands like Bon Jovi, Mötley Crüe, The Cult, Duran Duran, and Billy Idol on the stage of the Forum. For me, Megadeth with Scorpions at the Forum was another 'pinch me' moment of my career.

Back home in Arizona a week early, I had another event to prepare for: the relaunch of Ellefson Coffee Co. at Kat's Hog Heaven during the second week of November, which also doubled as my birthday celebration. Legendary vocalist Ron Keel, newly signed to EMP, performed at the event with his band, and the press and local media ate it up. Somehow, despite our enforced relocation following the closure of Coffee Choices, we had landed on our feet.

Usually, when I come off tour, I set the bass down and let my body relax. Not this time! My friend Glen Sobel hit me up and asked if I would be available to play bass for Rob Halford and Alice Cooper's set at Alice's annual charity event, Christmas Pudding, at the Celebrity Theater in Phoenix. Not only was I honored, in a strange way this was a way to reconcile myself with not jumping on the Alice Cooper tour offer in 2002.

Being a major Judas Priest fan, I knew most of Rob's songs already, but Alice's songs were a bit more tricky, largely because the original bassist, Dennis Dunaway, is such an amazing player, and the tunes were from the early 70s, a time when bass playing was a bit more melodic and even more progressive than what followed in the 1980s. I love being challenged by learning new songs that I've heard on the radio my whole life. It's one thing to *hear* them—it's a whole other thing to actually *play* them!

My dear friend Slash was joining us for several songs, and I hadn't played with him since the late 80s. Add to that, Ace Frehley would be jamming with us on the encore, and although he had been in and out of KISS a couple times, he's still the guy whose poster was on my wall as a kid for many, many years. It was going to be like jamming with all my superheroes, all at once! Tell that to the fifteen-year-old David Ellefson. The honor was truly mine that evening.

We did one final coffee event to wrap up the year at a Scottsdale coffee shop known as Maverick Coffee. We had just signed Alice Cooper's son Dash and his band Co-Op to EMP, so we asked them and Doll Skin to be our featured musical acts. The event was a huge success, and once again we showed that one thing Ellefson Coffee Co. is good at is throwing a hell of a party!

It was after this event that thee Hydra Beer Company from neighboring Sioux Falls approached us about infusing one of their beers with our Urban Legend coffee to create the Urban Legend Coffee Stout. While I don't drink, I saw the merit of branching out into other areas of the food and beverage market. In my mind, coffee is great in the morning and after a meal, but not something most folks tend to enjoy at entertainment venues or in the middle of a hot summer rock concert. At the same time, we were introduced to Desert Rock Winery in Scottsdale, which would lead to some more amazing opportunities, including a line of Combat Wines. Our brands were really taking shape.

We wound down the holiday season with family, but also made plans to exhibit Ellefson Coffee Co. and EMP Label Group at the following month's NAMM show. It would be hard to relax, with so much to prepare for, but somehow, even as a small but growing company, we seem to find a way when there often seems to be no other way. That seems to be the EMPire way!

FROM WHENCE WE CAME

8.1 FROM THE CORNFIELD TO THE HALL OF FAME

DAN DONEGAN (GUITARIST, DISTURBED) *❝I don't want to diss anybody that's lived on the coast, but for us, I think there is this certain work ethic in the Midwest. Just that blue-collar mentality, really having to go out there and work your butt off, be a machine.*

I was a union carpenter before the band got signed, I was framing houses, and I think part of my drive was, I was sick of building houses in zero-degree weather, in the middle of winter. I was like, There's got to be something better …❞

The Midwest has changed a lot since my days growing up there. When I left Jackson in 1983, Prince was the 'next big thing' coming out of Minneapolis. Before that, the region mostly consisted of farmers playing country music in the background in their tractors, coupled with the outcasts who loved rock'n'roll.

It's ironic that all these years later, in 2018, I would be inducted into the Iowa Rock 'n' Roll Music Association's Hall of Fame at Lake Okoboji, by Spirit Lake, just over the border into Iowa, about forty-five minutes from my hometown of Jackson.

Okoboji is a great summertime lake area. I used to go there to buy 3.2 percent beer with my buddies on the weekend, as Minnesota was a dry state on Sundays. Lake Okoboji also had a great music venue called the Roof Garden, where I saw groups like Head East and Black Oak Arkansas perform as a teenager. In the years before, it had played host to other Midwest national up-and-comers such as Ted Nugent, Styx, and

REO Speedwagon, before they had the breakthrough hits that launched them into the sports arenas and FM radio.

This is also where the Hall of Fame is situated, and I am so proud to be recognized for my successes in this community. The hall also includes many other musicians from the area—even Slipknot!— but what takes me back is the relic of a corner booth they salvaged when they tore down the Fox Lake Ballroom, which used to reside in Sherburn, Minnesota, about fifteen minutes east of Jackson. My bands played Fox Lake regularly, and it was a key hotspot for weekend concerts and shows by Top 40 rock acts who were popular in the area.

I'd say a highlight for me was when my band Killers opened for a popular Minneapolis act called Chameleon, who sounded pretty much like early Bon Jovi. They had four albums out, a semi-truck for their gear, a road crew, a spinning drum kit (five years before Tommy Lee did it!), and a keyboardist named Yiannis Chryssomallis, who went by the much more pronounceable stage name Yanni. Yes, *that* Yanni.

But trying to start a rock band in that area in the late 1970s and early 80s was a whole other story. My dear friend Greg Handevidt, who now practices law and lives in Mankato, has not only remained one of my best friends over the years but was also the one with whom most of my band endeavors happened. I had the drive and he had the balls to actually go out and do it.

Greg and I moved to LA together after our high-school graduation in May 1983, and it was his idea to call the band Megadeth, after a song our new friend Dave Mustaine had penned called 'Megadeath.' It was Dave's first post-Metallica song, and was inspired by then California senator Alan Cranston and his views on global nuclear disarmament.

Greg and I first met by the lockers in the hallway of Riverside Grade School in Jackson during the fifth grade, when we had a conversation about the band KISS. Greg had just relocated to Jackson and was already known around the campus as a loud, rebellious troublemaker, which I was not, but music became our bond. It's funny that I was raised a decent and modest person, but I have this tendency of hooking up with loud, boisterous guitar players. I guess I am the yin to their yang, and that's what makes it work.

I had just started playing bass around this time, and Greg was taking up the electric lead guitar. We were a perfect fit—I was the levelheaded, business-minded guy with drive, ambition, and focus, and Greg was the bold, adventurous loudmouth who was never afraid of an audience, a good-looking girl, or a good fight. In short, he *was* rock'n'roll, and together we were a team.

GREG HANDEVIDT (FORMER GUITARIST, MEGADETH) ❝*David and I met in the hallway at school. I was walking one direction, in line with my homeroom class, and he was walking the other direction. And as he was passing by, I saw he had a KISS logo scribbled onto his notebook, and I looked at him and I go, 'KISS uses Gibson guitars and Pearl drums!' And David turns around and goes, 'And Marshall amps!' From then on, we were fast friends. We just started hanging out, because we had that common musical interest. And it just kind of grew from there.*

I started playing guitar shortly after that, and he was already playing bass. Then we just started sort of jamming together, little kids thinking we were cool. That's how it started. We played our first quote-unquote professional show I think when we were thirteen. I think we got, like, fifty bucks or something. We were always serious about, we were going to be rock stars. There was never really any question in our minds—that's what we were going to do. We were serious about it. When we would play, we would expect ourselves to be perfect when we played the songs. We had this drummer Justin Neunschwander—well, we had a couple different drummers. I think we called it Tombstone, or Polaris. We had a bunch of different iterations. We were, like, eleven or twelve when we started learning songs—BTO songs, Cheap Trick songs—and thinking we were really gonna do this.

We had an original song, 'Riverboat Queen,' which was like the first song Dave ever wrote. It was cool for, like, a twelve-year-old or a thirteen-year-old or something. It was, like, a D chord, and you kept sliding it up. I can still remember the riff. That was, like, the first rock'n'roll song he wrote for one of our bands.

One seminal moment we had, we set up and played in the grade school, because the grade school had, like, an auditorium in it, with a stage. We got permission to play in the school one day—I forget if it was some kind of an assembly or something, I can't remember for sure how it came to be, but we went up there and we played, like, three songs. And, oh my gosh, they were just appalled. I wasn't wearing a shirt, which they were absolutely horrified by, and we were loud, and we were playing rock'n'roll. That was like our first almost punkish moment, where we sort of came out as rebellious, anti-establishment types.

I think the first show that we played for money was either up at the Jackson County Fair, or it might have been at the Armory. Jackson used to have this really cool armory—it was like this huge basketball court auditorium, and they'd have dances in there. Usually they'd have country bands come through, maybe like some rockabilly kind of thing. There were these guys in town they owned Lusk Music, which was the record store in town—it was Larry and Davy Lusk, and they had this country band, The Lusk Brothers. I remember my grandma had their album, and I thought it was the coolest thing. But they headlined it, there was this other band called Tres Hombres, and us.

The first concert that we ever saw was KISS, up in the Twin Cities, and the tickets were, like, $7.50. Dave's mom drove us. She and her good friend Sherri Conlin took us, and they sat there with us and watched the show. Dave and I were just in awe, because we were both such hardcore KISS fans. And it was just an amazing show. It was the tail end of Destroyer—Uriah Heep opened. I think they played a few songs from Rock'n'roll Over, but it hadn't come out yet, I don't think, so we didn't really know them.

I think the next show we went to after that was Cheap Trick, out in Sioux Falls. Here's the cool thing about that show. We had just discovered AC/DC. At the time,

I was working at Lusk Music, and whenever the new albums came in, I would go through them and pull out all the ones that looked cool. Let's just say I never got a paycheck. They basically paid me in records. So we basically discovered AC/DC when If You Want Blood … You Got It *came into the store—the picture of Angus, with the guitar shoved through him, and blood spurting out everywhere. Oh. My. God. These guys must be cool. So I snatched that up, and I put it on, and by the first two notes of 'Riff Raff,' they're my new favorite band. Dave and I just started pounding that album. We couldn't believe it.*

Back then, a lot of times they didn't advertise the openers, so you had no idea. It would say 'Cheap Trick with Special Guests' or whatever. So we go out there, and it was a really cool place to see shows, because the floor was all general admission, so if you were first in line, you were front row. I think every show we saw out there, we were front row. We got there really early, there were maybe ten people ahead of us in line, we were right up there. They would open up the doors, it would be a mad rush—everybody would run to the stage.

We got there four hours before the doors were supposed to open—we didn't care, we were gonna be up front. So the word's going around: 'Who's opening for them? Who's the opening band?' And some guy comes up and says, 'I think it's some band called AC/DC.' And we were like, 'You've gotta be kidding, man.' And it turned out to be AC/DC on the Powerage *tour. So we saw Bon Scott, maybe eight months before he died. It was awesome.*

And we were right up front. We were planted right between center stage and Malcolm. And I'll never forget that show, ever, because of the shock—we were so into AC/DC, and they just happened to be on tour with Cheap Trick. We had no idea. To get out there and find out they were playing, we were totally surprised. And, to this day, it's one of the most awesome shows I've ever seen.

We saw some other really, really cool shows—we saw Talas opening for Van Halen in 1980, Rory Gallagher with Rush. Rush was just amazing. April Wine. We kind of grabbed every show that came through out there that we thought would be halfway decent. 🗨

Short of one brief stint in my senior year of high school, when our band Killers (formerly known as Toz) disbanded, and I joined a popular Iowa hard-rock outfit called Renegade, Greg and I were side by side from fifth through twelfth grade, which also meant through all of our bands.

Greg lived in town and had cable TV, so he had access to shows like *Don Kirshner's Rock Concert* and *The Midnight Special*. Plus he had lived in larger metropolitan cities and traveled to places like California. He also played sports and was much worldlier than I was at a young age. As a result, and probably because of his rebellious nature, he turned me onto bands like AC/DC, The Sex Pistols, UFO, Montrose, Cheap Trick, The Ramones, and more. As sheltered as my life was, living on a farm six miles north of Jackson, with most music coming to me from my mother and her record collection, Greg broke me out of the shell and helped put me on the path to rock'n'roll education. Our bands were very progressive in having original material Greg and I composed, and we quickly adapted to learn FM hard-rock songs that would allow us to perform around the area. Shows at Minnesota clubs, bars, and ballrooms like Fox Lake were the first steps to some sort of local notoriety.

From there, we branched out into Iowa and South Dakota. In particular, there was a band out of Iowa who helped us get gigs with them at the Bancroft Ballroom and other Iowa festivals. We used gunpowder for pyrotechnics, and on more than one occasion we set fire to low roofs, stage curtains, and anything else standing in our way! We knew what the likes of KISS, Angel, and the big boys were doing, so necessity was the mother of our invention.

GREG HANDEVIDT ❝*Throughout high school, we played a lot of shows. We had a booking agent, Greta. I remember she got mad because one of our promo pictures* we wanted to use, I was doing the metal horns, and she was like, 'Oh no that's the sign of the devil! You can't use that.'

I remember one show we played down in, like, Grettinger, Iowa, we're onstage and we look out and the whole place is in a huge brawl. Like, a huge biker brawl. We played a pretty cool show.

There was a band from Iowa who had a good following in the five-state area called Gray James. They were cool. They were a hard rock band, a cover band—I don't think they played originals—but they looked good, and they were cool, and they liked us, so we played with them fairly often.

There was another band, Chameleon. We played quite a few shows with them as well, but we had a little falling out with them, because there was a show that we played in Northern Minnesota, and the crowd was chanting 'Killers, Killers, Killers' while Chameleon was on, and they kind of got mad about that. At the next show we played with them, our sound guy, Greg Carlson, caught them unplugging the mid-speakers from the PA, sabotaging us. I think it was one of their roadies.

Yanni was always really cool. He was like the quiet dude that sort of hung out in the background. Really nice guy, always had a smile on his face. And then the bass player was this dude named Dugan, and he was kind of a squirrely, jumpy guy. He had a lot of personality. Johnny, the guitar player, he was a really good guitar player, and he had a really good, heavy guitar tone. But Chameleon was a big regional band back then. They had a couple of albums out; they had a pretty decent following. We played a lot of shows with them when we were in high school.

We had our 'get us hired' setlist, and then we had our actual setlist, which we would play. Our 'get us hired' setlist had all kinds of wanky songs in it—slow dances and, like, .38 Special songs. Stuff that would get us hired at school dances. And then we'd get there and we'd say, 'Oh, we don't play that one anymore, we replaced it with "Love Me Like A Reptile" by Motörhead.' Once we showed up, and they paid us, too bad. And then we'd turn their dance into a concert, where everyone is standing by the stage pumping their fist, instead of dancing.

Of course, the school people would be mad. We didn't care—we just wanted to play shows. We had songs on our setlist that we never even learned. 'Oh, let's play this song. It'll get us some gigs.' And then we never even learned it. 'Yeah, we replaced that with "Sanctuary" by Iron Maiden. It's got a good beat. You can dance to it.'

But by the time we were in high school, we were really serious. At one point, I know that Greta was billing us as 'The Youngest Hard Rock Band in the Five-State Area,' because we were, like, sixteen, seventeen. And we were good. By the time we were sophomores in high school, we were deadly serious. We were tight, and the thing about our approach was, we never bit off more than we could chew. Whatever we did, we did it really well.

We knew how good we were at each phase of our development, and we never tried to push too far beyond it. Except when we were rehearsing, and practicing, and trying to work new stuff up. And that helped us to be a tight, really good band who could go out and play. It helped us compete with all these other guys that are, like, thirty years old, and we're out there keeping up with them.

As we got on further into high school, we were playing really sophisticated metal, New Wave Of British Heavy Metal stuff. We were playing Judas Priest stuff, and not just 'You've Got Another Thing Coming'—we were playing 'The Hellion,' 'Electric Eye,' Maiden songs off the first two albums. We played 'Killers,' we played 'Murders In The Rue Morgue.' We played B-side stuff.

There was a time when David went off and was with this band down in Iowa, Renegade—I got mad at him, I was jealous, and all that. We went through that little crap. But then Bill Heller, the guitar player in Renegade, was really good. And David sort of snagged him away from them, and he came and started jamming with us in our senior year of high school.

By the time we graduated, we knew what we wanted to do. We were sitting around trying to make a plan, figure out what we were gonna do, and that's when we decided, you know what, we gotta go to LA, man. So that's what we did. 🙶

CUB SCOUT DEN #1--

Cub Scout Den #1 won the trophy at the Blue and Gold Banquet last Monday night for having the most parents at the annual banquet. Members of Den #1 include David Ellefson, Jeff Olson, Mark Nelson, Kevin Trosine, Mike Kielty, Brian Mix, Bradley Schmidt, and Paul Nielsen. Bryan Johnson and Paul Jones are missing from the picture. Mrs. Daryl Olson is the Den Mother and Mrs. Dallas Schmidt is the Assistant Den Mother.

(PILOT PHOTO)

Vol. 1, Issue 3 - Jackson High School

KILLERS

THE KILLERS SONGLIST
November 1982

KILLERS

David Ellefson - Bass Guitar
Greg Hier - Vocals
Brett Frederickson - Drums
Brad Schmidt - Guitar

1. No Secrets (Angel City)
2. Everybody Wants You (Billy Squier)
3. I Think I'm In Love (Eddie Money)
4. Just What I Needed (The Cars)
5. Tough Guys (REO Speedwagon)
6. Take It On The Run (REO Speedwagon)
7. Just Between You And Me (April Wine)
8. I Like To Rock (April Wine)
9. Arizona (Scorpions)
10. Hang On For Your Life (Shooting Star)
11. Talk To You Later (The Tubes)
12. My Kind Of Lover (Billy Squier)
13. Midnight Rendezvous (The Babys)
14. Rockin' Into The Night (.38 Special)
15. Caught Up In You (.38 Special)
16. Fantasy (Aldo Nova)
17. Wasted (Def Leppard)
18. Rocks Off (Def Leppard)
19. Rock And Roll Party In The Streets (Axe)
20. Eye Of The Tiger (Survivor)
21. No One Like You (Scorpions)
22. Paranoid (Black Sabbath)
23. Transylvania (Iron Maiden)
24. Sanctuary (Iron Maiden)
25. Murders In The Rue Morgue (Iron Maiden)
26. Another Life (Iron Maiden)
27. Workin' For The Weekend (Loverboy)
28. The Hellion (Judas Priest)
29. Electric Eye (Judas Priest)
30. The Green Manalishi (Judas Priest)
31. On The Run (Judas Priest)
32. Headin' Out To The Highway (Judas Priest)
33. You Got Another Thing Comin' (Judas Priest)
34. You Really Got Me (Van Halen)
35. Somebody Get Me A Doctor (Van Halen)
36. Pretty Woman (Van Halen)
37. Where Have All The Good Times Gone (Van Halen)
38. Are You Ready To Rock (Michael Schenker Group)
39. No You Don't (Pat Benatar)
40. I Don't Know (Ozzy Osbourne)
41. S.A.T.O. (Ozzy Osbourne)
42. Flying High Again (Ozzy Osbourne)
43. Let's Get It Up (AC/DC)
44. Power (Rainbow)
45. Only One Way To Rock (Sammy Hagar)
46. Burnin' For You (Blue Oyster Cult)
48. Let It Go (Def Leppard)
49. Sin City (AC/DC)
50. Who Made Who (AC/DC)
51. Boom Boom (Out Goes The Lights) (Pat Travers)
52. Back On The Streets (The Blackhearts)
53. Lightning Strikes (Aerosmith)
54. We Don't Want No Anymore (Steelbreeze)
55. Don't Fight It (Kenny Loggins & Steve Perry)

ABOVE An early band photo shoot in front of my family farmhouse in Jackson. The River City Band featured high-school students much older than me. I was twelve. **TOP RIGHT** Winning a trophy with the cub scouts as a young boy. **CENTER RIGHT** With Killers, my last band in Jackson before I moved to Hollywood. *Left to right:* me, Greg Handevidt, Jerry Giefer, Brett Frederickson. **BELOW RIGHT** A Killers song list, which sported numerous Top 40 radio songs in order to get us gigs.

SKULL SPLITTING METAL!!!

FAST...LOUD...AND RUDE!

FEB.17th
BERKELEY, CA.
RUTHY'S INN
2618 San Pablo Ave.
(415) 849-3258

FEB.19th
SAN FRANCISCO
THE STONE
412 Broadway
(415) 391-8282

ABOVE Onstage during the *Peace Sells* world tour. This Jackson bass guitar provided the impetus for my current signature models. Photo by Harald Oimoen.
LEFT An ad for the first two Megadeth shows, in Berkeley and San Francisco, February 1984.

Hey Brad,

What the fuck!!! How have things been lately? I got your letter from back in January sometime + haven't had a chance to get back to you. How's the playing coming? Are you planning to come back here or go east?

We went to debut in San Fran on Feb. 17 in Berkeley, + the 19th right in San Francisco, + it was FUCKING GREAT!!!!! I'm telling you, the crowds are NUTS!! Have you seen all the slam dances, + punk crowds on T.V. well, it was that INTENSE!! People were yanking on us, the mics + thrashing everything else in sight. In San Fran, someone in the crowd reached right up + broke the E string off my bass!! They're fucking crazy thrashers!!!!

We had a helluva good time + got stoned + caused all kinds of trouble. We took a band called ABBATOIR up there with us + they went down all right. Supposedly, there's tapes of that gig all over the world. One kid sent his to Germany!!

The other night Dave talked to a producer from Roadrunner records from Holland (they handle Mercyful Fate) + they want to start negotiating this week. So that's good. A producer from Shrapnel keeps calling to sign us, too, so now we will definitely sign with someone. Probably Roadrunner, + record with Megaforce in New Jersey. I'll keep you posted.

We're going to move to San Fran. in May cause you know how bad it sucks here!! Frisco was cool. It's such a clean city. At least you see trees + grass, unlike down here. We have to play 3 nights (April 14, 15 + 16) at the Keystone in San Fran, Berkeley, Palo Alto so we definitely need a killer crew. It wasn't too bad, but it would be great if you wanted to work with us!! We hope to go to N.J. in June or July to record, depending on what happens with Roadrunner.

This is a rough drawing of our stage. It's pretty heavy, huh?! I had 6 bass cabs plus Matt's 2 Marshall cabs, Matt's head + a 200w Marshall head. Dave had 9 heads + 6 cabs + so did Kerry (the other guitarist). Believe me, it was POWERFUL not as loud as powerful, so it sounded good.

So ANYWAY enough about Megadeth! say hello to Yonker, Carlson + whoever else. Write back + let me know what's up with you, your plans + whatever else. Expect to hear from you soon. Same Address!!

THRASH TILL MEGADETH!!
David

THIS PAGE A letter I wrote to my friend Bradley Schmidt in 1984, after he moved back to Minnesota. These letters home helped me maintain some ballast while I was sailing forward with my new career in Megadeth. Note the stage set design on the second page. My return address was just one of many temporary landing spots Dave and I found when we were getting the band off the ground in 1983–84.

RIGHT In 1986, Dave and I stopped back at the farm in Jackson after finishing the *Peace Sells* album for some much-needed rest and relaxation. We are pictured here with my lifelong friend Bradley Schmidt. BELOW Mom, me, and Dad backstage at Roy Wilkins Auditorium in St. Paul, Minnesota on the *Countdown To Extinction* tour 1992. OPPOSITE On the *Peace Sells* tour in 1986, around the time Chris Poland joined the band as second guitarist. Photo by Harald Oimoen.

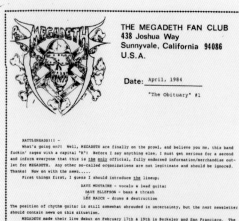

THE MEGADETH FAN CLUB
438 Joshua Way
Sunnyvale, California 94086
U.S.A.

Date: April, 1984

"The Obituary" #1

RATTLEHEADS!!! -
What's going on?! Well, MEGADETH are finally on the prowl, and believe you me, this band
fuckin' rages with a capital 'R'! Before I say anything else, I must get serious for a second
and inform everyone that this is the only official, fully endorsed information/merchandise outlet for MEGADETH. Any other so-called organizations are not legitimate and should be ignored.
Thanks! Now on with the news.....
First things first, I guess I should introduce the lineup:

DAVE MUSTAINE - vocals & lead guitar
DAVE ELLEFSON - bass & thrash
LEE RAUCH - drums & destruction

The position of rhythm guitar is still somewhat shrouded in uncertainty, but the next newsletter
should contain news on this situation.
MEGADETH made their live debut on February 17th & 19th in Berkeley and San Francisco. The
first night was at Ruthie's Inn, Berkeley, but unfortunately the show was not advertised and only
130 bangers managed to make it. Also, horrendous sound problems plagued the band all evening.
However, the Ruthie's fiasco was quickly forgotten when MEGADETH hit The Stone in S.F. two days
later (Dave's old stomping ground with METALLICA)! A near sell-out crowd of 500 Bay Bangers
(The Stone holds 600) turned up and gave Mr. Mustaine & Co. their true baptism of fire. As
mentioned earlier, the band is without a permanent rhythm guitarist, but kindly appearing as
"guest" rhythm axe was KERRY KING of SLAYER fame. Although the attendance figure is down impressive (Remember, this was only the second time they'd been onstage together!), since the gig
was on a "school night", many of the "school age" Metalheads were unable to attend, so rest assured the next time MEGADETH invade The City By The Bay they'll have a sold out house on their
hands!
Now on to the important thing: THE TUNES!!! Here's a quick rundown of the MEGADETH ar-
senal: "Hook In Mouth", "Burnt Offerings", "Chosen Ones", "Skull Beneath The Skin" (the band's
theme song), "Lookin' Down The Cross", "Love To Death" (Dave's ode to an ex-girlfriend), "Next
Victim", "Bad Omen", "Devil's Island", and "Rattlehead". Among the new songs that have just
been completed are "Conjur Me" (an instrumental) and "Black Friday". The band's sound is fast

(2)

and heavy of course, but what puts them ahead of many other "thrash" bands is their use of
interesting and unique chord progressions and scales, making the songs musically impressive
and thrashable! The boys also have some of the most outrageous lyrics around; if you're a
fan of George Romero or Herschel Lewis, you'll take to this band immediately.
Anyone who's seen or heard Dave's work with METALLICA already knows of his fast fingers
and song writing ability. However, on top of his musicianship, his vocals are amazingly
(SURPRISINGLY!) good! Also, the other members surprised the hell out of me too! Instead
of third-rate, poser players like I was half expecting (Sorry Dave!), they're attitude, playing, and onstage aggressiveness is far superior to more than a few of the "big name" bands
I've seen. "Aggressive" is an adequate catchword of MEGADETH; instead of standing around
up onstage like so many old and new fart bands, these guys take the show to the crowd! In
short, they're damn impressive, especially when you consider they've only really existed
for a mere three months! "THAT'S INCREDIBLE!!!" (cough...)
Anyway, that's it for now. Merchandise, tapes, etc. are all being planned even as we
speak. However, rather than spreading some rumors and raising false hopes, I'll just leave
it at that until things are confirmed. Rest assured though, these things will be available
in the coming months, which you will all be informed of A.S.A.P. Sure, MEGADETH are just
another one of those countless new bands on the scene, but I'm not bullshitting when I say
this band is a pure example of unadulterated Power Metal at it's most extreme. So stay in
touch and get in on the ground level of this organization.... RAGE 'TIL DETH!!!!!!!!!!

BRIAN LEW

STOP PRESS!!! MEGADETH will be making their second S.F. Bay Area trek on April 15th,
16th, & 18th in Berkeley, Palo Alto, and San Francisco respectively. Be there or die!
Kerry King will once again be playing rhythm.

ABOVE The original Combat Records *Bullets* compilation from 1986, featuring Megadeth's 'Peace Sells.' **LEFT** The *Obituary* newsletter was our earliest fan-club mailer, facilitated by our friends who pitched in to help us offer fans updates on our band activities. This was the very first letter, issued back in early 1984 as we launched the group.

ABOVE Onstage with Dave during a sort of homecoming gig at First Avenue in Minneapolis during the *Peace Sells* tour in 1987.
LEFT Taking a bite out of our debut LP for Combat Records, *Killing Is My Business … And Business Is Good.* Both photographs by Jeff Yonker.
FOLLOWING PAGE An ad for the *Kill For Thrills* US tour of 1985.

My father, Gordon, used to let us rehearse in our basement on the farm. He was super-supportive of me and my musical endeavors. God bless him for his tolerance, as he had not one musical bone in his body. But I think he admired that I found a passion, and that the guys and I were dedicated to our cause.

He put up with our loud music in the house, as well as our screaming, ranting and raving whenever there were band disagreements. On some level, I think he understood that that was all part of being an organization, learning how to get along. He eventually dedicated one of several farm sheds exclusively to becoming a band practice hall. He paid a professional to insulate the building and move a large furnace in so we'd be warm in the winter months. The shed had a large roll-up door, which allowed us to easily load our gear in and out and was large enough for us to store our gear, sound, and lights, as well as work on our stage performances.

I think the only time my dad got really furious with me over our music matters was not really over music at all. He would buy a full side of beef from a neighbor, so we'd have plenty of beef on hand for the year in our deep freezer. But in the summer of my junior or senior year of high school, we would rehearse in the evenings most every night. Someone would always have a few beers, and a few girls would be hanging about. I'd go fire up the outdoor grill and dig into the family deep freeze to graciously grab some steaks to feed the band tribe at our house. However, one evening my dad wanted a nice steak dinner for the family, and he was furious to discover that all the meat was gone. I had to confess that it was me who'd offered the family holdings to be devoured that summer during our band rehearsals. Oops … never again!

8.2 UNLEASHED IN THE MIDWEST

The day I bought Judas Priest's *Unleashed In The East* album on vinyl at age sixteen is the day my life changed. Until then, I had been searching out the heaviest and hardest music I could find, which was mostly American hard rock like KISS, Van Halen, Boston, and Aerosmith. But once Priest's live album landed on my stereo turntable, it was a whole new ballgame for me. I had never heard guitars so heavy, solos so blistering, pounding double-bass drums, or screaming vocals that were out of this world.

Like a lot of albums that changed my life, the cover photo was similarly important. With K.K. Downing's flying V and Rob Halford's total metal look, Judas Priest were like a gang of dangerous bikers—and I wanted in.

From there, Justin, the drummer in Toz, began turning me on to things like Black Sabbath's *Heaven & Hell* and Scorpions' *Lovedrive*. These were more melodic records, but they also had searing guitar tones, and, in the case of Sabbath, some amazing bass lines, too. The door to *real* heavy metal had been opened.

Shortly thereafter, we hired a new guitarist named Jerry Giefer, who came from the neighboring town of Windom. Jerry had only been playing guitar for about two years, but he was amazing—he had real natural talent, and he could play anything you put in front of him. His ear for music was incredible.

Jerry turned me and the Toz guys on to things like Motörhead's *Ace*

Of Spades and *No Sleep 'Til Hammersmith*, as well as Venom, Diamond Head, and the first two Iron Maiden albums, *Iron Maiden* and *Killers*. Around that time, Justin brought in the brand new Def Leppard LP, *On Through The Night*, and at that time I think vocalist Joe Elliott was the oldest member at only nineteen or twenty years old. Their drummer, Rick Allen, was only sixteen!

This was the New Wave Of British Heavy Metal (NWOBHM), and it changed our lives—so much so that we changed the name of our band from Toz to Killers …

BRIAN SLAGEL (FOUNDER, METAL BLADE RECORDS) ❝There's no doubt in my mind that none of us would be doing what we're doing without the NWOBHM, because we were all so heavily influenced by that. And then, obviously, we all grew up on the 70s stuff. And certainly Priest was one of the top ones there—AC/DC, KISS, you name it—but that whole scene that happened around 1979–80 that was going on over in Europe was a massive influence. You talk to any band that started in that same time and had success—they'd all say the same thing. If that scene didn't happen, I don't know if it would have gotten the American scene, and who knows what would have happened. ❞

It's because of this that I appreciate it when I see bands that name themselves after Megadeth songs. I get it! I was once that guy myself, and I take it as a nod of respect and appreciation for the music we created. Imagine how thrilled I was, then, so many years later, when we were offered the role of direct support to the mighty Judas Priest. This was in 1990: I was newly sober, and it was like a gift from the metal gods. The bill was Testament (supporting their *Souls Of Black* LP) as opener, then Megadeth, and then Priest, who had just released *Painkiller*, as the headliner. That tour took us across the USA and Canada in the fall of 1990 and into January 1991.

Soon after that, we made our first break into South America when we performed to over 140,000 people at Rock In Rio in February 1991, which really set the stage for Megadeth to break big across the continent in the decade that followed. It was also the show where I finally got to see Sepultura, who were from São Paulo, for the first time. Nick Menza was the guy in Megadeth who would often discover new cutting-edge metal bands, and Sepultura were one of his faves—he would often crank them out on the stereo in the back lounge of our tour bus on the Priest tour.

We played the metal day at Rock In Rio, on a bill featuring Sepultura, Queensrÿche, and Judas Priest, with Guns N' Roses as the closer. It was a monumental show, and it was also a monumental day for me, to have so many heroes on that stage.

K.K. DOWNING (FOUNDING GUITARIST, JUDAS PRIEST) ❝I've known David Ellefson for many years. Judas Priest and Megadeth have been on many, many shows together, we've toured pretty much everywhere—Europe, the UK, the States, and actually we did some shows in Mexico where we were supporting Megadeth, when we had Ripper in the band. I remember those shows pretty well. I think Megadeth were in their prime right about then. And when we played those shows in Mexico with Megadeth, with Priest supporting them, it was good, because I got to really watch the whole show.

When you headline, you don't always get to see or particularly appreciate what the opening bands are doing, because you're doing your own thing—interviews, getting ready for the show, warming up, stuff like that. You might get to pop out and catch a couple of songs, but that's not really what the show's all about. With Megadeth, for once, I had the chance to take in the whole show, and get the chance to really appreciate what they were able to do.

Rock In Rio was completely mad—it's one of those shows that you get bloody nervous about doing, you know? Brazil, Rock In Rio, so many fans there, and being televised throughout South America … you've got to be careful to put on a really good performance. You're out there, in a party town, in Rio De Janeiro, and then you get out the night before, you're pumped up for the gig, Brazilian girls everywhere, fans everywhere—it's pretty tough to sleep before an event like that. Priest did a lot of big shows, like the US festival, or Live Aid in Philadelphia—you get these big gigs that are more than just a festival. You get used to playing festivals, but some of these shows are so big, you just don't want to blow it by partying too hard the night before.

In fact, when we did Rock In Rio, I think Glenn [Tipton, guitarist] did party hard the night before, but obviously it didn't affect the gig—he managed to play well, but I don't think he slept the night before. I think he was afraid to move onstage for fear of being toppled over. I guess we can burn the candles and both ends and still put on a good performance. Guns N' Roses, I don't think they had a very good gig there. I didn't watch the band, but that was the feedback I got. I don't know what happened there, but … 🗨

KIKO LOUREIRO 🗨I always talk about this specific concert I went to, and I have so much fun watching this concert now—you can find it online. I was there as a big fan. I will never forget that concert. I saw Megadeth other times when they came in the 90s, but that specific concert was amazing. The lineup was great. I remember Marty Friedman on guitar was so loud. Mustaine's singing, and those complicated riffs. And Ellefson was such a great player. I was, like, eighteen, nineteen, and I was playing guitar already—I was just starting to have a band—and seeing them play with such energy …

I always tell people my impression of Megadeth is more from this period. The really early days, those albums were really hard to get in Brazil, so it was not the same thing as here in the US. I had friends, and we were into Slayer, or European bands like King Diamond, and then it was, like, tapes. Then music videos like 'Peace Sells'—that was huge for me—but that concert in '91, when you see a band live … back in the day, we didn't have that many concerts in Brazil, so seeing Judas

Priest Painkiller, Rust In Peace Megadeth, that was huge for me. They were a huge influence on me. 🙶

K.K. DOWNING 🙶*I think Megadeth are a band that are pretty disciplined, like me. Never, ever have I been on that stage and had a drink before I played. I really looked forward to having a few beers when I got offstage—that was a big reward for me. I think it's because of the intricacies of what they do musically—the guys all really need to be on the ball, and every time I've ever seen them, that was my observation.*

We've got some pretty tricky songs, too—if we're playing 'Ram It Down,' or 'Screaming For Vengeance,' or 'Painkiller,' it's physical and mental, with such fast, alternate picking, you can't really be wasted or you'll fall apart. Some bands we know and love are just rock'n'roll—they'll just go out there, cigarette in their mouth, Jack Daniels or gin and tonic in their hands, and if they're not quite in tune, or playing in time … whatever. There are bands that can do that, but for us, we have to deliver what the fans expect from us, which is the songs played properly, and how they should be. We had to be pretty cautious about our lifestyle, and how we handled everything.

With bands like Megadeth coming through, there was a new movement, obviously a very substantial and prolific one, in the States, bringing a unique brand of metal to the audiences. When I started listening to Megadeth, I'm thinking, wow, this band … because we were supposed to be the iconic heavy-metal band, but with a band like Megadeth, it's a much more intricately detailed, and somewhat more complex version of metal, with great instrumentation. It was something that definitely made our ears prick up. I can say, honestly, as much as Priest influenced a lot of bands, so many musicians in the world are walking in the footsteps of Megadeth. 🙶

8.3 METAL MASSACRE

By the time I got to LA, the Hollywood bands like Mötley Crüe, Quiet Riot, WASP, and Ratt had all begun their ascent into megastardom through their tireless work on the Sunset Strip. But the next generation of metal, which I would become a part of, was built on a more underground work ethic—one that was driven exclusively by its diehard fans and supporters. One of the earliest supporters of this was Brian Slagel, who founded Metal Blade Records.

Brian was always on the scene at metal shows in LA, and he was becoming well known as a young record-company mogul. His notoriety grew with the release of his *Metal Massacre* compilation albums, which featured the up-and-coming talent of the underground LA metal scene. A fun fact is that a few years earlier, Brian had become fast friends with the young Danish transplant, Lars Ulrich, who had relocated from Denmark to Orange County in hopes of following in his father's footsteps as a pro tennis player. Brian was an encouraging factor in Lars starting a band … a band that would become the global sensation known as Metallica.

Brian featured Metallica on his first *Metal Massacre* release in 1982, alongside Steeler, Bitch, Malice, Pandemonium, and more. (There were actually two versions of Metallica's featured song, 'Hit The Lights'—one with Lloyd Grant on guitar, and another on reissued versions of the album with the band's new lead guitarist, Dave Mustaine, recorded a year or so later.) Brian's passion for the harder metal scene drove the success of his label, which as a result is still thriving today and continues to launch metal bands from all corners of the world. The *Metal Massacre* albums were a real juxtaposition to the Hollywood hair-metal scene, and they really gave rise to our generation of thrash, power metal, and the LA underground scene.

BRIAN SLAGEL ❝*I didn't really do any of this to start a label, that's for sure. I was just a really huge fan of what was going on in England. I started the first ever American heavy-metal fanzine, The New Heavy Metal Revue—don't ask me why we spelled it that way. And then I got lucky enough to work at a record store in LA and started bringing in all that New Wave Of British Heavy Metal stuff, and started turning everybody in LA on to it.*

I started doing the local radio shows—giving them records to play on the metal show. I was doing a lot of journalistic stuff. We did an article in Sounds, which was a weekly magazine over in the UK, on Mötley Crüe. And then I actually ended up writing for Kerrang! I was doing all this stuff and I didn't really think I was going to start a label. But, around 1981, '82, there were all these bands playing in LA and no one knew they existed, because this was a million years before the internet. So I kind of got the idea from talking to all these importers that I was buying all the records from: 'Hey, if I put together a compilation of local LA heavy-metal bands, would you sell it?' And they all said, 'Sure!' I saw all these compilation albums that came from the New Wave Of British Heavy Metal, and I thought if they did it over there, maybe I can do it here.

So I started to go to a bunch of bands. Mötley was supposed to be on it, but they ended up putting out a record, so they didn't. But obviously Ratt was on it, and Malice, and Steeler. And then my friend Lars called me up and said, 'Hey, if I put together a band, can I be on your record?' And I said, 'Sure.' And that ended up being Metallica. The first version was just James and Lars doing 'Hit The Lights,' and then Lars's friend Lloyd Grant did the lead. And then, eventually, that sold out really quickly, and I had to repress it—a whole big long mess of that. ❞

JAY REYNOLDS (GUITARIST, MALICE) "I started Malice in 1981. There was a whole bunch of bands just starting out in LA, and the very first thing I did was, I got Malice set up on the Metal Massacre 1 record. I literally helped Brian Slagel put together his very first Metal Blade record. Metallica was on that one. Dave was in the band, and that was the first thing they released, was 'Hit The Lights' on Metal Massacre 1. Then, on Thanksgiving of '82, we played a Metal Massacre show—that was the first gig we played. That was pretty much when I met Mustaine. I had known Lars before that. "

RON KEEL (VOCALIST, KEEL/STEELER) "Steeler was up and coming on the Hollywood scene, and Metallica were just getting started, and they opened for us at the Whisky. I've got a photo of the marquee—definitely one of my favorite marquee photos. You always took a picture of the marquee, and I'm so glad we took a picture of the marquee that day, on the Sunset Strip in Hollywood.

I think we met Dave Mustaine at that point, and we were both just around in Hollywood. We were also on Metal Massacre 1 with Metallica. Brian Slagel was a huge Steeler supporter, and he did a lot for us at that time. We actually headlined the first Metal Massacre concert, and RATT was our opening band. The compilation had RATT, Metallica, Malice, Steeler … we had just released the 'Cold Day In Hell' single, and it was getting a lot of buzz, in the US and especially overseas. Sounds had given us a stellar review, and all of a sudden we were a force to be reckoned with. And Brian Slagel was putting together this compilation album, and he offered us the lead track on side one. The first track on the album. We gave him our 'Cold Day In Hell' single to use. It was only on the first pressing. I don't know why I did this—I thought it was a good business move, but looking back I wish I hadn't done it—but we limited his use of that track to only the first pressing. So after that first pressing, all consecutive versions had Black N' Blue's 'Chains Around Heaven' in place of the Steeler track. "

BRIAN SLAGEL "When we did the repressing, that's when they had the demo

185

together with Mustaine on it, and the proper band, so we put that version out on the second version.

One of the distributors who distributed the record was called Greenworld, and they eventually later became Enigma. But they came to me, because they knew I had no money—I had barely scraped up enough money together to make the first 2,500 copies of Metal Massacre. And they came and said, 'We know you don't have any money, but you might know what you're doing, so we'll give you a pressing and distribution deal, which means if you bring us something we'll manufacture and put it out.' I go, 'Well, I could probably do that.' So I just went to bands I knew, like Bitch and Armored Saint, and we started putting out records. And slowly but surely, over time, it turned into an actual record label.

Obviously I knew Dave from Metallica. And then, when he was not in Metallica anymore, I kind of figured he would do something else. I don't remember speaking to him directly about when Megadeth was forming, but I definitely heard from people around that he was forming another band, and that eventually became Megadeth. They started to play around and look around, so I was pretty well aware of them, probably before a lot of people, just because I knew people associated with David, and Dave Mustaine as well. Obviously he was going to form something, and that became Megadeth. **”**

8.4 HOLLYWOOD SQUARES

When I was sixteen years old, still living on the farm in Jackson, there was only one real guitar publication, and it was *Guitar Player* magazine. I hung on every word spoken through that publication—every interview and each advertisement was a pipeline of truth conveyed to me from a world of professional music experts beyond my realm.

Around this time, a Hollywood-based vocational music school called Musicians Institute started to run advertisements in *Guitar Player*. It boasted a 'real-world education' from respected top-level musicians in Los Angeles, including the guys from Toto. That got my attention! The school also seemed like the perfect vehicle for talking to my parents about making a legitimate move to LA to pursue a higher education in music. After all, what parent doesn't want their kid going to college—especially one that could lead to a real job? Musicians Institute was my ticket to LA, and, once I got there, I could quickly find or start a band and pursue the climb to the top of the rock'n'roll ladder.

Fortunately, my parents were on board. I soon discovered that my father had had his own explorations in California sometime after his high-school graduation, which is no doubt why he supported me leaving the farm to pursue my ambitions in LA. Soon, my three friends and I began to prepare for the pilgrimage westward. It was me, my childhood friends Brad Schmidt and Greg Handevidt, and a neighboring young bassist named Brent.

As a parent now myself, I can't even fathom letting my kids run off to the showbiz capital of the world without any parental supervision. I know now the sleepless nights our parents must have had while their teenage sons packed up and left home only five days after their high school graduation!

However, once we arrived in LA, a sobering reality quickly set in. In Minnesota, rock'n'roll stardom was an untouchable dream—something only my idols in the posters on my bedroom wall had achieved. Now we were in their backyard, in Hollywood, and it was time for me to suit up and show the world what I had to offer as a bassist and an entertainer. Suddenly it seemed like moving to LA was maybe not such a great idea. But fear can only hurt you—it usually doesn't help you.

It was one evening after Greg and I had met Dave Mustaine for the first time, in June 1983, that we sat in our downstairs apartment and he looked at me and said, laughing, 'Dude, lets face it … we're hicks!' It was true: we were small-town kids living in a big-city world now. It was time to get hip and get with the plan.

GREG HANDEVIDT ❝We had seen an ad for GIT—Musicians Institute, it's called now—and we were like, 'Dude, we need to do this. This would be so cool.' We had heard somewhere that once in a while Eddie Van Halen would come by and do clinics, and we were like, 'That's what we have to do.' So went out there to make our bones, and we intended to go to Musicians Institute, but whatever came, came, you know? And what came was Dave Mustaine.

That's such a wacky story, too. David's dad, Gordon—I don't know if it was a relative or a family friend, but he knew someone out there that she owned a building, and he got us an apartment in Hollywood. From back in Jackson, Minnesota, he gets us an apartment in Hollywood, we go and move in, and there, lo and behold, we move in right below Dave Mustaine. He literally lives directly above us. We get in there, we get moved in, and we're trying to get our feet back under us. We moved out there with two other guys, Brad Schmidt and Brent Giese, and they moved in the apartment upstairs, next to Mustaine. ❞

BRADLEY SCHMIDT ❝David and I have known each other since we were five or six years old. We were cub scouts together, so I've actually known David longer than Greg. I was born in Jackson, but I moved away after third grade, and then we reconnected when we were in high school, after we were all able to drive. I'd moved to Windom, which is just, like, seventeen miles away, but it might as well be the other side of the universe when you're a kid. My mother was best friends with Justin Neuenschwander's mom, though, so I always kind of knew what was going on in Jackson.

I was probably fifteen when I reconnected with David again—because of Jerry Giefer, who was the guitar player from Windom that joined up with Greg and David in their band, Killers. I don't know if the band was officially called Toz at the time, but it eventually became Killers. So David and I reconnected, and I met Greg. I don't know if Jerry was fired from Killers or he quit Killers, but they were looking for another guitar player, and I was his replacement. However, it never really came to be, because David, shortly thereafter, joined up with Renegade, a band from Estherville, Iowa.

Of course, if you talk to everybody else involved, there are probably little branches that go off and tell a whole other story. But David goes off and joins Renegade, and we're all still friends, we're still doing stuff together. This was all in our senior year of high school. Somehow, Brett Frederickson—the drummer for Killers, who was also from Windom—myself, Greg, David, and this other bass player friend from Windom, Brent Giese, we all started talking about going out to California to go to Musicians Institute. I don't know how deep the other guys got into it, but I actually applied and was accepted, and I got a grant from the Pell program to actually go to GIT. Brett actually didn't end up going out there with us, but all of us told our parents that we were going out there to go to school. I think that made it easier for the parents to accept.

For myself, though, I actually did go through the process of applying, and I got accepted. So we all moved out to LA, and we moved into the apartment upstairs from David and Greg, right next door to Dave Mustaine. 🎔🎔

GREG HANDEVIDT 🎔🎔*So we're out there and we start rehearsing, in earnest, down in our little apartment. And we were like, 'It's 9:30 in the morning, we can start cranking now, it's late.' You know, having grown up back here on the farm, where you're up at the crack of dawn. Nine o' clock in the morning, we're up, and we're tearing up Maiden songs. And Tracy, this girl that lived with Dave upstairs, throws a flowerpot down and it smashes onto our AC unit, and she's screaming at us to shut up. So we stop playing.*

The thing is, the buildings were so close that you could see the reflections of the other apartments on the windows of the building next to us. And I would see Dave, hanging out the upstairs window, listening to us. We'd be standing there, playing, and you could see him hanging out the window, listening. So we knew he was up there, and we knew he had to be a metal guy, just because of how he looked.

I can't remember if it was the same day, or a day or two later, that we ran out of cigarettes. We didn't know anybody—at that point we hadn't really even ventured out of the apartment yet—and now we're out of smokes. So we're like, 'Let's go up and talk to that dude upstairs.' So we go up and we knock on his door, and he answers the door, and we go, 'Hey, do you know where we can get some cigarettes?' He looks at us like we're aliens, with that Mustaine sneer, like, 'What are you talking about, you idiots?' He kind of looks at us a second, and he goes, 'Oh, are you the guys from downstairs?' And we're like, 'Yeah.'

So then he invites us in, and we tell him our story, and here we are. He takes us down Hollywood Boulevard, over to the little liquor store, and we get our stuff. We ended up hanging out with him all night that night—we sat up in his apartment till, like, three o' clock in the morning, just talking about stuff and getting to know each other. It was a blast.

We knew from like the very first time we met him that there was something special about him. That first night was great. We sat up there, drank Heinekens, smoked weed, and got to know him. And from that moment on, we just started hanging out, we were just friends. 〟

BRADLEY SCHMIDT 〝*I was only out there through the summer, and then I moved back, after I didn't go to school, and the only jobs available were these phone-soliciting jobs. We did a couple of those and were like, 'Oh, God, this sucks.' But the whole time I was out there, Dave never had a guitar. He had a BC Rich Bich, but if I remember correctly it was at the factory having some work done. So he would come over and play my Gibson Explorer, and of course David and Greg lived right below, on the first floor. Brent Giese and I lived on the second floor, right next door* to Mustaine, so he would come over and play my guitar—I'm sure he did the same thing to Greg.

I think I may have actually been the first one that he asked to audition, not because I was great or anything, but he was over playing my guitar, I had a 1978 Explorer, and, like, a fifty-watt Marshall stack, and he's explaining what he wants to do. This was shortly after we had met him. But he's like, 'You know, you got the right look, and you're skinny, and you've got long hair, and you're a good guitar player. If you're interested, you can come and audition for my band.' Then he proceeded to say that, in the studio, he was going to be doing all the guitar stuff. So my thought was, like, 'Oh, okay.' Because who was Dave Mustaine? He was just another guy. Who's Metallica? I'd never heard of them. Of course, my initial thought was that if I'm going to be in a band, I want to contribute, you know?

The follow-up was something like, 'As a matter of fact, all of you guys are welcome to audition—Brent, Greg, and David.' My first thought was, and I asked Dave, 'What about Matt?' And he said, 'Yeah, that's gonna be a problem ...' 🙶

GREG HANDEVIDT 🙶So we met Mustaine and we all started hanging out, just as friends. And then I started learning his songs, because, I could hear him play. I would hang out of the window and I could hear him play, and I started learning the riffs. I was like, 'Wow, that's really cool stuff he's doing.' We didn't have any idea of who Metallica was, but he told us the whole story, of what happened and what happened between them.

I learned his songs, and after a while I was like, 'Dude, let me try out,' 'cause I knew he was trying to put the band together. And he had this dude named Matt Kisselstein—great dude, really nice guy, but he couldn't play. Dave was trying to teach him how to play bass so that he could be in his band. And David was so much better. His first reaction was, 'So, what about David?' And I said, 'Ah, don't worry. David and I have an agreement. If something comes along, it's cool. Whatever.' I knew that David was going to be playing bass for him before long.

So I go up and I jam with him, and I already knew his songs. It was nothing special—just over time, from hearing him play, I learned the riffs. He was like, 'Oh my God, you already know my songs.' And I'm like, 'Yeah, I've been listening to you play them now for weeks.' So from then on I started jamming with him.

Maybe, a day or two after that started—it may have even been the same day—I was like, 'Man, you need to listen to David play bass. Seriously, dude. He's really good.' And the same thing happened: he sat down with David one time, and he was like, 'Oh my God. You're the guy.' And that's how it went down. 〞

BRADLEY SCHMIDT 〝Dave already had a bass player at that time—a guy named Matt Kisselstein, a California kid. He was just kind of starting to learn, but he wasn't really that good, and he never really did music after that. That's why I say I might've been the first one that he asked, because he said we'd all be interested, including David. Matt was just into music, and I think he had the right look, but then we came alone, and we were all good players, but David was fucking awesome, of course. 〞

GREG HANDEVIDT 〝It was a combination of stuff that evolved into songs that range from Killing Is My Business all the way up to So Far, So Good … So What! 'Set The World Afire' was one of the very first songs. But that song was called 'Megadeath' at the time, 'cause there was no band name yet. At that point, when we first started, we were trying to figure out what to call the band. I suggested we call it Megadeth. It's funny, because I listen to the first couple Metallica albums, and some of the riffs that we had in Dave's songs back then ended up on Ride The Lightning. Then Dave hears that stuff, and now he's got to rewrite the songs. He has to go through and rewrite his own songs, because Metallica used those riffs.

Dave's got his issues—he's Dave—but in my opinion it's totally understandable why he was so bitter about what happened with Metallica. Because, first of all, the way that they did it, the way they kicked him out of the band, was so shitty, and then for them to sort of scoop up a lot of his riffs, on top of all that, and then just sort of give him the finger when he goes back to say, 'Hey man, what's up with my riffs?'

That would make anybody pretty mad. The thing about it is, I listen to Metallica, and they are a great band. But the level of sophistication in the guitar playing in Megadeth, compared to Metallica—to me, there's no comparison. The guitars in Megadeth are so much more sophisticated than what Metallica did. And don't get me wrong, Metallica is a great band, and I love them, but for me, as a guitar player, there's no comparison.

David and Dave never really told me why they wanted me out of the band. I don't know why. I haven't read his book, but an attorney buddy of mine, read it and said that Dave said he didn't like my hair. And that could absolutely be true. I would not be shocked at all if that were true.

They came down one day, into the apartment, and they sat across from me, and I'll never forget it. They sit down, and David never looked at me, he looked down at his feet the whole time, and Mustaine told me, 'You don't have good enough equipment.' And he told me I smoked too much pot, and I was kind of like, 'Are you kidding? Who do you think I do it with?'

And he just kind of moved on through that. I'm like, 'C'mon, dude.' But that was it. 'Okay, I'm out.' But Kerry King was calling him every day—'Hey man, let's do something'—he wanted to do something with Dave something fierce. And I know at one point they did end up jamming with Kerry for a while.

So I'm out, and they got another guitar player to come in. A week later, I'm sitting in the apartment—David had moved out at this point, and moved in with Dave—and I hear a knock at the door. It's Mustaine. 'Dude, would you consider coming back?' I guess the guitar player wasn't working out. The first thing out of his mouth, though, was, 'David said you hate us.' I was like, 'Dude, I don't hate you.' You know what it was like though back then—I was immature, like, 'Fuck you guys.' Just young kids being idiots.

I guess the other guitar player couldn't play the parts. At that time we were doing 'Looking Down The Cross' and 'Set The World Afire,' which was then called 'Megadeth.' We were also playing 'The Mechanix,' 'Jump In The Fire'—some really complex stuff. So, anyway, I was like, 'Okay,' because I wanted to go back,

I wanted to be in that band. So I went back and rehearsed with them twice, and it just wasn't the same. It felt weird. I don't know any other way to explain it. I didn't feel comfortable at all. And that was it.

A couple of days later, I said, 'Look, I'm going back to Minnesota.' Here's the other thing: I had a kid back here at the time. I have two grown kids, and my oldest daughter was, like, a year old, and I barely knew her. That was also bugging me. I wasn't making any money. I wasn't contributing to my daughter. She's growing up and I'm not there. So that was another big pull for me to move back.

Dave tried to talk me out of it, and I said, 'No. I'm going.' I went back to Minnesota. We all did—everybody but David. I got married, I went to school a little bit, and I formed Kublai Khan. 🎵

BRIAN SLAGEL 🎵*There was always this underground of really heavy stuff that was going on in LA at the time, Metallica obviously being the first. And they didn't last too long in LA, just because they were so heavy that none of the promoters knew what to do with them. The only band that really made sense to play with them at that time was Armored Saint. But then I started finding all these other bands like Savage Grace and Omen and Cirith Ungol—all these bands that were really super-heavy, hanging around.*

And then obviously, you know, Bitch was playing shows. In fact, the first time I saw Slayer was opening for Bitch, out in Anaheim. And Anaheim had a little bit more heavy stuff going on out there than they really did in LA. There was this really big underground of super-heavy stuff, but it didn't get lot of a whole lot of credit in the mainstream, because all the big bands ... you got Guns N' Roses and Warrant and all this other stuff that came out of LA, and that's what it became known for.

But there was always a good solid underground of metal. Both Metallica and Slayer definitely came from LA, and you'd probably say, for all intents and purposes, Megadeth came from LA. So, really, three of the Big Four came out of out of southern California. That's always been lost on a lot of people. But it was a really great time, because there were so many amazing bands playing around, and a lot of musicians. And, obviously, bands were moving from other areas, too, because they saw that there was an opportunity in LA. It was a great time to be there, for sure. **"**

JAY REYNOLDS **"**I kept bumping into Dave Mustaine around when he got kicked out of Metallica and started Megadeth, and I met Junior backstage at one of their first shows. All the bands in LA, we all grew up together. It's kind of like we went to college together. After high school, we all left our hometowns and moved to Los Angeles to go to Heavy Metal Debauchery College.

It was amazing, dude. It was the post-Starwood period, as I put it, because when I was kid going to high school in Portland, I used to come to LA and see bands and stuff, and I used to come to the Starwood a lot to see Quiet Riot, Van Halen, all that stuff. I was good friends with the Mötley Crüe guys back in the day—I hung with Tommy. Got in lots of trouble with those guys.

That's the weird thing—all the bands, the whole gamut of bands, we all hung out together. The early 80s in LA was pretty magical. The heavy-metal thing. The New Wave Of British Heavy Metal thing had already happened, and then the New Wave Of LA Metal happened, and it was on fire right then. Everybody got a record deal, and some people made it instantly, and some people slugged it out and made a living. But we all lived it 24/7. There was nothing like it. It was like Ancient Rome. It was pretty decadent. Anything you could possibly ever imagine, pretty much happened. **"**

9

BEHIND THE CURTAIN

9.1 NO BIG DEAL

One evening back in 2016, Thom called me up and excitedly told me, 'I think we can acquire Combat Records!' He was thrilled. I was lukewarm about the idea. Combat had been the home of Megadeth's first commercial release back in 1985, but we had a hostile relationship with the label, if only for their shoestring budgets and poor business decisions, like changing the artwork to *Killing Is My Business* without consulting us.

However, as an outsider to the Megadeth camp—and as a record-label founder himself—Thom thought the move to relaunch the label would be a good one. He also felt that as the man whose band largely put the label on the map in the first place, I deserved the right to own the imprint that put us there. Thom may have crazy ideas, but most of them really do work! So I agreed.

Next, we set about securing the trademarks and carefully staging the launch of the new Combat Records. It was important that we not dilute the brand, which is what had happened in the 2000s, when some not-so-thrash albums were released under a rebranded version of Combat label. To Thom—and seemingly the rest of the world besides me—Combat was held in high esteem as the original and best thrash/punk record label.

Our relaunch would have to pack a big punch to carry forward the image it left in so many young thrash fans' minds all those years ago. I was determined to do things differently, now that the brand would be in my wheelhouse. I was driven to make sure that *my* Combat would be a much better experience than the one I had to endure back in 80s.

•

After we formed Megadeth, in June 1983, we went through a procession of band members, all the while receiving major interest from record labels. The usual label suspects in those days were Metal Blade and Megaforce. Metal Blade had released the *Metal Massacre* series compilations, which served as Metallica's introduction to the world via an early version of 'Hit The Lights,' recorded prior to Dave joining the band. Since Metallica had just released their first album, *Kill 'Em All*, on Megaforce, the that label was viewed as a potential suitor, too, although it seemed less likely, since the label's president, Jon Zazula, had also been also part of the decision to sack Dave from Metallica earlier that year.

Our initial five-piece lineup—me, Dave, guitarist Greg Handevidt, drummer Dijon Carruthers, and short-term vocalist Lor Caine— quickly transitioned into the trio of me on bass, Lee Rausch on drums, and Dave handling both guitar and lead vocal duties. We were steadfast in our pursuit of a second guitarist, and we happily accepted Slayer founder Kerry King for the role when we debuted the band in San Francisco in February 1984. But then, after a second run of dates in the Bay Area in April, Kerry went back to pursue Slayer, and Lee returned to his native Ohio.

BRIAN SLAGEL ❝I remember seeing the LA shows, and I actually saw one of the San Francisco shows with Kerry King, too. I think that's the first time I saw them. I don't think they played any shows before then. Seeing them with Kerry was pretty interesting because, you know, there was Slayer happening, and Kerry got this opportunity to play with Dave in Megadeth.

It was really interesting for me to see Kerry playing something other than Slayer.

It was actually really cool, but I know it was a tough thing for Kerry because he probably wanted to be in both, if he could, but eventually you've got to choose one and we see where that goes. 🎵🎵

A guy named Jay Jones soon entered the picture. He was a fast-talking, name-dropping sort of guy who was highly strung and always had nose candy at the ready, be it white or brown. He suggested we bring in jazz/rock fusion drummer Gar Samuelson and guitarist Chris Poland, whom he had managed when they were members of a progressive-fusion outfit in LA called The New Yorkers. The New Yorkers had apparently been quite popular in the area but couldn't land a record deal, and had thus disbanded by 1982.

Gar was a likeable if somewhat peculiar guy. He was tall and lanky, but when he sat down behind the kit, it was clear his talents lay beyond that of heavy metal. As I had been in my high school's jazz band as a teenager, I had played with some very adept jazz musicians, but Gar was on the next level. He also was also a general manager at BC Rich guitars, which was quite convenient, since Dave and I both played them by choice. This made for a sudden burst of cool guitars that Gar would bring into rehearsal from time to time, while also quickly expanding my collection of basses.

BC Rich had become suddenly popular in the recent explosion of the LA metal scene as the guitar of choice for such heavyweights as Mötley Crüe, Tony Iommi, Rick Derringer, WASP, Lita Ford, and more. In fact, I recall accompanying Gar one evening as he took some guitars to Rick Derringer at Cherokee Studios on Fairfax in Hollywood. Rick was producing a new band called Madam X for Jet Records/Epic, the label made famous by Ozzy Osbourne and his first two solo albums. Rick was enjoying major success at the time with pop singer Cyndi Lauper and wrestling star Hulk Hogan. They were recording their debut album, *We*

Reserve The Right, which, ironically, EMP would release the follow-up to some twenty-five years later.

Meanwhile, back in Megadeth, Dave and I began working with Gar, but as a three-piece. We played some more shows up in the Bay Area, as well as the Water's Club in San Pedro. It was interesting to play our music with only one guitar, and for a few months we made it work.

By mid-1984, the record-deal chatter was ramping up, especially now that we were playing the band to packed houses around California, with interest mounting around the world. In the end, it came down to two suitors: a Dutch company called RoadRacer Records (which later became Roadrunner Records), and Combat Records out of Jamaica, New York. Dave and I took a meeting with RoadRacer president Cees Wessels (pronounced 'Case') at Le Parc Hotel in West Hollywood, but as much as we liked Cees and his presentation, we felt that signing to a foreign label could lead to trouble with contracts and getting paid.

Our discussions with Combat A&R man Walter O'Brien seemed to move along well. Walter would of course go on to form the iconic Concrete Marketing with his partner, Bob Chiappardi, and would later manage Pantera. He seemed to understand our band, and by the fall of 1984 we had inked a deal with him and Combat, which included a modest $8,000 advance to produce and record the album.

Something else happened around that time that I'll never forget. I remember walking past the Supply Sergeant, a famous army-surplus store on Hollywood Boulevard, and in the front window were two mannequins wearing military T-shirts. One said 'Kill 'Em All … Let God Sort 'Em Out.' The other one read 'Killing Is My Business … And Business Is Good.'

JUAN GARCIA (GUITARIST, ABATTOIR/AGENT STEEL/BODY COUNT) ❝*I first met Dave Mustaine when Abattoir played the Country Club with Metallica. It was on the Kill*

'Em All tour, I think it was late '83. [November 4, to be exact.] We had a song called 'Screams From The Grave' that was coming out on Metal Massacre IV and getting rotation on the Mighty Metal Hour on KMET. We were doing well locally, so they had us open for Metallica.

I met Mustaine in the back of the Country Club. He was on a moped, and he was saying, 'Where the fuck is Lars?' He was all pissed. At the time, I didn't know who he was, but I think it was when he was freshly out of Metallica. He seemed like a totally cool dude. I obviously knew my history—that he was in Metallica, and that he wrote songs with them and stuff. So I started hanging out with him, and through Dave I met David Ellefson, when they were living in an apartment together, before they recorded their demo. It was right around the time they were going in to record their first demo.

We were doing some demos, too, and we went in to record some more stuff with this guy named Jay Jones. Jay was this guy from the San Gabriel Valley, which was like a suburb of LA, and he would get us BC Rich Guitars. Mustaine played a BC Rich, and obviously Ellefson played a BC Rich bass, and that was kind of our connection, the BC Rich thing. Jay produced and paid for some Abattoir tracks, and we went on and got a deal through Combat. Jay started hanging out with Mustaine and Ellefson, and he produced their first three-song demo. He may have managed Megadeth for a very short time, too, before they got the deal with Combat.

Megadeth also invited us to play their first ever show, up in San Francisco, at Ruthie's Inn in Berkeley. It was Abattoir, Trouble, and Megadeth … the first shows we did up in the bay. We combined backlines, so we had this wall of Marshalls. It was incredible. Kerry King played rhythm guitar for Megadeth for those shows—it was fucking crazy.

We had a big U-Haul, so, like I said, we took a wall of amps. The guys from Exodus showed up—Paul Baloff and all those guys were at the show—and they were, like, tripping out. Ruthie's Inn isn't a huge place. It's a pretty decent-sized club, but to have a wall of amps behind you is kind of nutty. And it was a good crowd, man. I had no idea that they already had a big following.

There was another show in the city, at the Stone. That place was completely packed, and Megadeth just totally slayed. It was incredible to witness that. Kerry King brought a Nerf football with him, and we all played football in the park. We destroyed that ball. It was Abattoir vs. Megadeth, playing football in the park in San Francisco, and we had a really good time. It was cool to be involved in all that.

The next day we went to the Record Vault, which was the record store up in the Bay where all the metalheads used to go. I stayed with Megadeth [rather than] drive back with Abattoir. I was like, 'Man, these guys are totally, hella cool,' and I was really getting along with Ellefson and Mustaine, so I just kind of stayed up there with them and drove home with them. There was no sense in me driving back to LA—I figured I might as well stay and hang out, and check out the city, so I did. And I got along with them really well. It was awesome.

We shared a rehearsal studio a couple times, when they were just getting stuff going, before they had Chris Poland in the band. They had Gar Samuelson on drums, and they were just about to get Chris in the band. They helped run the studio and stuff, and I always got along with them. I thought they were awesome guys. And, obviously, metal as hell.

My experience with Combat was a real positive one—they were all hard-working people over there. They put out some iconic stuff, man: Mike Schnapp; Steve Sinclair, before he did Mechanic Records. They had a great staff, and they worked really hard for us. 🗲🗲

In December of 1984, we entered the Indigo Ranch studio in Malibu—a haven of recording once used and part-owned by the British group The Moody Blues—and started work on our debut album, *Killing Is My Business … And Business Is Good*. Guitarist Chris Poland came on board a few months before that, and this was the beginning of the famously mounting drug use inside the band. In fact, never was there a rehearsal or recording day that went by without drugs being snorted (and eventually injected) by someone.

Gar and Chris had girlfriends. I recall having to keep my heavy drug use off the radar when I went on dates with more 'normal' girls, with whom I'd keep to beer and the occasional joint. It was not until a year or so later that I had turned my attention to racy rocker women who fully embraced the seedy underbelly of the Hollywood rock'n'roll lifestyle. By then, I was deep into my addiction, which was seemingly all part of the journey of being in an 80s metal band in Los Angeles.

Jay Jones was continually fired and rehired during 1984–85, usually at the urging of Gar and Chris. He supplied us with a lot of party favors—he bought me and Dave cheap hamburgers—and took us under his wing, but his days were clearly numbered.

Jay had of course helped broker the Combat deal, secured the studio, and brought in Karat Faye to engineer and co-produce the album. Karat had been a staff engineer at the famed Record Plant studio in Hollywood, which laid claim to hit records by Rod Stewart, The Blues Brothers, and so many others during the 1970s and early 80s. We trusted Karat and his expertise in recording the band, but with little money at our disposal, we were soon running low on funds, which is why we ended up moving to Crystal Sound Labs in Hollywood to finish the overdubs for and then mix the record.

We delivered the masters to Combat and then weeks went by as we anxiously awaited the final product. Imagine our surprise when it showed up in the mail and we discovered that Combat had completely disregarded our artwork and instead chosen to reshoot and reassemble the entire package with *their* concept instead. Gone was our logo, which was replaced with a gothic font, while the hand-painted image of our mascot, Vic Rattlehead, had been replaced with a monkey skull dripping with strawberry jelly intended to look like blood.

We were furious. By this time, Walter O'Brien had left Combat, and new faces were driving the bus. Things only got worse as we ventured out on the *Kill For Thrills* tour to support the album, alongside Combat labelmates Exciter, who hailed from Ottawa, Canada. The tour was at best a financial shortfall and at worst a complete and utter debacle. Dates were quickly canceled—or simply failed to happen—due to negligence on the part of the agents who booked the tour. But we had to make at least one full trip across the USA. I've since followed the same mantra with all the other bands I've worked with: *If you don't at least throw a line in the water, you'll never get a bite.* That's what the *Kill For Thrills* tour was for us.

9.2 KILLING IS MY BUSINESS . . .

JASON McMASTER (VOCALIST, DANGEROUS TOYS, WATCHTOWER, BROKEN TEETH) **"***I think it was about 1985: my friends Militia were opening for Megadeth and Exciter. I saw them at the Back Room in Austin, but they were also on a bill at Randy's Rodeo in San Antonio. It's an infamous club. Everybody's fucking played at Randy's Rodeo: The Sex Pistols, The Ramones ... anybody who is anybody in my book.*

I was tech'ing for Militia—they're a Texas thrash band, they reformed about ten years ago, they do a lot of gigs with Helstar. After Megadeth played, I went back in the backstage area, which was more like a three-foot crawlspace between the stage and the back door.

I went back there and Mustaine was partied down. I was, like, nineteen or twenty years old, and it was interesting to see. He was still coherent enough to converse with me, but of course I have no idea what we talked about. I remember talking to Ellefson ... I want to say it was in Corpus Christi around the same time.

They were still in a van, and [Peace Sells] was brand new. I was way into Killing Is My Business, so I got Peace Sells the first day.

A friend of mine, the singer for Devastation, Rodney Dunsmore … him and some other dudes brought [Megadeth] down there to play. I had just gotten Doug Keeser from Watchtower an audition for Metallica, and that would've been October of '86, 'cause Cliff passed in September of '86. It was a crazy time. It's a little bit hazy right now, but I remember talking to Junior and Mustaine—I feel weird calling him Junior now, but that was his nickname, that's how I could tell them apart—and I'm telling them, 'Hey I just got Doug from Watchtower an audition for Metallica.'

And Mustaine kind of drifted off, like, 'I don't give a fuck, why are you telling me that?' Which is very Mustaine. Junior was like, 'That dude's good. I could see that, that could work.' Something positive about Doug. Ellefson was always cool, just a nice, positive guy. But I was a huge fan of Megadeth and the first couple of records, and when they popped up in South Texas I saw them as much as I could.

The Back Room is the same place Dangerous Toys was discovered, just a couple years later. But at this time I was still in Watchtower—Dangerous Toys didn't even exist yet. I didn't start working with Toys until maybe a year later. Things started to happen, these guys needed a singer, I told them I'd fill in … that was in October of '87. By March of '88, Toys was signed to a major label, and they basically bought me out of Watchtower, and I severed ties. It was very strange, because I was in Watchtower for, like, eight years, almost a decade. And I feel like we were really part of something—I was a pioneer of something—and I also feel Megadeth was part of that. There was some crazy time-changing shit going on at that point. 🙶🙶

I remember Jason coming out to early Megadeth shows in Texas when he was in Watchtower, and talking to him, and then, just a few years later, I see him burning up MTV.

There were two notable people in my mind: Jason and Kip Winger. When we went out with Alice Cooper in 1987, Kip was his bass player. And they were in a nice tour bus, staying at the Four Seasons, being treated like rock stars. He comes up to me one day, and he said, 'Man, you're so much farther along than I am.' I said, 'What are you talking about? You're the headlining band, playing to sold-out arenas every night.' And he goes, 'Man, but when this gig is done, I'm done. You're at least starting something new.'

As broke and scrungy as we were, he was right. He was flying off on weekends from that tour, recording and writing what would become that first Winger album. And Dangerous Toys, simultaneously, were doing the same thing. I remember turning on MTV, seeing Kip Winger doing 'Madalaine,' and going *Wow! Check this out!* And then Dangerous Toys came out, and both bands just tore up MTV that year. I mean, two different genres, but both artists absolutely just blew up out of nowhere. And I was just like, *Wait a minute, that's that dude I remember talking to when we were loading in and soundchecking at those gigs in Texas!*

•

The *KIMB* tour kicked off in June 1985. Having a tour to support the album was a good idea, although the booking agent was questionable to say the least, and the budget was upside down before we'd even left LA.

The tour began at the legendary Baltimore rock club Hammerjacks. We would open the shows and Exciter would headline. The first night pretty much set the tone for the ill-fated tour, however, as Gar showed up late, so we had to swap spots with Exciter, leading to them opening and us closing the show. Gar was still working for BC Rich guitars at the time and had been exhibiting with the company in New Orleans, at the summer NAMM show. His flight in from New Orleans was delayed, and for the show to happen at all we had to swap our positions on the bill. Fortunately, Exciter were gracious about it.

The next show was in Upstate New York, and after a quick appearance at a nearby record store, the show went off without a hitch. But what followed that evening couldn't even be written into a movie, it was *so* bizarre and harrowing.

After the show, we were driving to our next stop in Cleveland, Ohio. Sometime after midnight in eastern Pennsylvania, the van seized up, and we had to pull over to the side of the road. Because the van was from a local New Jersey rental company, we had no national support, like you would from a company like Avis or Hertz. So, after a few failed attempts to revive the engine, our tour manager Frank and I set out to hitchhike our way along the Interstate to assess our options.

We suddenly happened across an exit called 'The Promised Land,' and, lo and behold, there was literally one streetlight along a small main street parallel to the freeway, and under it was a National Rental Car. It was actually open, and they had a Chevrolet Caprice in stock. I had a Visa credit card my father had given me when I left home back in 1983, for *emergency use only*—one I never used for *anything*, because I didn't want to rely on my family for financial support. This was an emergency, though, so I swiped the card and rented the car. Ironically, that Visa card would end up financing the remainder of the tour, as well as several more cars and vans over the next five weeks.

Frank and I went back to the van to pick up the guys and cram our luggage into our new set of wheels. With four band members and two crew guys, we would take turns driving. A few hours into the drive, Gar was at the wheel and I was behind him in the back seat, trying to get his DW kick pedal out from between my feet. Gar reached around behind him and apparently took his eyes off the road. Suddenly, at 85mph, we drove straight off the road, full speed ahead. Grass was flying everywhere as we took out a signpost, which then flew overhead. We were all screaming as Gar tried to gain control of the car, which was now flying into a ditch, ready to do cartwheels. I have never been so scared in my life. We all knew we were as good as dead.

And then suddenly the car came to a dead stop. We were speechless. A boom box cassette player slammed against my neck and gave me whiplash. In disbelief that we were even still alive, we pushed the dented doors open and got out of the car.

Full of pain, I walked up to the top of the ditch, where the driver of a semi-automatic truck had pulled over after witnessing our near fatal crash. Embarrassed, I tried to offer a quick explanation. 'Must have been a deer that jumped out in front of us,' The driver was amused, of course, since he knew better. He offered to pull the car out of the ditch with his winch. The sad state of the car became clear as we replaced the front driver's side tire with the little spare from the trunk, with which you could travel at no more than 45mph.

After a further four-hour drive, we limped into the promoter's house in Cleveland. Weeds were sticking out of the car, and we looked like a bunch of low-rent hillbillies as we parked up and made preparations to rent a new van before the show. And this was only the third show of the tour! What next? Soon we would have our answer. More dates were canceled, and money was so tight that we were having kind-hearted fans buy us food, beer, and cigarettes, and take care of us when we could afford a motel for a shower.

Having reached our wits' end, Dave called the Combat Records headquarters in Jamaica, New York. He got our A&R man on the phone, but after listening to our sympathetic cry for help, the guy simply replied, 'You guys need to go home and get jobs.' *What?* They were our *record label*, and this is the response we get? That was it. From that moment on, we were driven beyond *anything* to make the band a success.

The *KIMB* tour budget had been tight to begin with, and guitarist Mike Albert, who replaced Chris Poland, had warned us about a potential shortfall. He was a salaried sideman on the tour, so he was keeping his eye on the budget to make sure he would even get paid. In fact, he'd warned us not to even *do* the tour, because even when a tour shows a slight profit on paper, somehow things always come up to eat away at the profits and leave you with a negative cash flow. In this case, we were leaving town knowing we were going to be possibly $10,000 in the red!

Fortunately, we'd got a $10,000 merch advance from a startup in the San Fernando Valley. The idea came up that we should use half of the money to buy pot and then, by selling it along the way, we would double our money. But naturally we became our own best customers, and somehow those profits never materialized.

Around this same time, we got a call from a young hustling New York booking agent named Andy Somers, who expressed great interest in Megadeth. Although he resembled a square-cut Jerry Seinfeld more than a heavy-metal hellion, he seemed to understand our mission and what we stood for. We quickly brought him into the fold, and he tried to salvage some of the remaining dates for the tour.

After the tour wrapped in Seattle and Portland, I drove from Los Angeles to drop the van off in Denver, and then back home to the farm in Jackson, to recuperate from the tour. I needed it. We were beat up, and we needed time off to regroup.

After a month in Minnesota, I flew back to LA to join back up with Dave. By this time, he was using my van to get back on his feet and conduct band business. He had a new apartment he shared with a woman named Nancy, the combination of which would provide the impetus for the song 'Wake Up Dead.'

With Chris Poland back in the fold, he, Dave, Gar, and I began writing at a rented rehearsal room in downtown Los Angeles. We built a loft there that doubled as a crash pad when one of us was homeless, which was often. It was there that we wrote the songs for our second album, *Peace Sells … But Who's Buying?*, which was to be recorded for Combat Records.

Around this time we got an offer via our new agent to do a set of double-header shows with Slayer at the now-infamous L'Amour in Brooklyn and the City Gardens in Trenton, New Jersey. The two bands would travel from LA to NY together as a co-headlining package. We would play first and then Slayer would close the shows. I recall after Slayer soundchecked at that first show, Gar asked their drummer, Dave Lombardo, to move his drums from the riser so he could set up his kit, to which Lombardo replied, 'No way! One day you'll be where I'm at, and then you won't want to take your drums down either.' Oh boy, young band egos and silly pissing matches.

Clearly Gar wasn't having any of this nonsense—he was older and, quite honestly, deserved all the respect in the world as a class act and a world-class drummer. Somehow, the squabble was settled before the show, but the rift between Slayer and Megadeth would be sustained for years to come, eventually shifting to Dave and Tom Araya exchanging sparring words in the press around the time of the *Clash Of The Titans* tour in 1991. Such is heavy metal.

A few weeks later, we got an offer to play with Motörhead and Wendy O. Williams at the Santa Monica Civic Center, and at a theater in San Diego. This was a huge deal for Megadeth, as Motörhead were icons to us, while Wendy O. Williams, a legitimate NYC punk-rock icon, had just left The Plasmatics to go solo.

We kept writing through late 1985, and with a new album's worth of material in the pocket, Andy booked us on a three-week cross-country tour in early '86. Now upgraded to a U-Haul RV, we have a bit more comfort and legroom than we'd experienced with the ill-fated vans and rental cars of the previous year.

The tour also provided us with a way to tighten up the new songs for what would become *Peace Sells* a few months later, but it was still very much a low-budget affair. One night in Milwaukee, we finished soundcheck and went over to see what the promoter had provided for our dinner. To our shock, we discovered a small electric hot plate with a pan full of Dinty Moore Beef Stew. We were aghast!

THOM HAZAERT ❝*I actually got the real story from the promoter, Jack Koschick. His sister made a nice batch of homemade beef stew for the band and the crew, but everyone else ate it, so there wasn't enough to go around, so they added a few cans of Dinty Moore to stretch it out. Drama queens!* ❞

I remember that night because it was also the show where we introduced a new song we had recently written called 'Peace Sells ... But Who's Buying?' Gar would begin the song with a quarter-note kick drum pattern, and after a few bars I would join in with the bass intro riff. Immediately, you could tell we had a hit on our hands.

A few shows later, we made our way to NYC, where we performed at the famous Irving Plaza. Andy had invited Capitol Records A&R talent scout Tim Carr down to the show, and he liked what he saw. A bidding war ensued, with Elektra Records and MCA also getting involved. Tim and Capitol won out, and within a few months had signed the band to a seven-album deal. By then, we had already begun recording our next album (*Peace Sells*) for Combat, but fortunately Capitol bought out the contract, allowing us to transition over to the new label in time for its release.

As the *Peace Sells* album was being readied for release, we spent the summer of 1986 on tour with King Diamond, who had just gone solo from his band Mercyful Fate. Then, in early 1987, our lucky break finally came when Alice Cooper invited Megadeth on his *Constrictor* tour, which would have us playing the largest sports arenas across the USA.

While Alice's audience was a bit older and a little more 'classic rock' than ours, the tour gave us a real education in how to work the big stages and prepare for becoming an arena band. Metallica had inked a deal with Elektra Records a few years earlier and were touring with Ozzy Osbourne. Anthrax had signed to Island Records and were beginning to tour with Ozzy and Iron Maiden, too. Slayer were settling in with Def Jam. Megadeth, now on Capitol, needed this big break with Alice to make the leap to arenas and major-label success.

ALICE COOPER ❝When I first heard Megadeth, it was during the period when that type of band was coming out, and I totally got it. I loved the energy of that band. I said that they get out there, and they bring it. And you could hear that Dave's guitar playing was so great. And Ellefson was so solid. You now, I even brought up Ellefson's name for (Hollywood) Vampires, when we needed another bass player. They were out on tour, but I said, 'Hey, man, he would be awfully good to play bass for the Vampires.' If we could've caught him on an off time from Megadeth, I think he would've been in the Vampires.

But anyway, it was one of those things where, you know, a band either has it or they don't. I've gone and listened to bands, and I go, 'Yeah, they're good, but do they have it? Do they have that thing that nobody else has?' Most of the time they don't. Whereas I think Dave's, at that time, anti-establishment attitude and that anger that was in him, was very, very good for the band. It didn't play out well for him personally, but when he got that under control, I think then the band really became a classic band.

Him, both of the guys … it was something that you could really look at and go, 'He has a history, he was this, now he's this, and the band is better.' That was a band I was really very proud to say we got on tour before anybody else did. We also did the same thing with Guns N' Roses, ZZ Top, AC/DC, Blondie, Billy Squier, Eddie Money—those were bands that opened for us, that went on to be really big artists. They were just starting out, but when they got in front of an arena, they learned how to do it. ❞

212

Alice was kind enough to offer us some sage words of wisdom about our own drug and alcohol use, warning us to slow down so we didn't burn out. When Alice spoke, we listened. Unfortunately, we were young, and as our careers were taking off, so were our habits and addictions. The next two years would wreak havoc on our band, the members, and my personal life.

9.3 MORTAL COMBAT

We made the announcement about the return of Combat Records in November 2017. It was the shot heard around the world, with everyone from *Billboard* to the Grammys reporting on the news. It was incredible to have such overwhelming and unanimous support from industry folks, and it really set me, Thom, and our Ellefson Brands on a new course of being able to truly stand on our own, away from just my role in Megadeth. After fifteen years of rebuilding my name and legacy since Megadeth disbanded in 2002, it seemed I had squarely arrived as an adult man on my own two feet in the record business.

I was no longer just a bass player in the music business. I was still a member of the group I co-founded, but I had also successfully helped launch Metal Allegiance, Altitudes & Attitude, EMP Label Group, Ellefson Coffee Co., and even a merchandise company called MerchLive, not to mention a growing list of signature gear and musical equipment, plus the beer and wine partnerships with Hydra out of Sioux Falls (for the Urban Legend Coffee Stout) and the Desert Rock Winery in Scottsdale (for the Combat Blood & Bullets Cabernet and Combat Hard Cider).

As with any good partnership, Thom and I have had our disagreements, but I've also learned over the years that we have different roles inside the Ellefson Empire. Sometimes I dream things up and he makes them happen, other times he dreams them up and together we make them happen. It's a true partnership—each of us knows our place, stays in our lane, and trusts the other to get the job done.

THOM HAZAERT ❝Through the 80s and into the 90's, Combat was one of the dominant forces in metal—essentially part of the 'Big Three' of classic thrash labels, along with Metal Blade and Megaforce. (And joined shortly thereafter by RoadRacer, which would become Roadrunner.)

While Megaforce had Metallica and Anthrax, and Metal Blade had Slayer, the tiny Combat imprint found its way onto the map by releasing Killing Is My Business … And Business is Good in 1985. While the Combat logo appeared on all Megadeth releases through Countdown To Extinction, within a year Megadeth had moved on to greener pastures at Capitol Records. But Combat stayed active through the late 90s, releasing classic LPs by Mercyful Fate, Sword, TKO, Death, Nuclear Assault, Circle Jerks, Exodus, Virus, and tons more.

Eventually, the catalogue was sold off, with albums reissued by a range of different labels, while Combat itself officially ceased to exist. In the 2000s, the label was briefly resurrected, albeit in completely rebranded form—and with a terrible new logo—and churned out just a few releases before going dark again for over another decade. Then, in 2016, after we launched EMP, I hatched a harebrained idea to acquire the trademarks and intellectual property for Combat Records and relaunch it as an imprint of EMP. David wasn't immediately thrilled with the prospect, as time and time again he had regaled me with tales of his displeasure at the hands of the label. But I convinced him of the strong legacy of the label, and that him re-launching Combat, as a co-founder of the band that put it on the map, would be just the kind of poetic justice heavy metal needed. And I think I was right.

So I set out to plan the resurrection of Combat Records. To me, the most important thing with Combat was keeping with the original spirit of the label, with a slightly updated bent. I commissioned a flawless recreation of the original Combat logo and set out to create branding that would not only invoke the original spirit of Combat but also bring it into 2018. As for the bands, I set out to sign the best modern thrash and metal artists—Bay Area Thrashers Hatchet, Soulfly guitarist Marc Rizzo, Israeli metallers Black Sachbak, as well as Green Death and Dead By Wednesday, who moved over from EMP—while also securing some of the original Combat artists, like Helstar, Sword, Virus, and 80s underground thrash icons Wrath.

Just at the right time—in another unprecedented display of divine intervention—I met Melody Myers, one of the most amazing graphic designers/visual artists in the world, who became my right hand when it came to the marketing and branding for the revived Combat. Together, literally, on the eve of the announcement, we created Charlie Tango, the bullet-toothed skull that became the 'face' of the new Combat. Melody also designed the labels and branding for the Combat Beer and Wine, a stunning collection of amazing branding materials, videos, and visuals, and basically everything else under the Ellefson umbrella, since.

In our discussions about how to relaunch Combat, David and I got to talking about the Combat Bullets sampler, an 80s compilation that included tracks from Megadeth (the original version of 'Peace Sells'), Helstar, Agnostic Front, and others. Like another swift blow from the divine hammer, less than a week later I found a pristine LP copy at my local used record store, Rock'n'roll Land in Green Bay, Wisconsin (also an Ellefson Coffee Co. retailer), and we hatched the idea to do an updated version.

We celebrated the relaunch of the label with Band To Band Combat, a massive online 'battle of the bands' competition that was so massive it crashed our website over a dozen times in the course of receiving over a million votes cast in just over two weeks. The top twenty-five artists got a spot on Combat Bullets Vol. 1.0, with one artist chosen by me and David, underground thrash/punks Throw The Goat, also ending up on Combat.

To call the Combat relaunch a stunning success is really an understatement of the highest order. The reaction from bands, fans, and the industry has been unanimously over the top. And, really, it could have gone either way. Thinking about it, in hindsight, messing with a brand that people love and cherish, and that is tied to some of their fondest and most important musical memories, can be dangerous business. So we just tried really hard to do it right. **"**

CHRIS CANELLA **"**This may sound weird, but David and I always seemed to cross paths, and I always knew we would be working together in one way or another. Not only because we both live in the Phoenix Valley, but little kismet style moments along the way. All the way back to when I was tracking the very first Autumn's End demo, Villain Recording was really a two-bedroom home studio, but it had a vibe that everyone like to go to, including David. I was borrowing a bass from my friend at the chain music store in the area, and I had to bring it back in two days, so of course I left all the tags on.

During the session, David came over to meet with Byron [Filson, owner and engineer], and he looked over and said, 'Hey! Going with that Minnie Pearl look, huh?' At the moment, the timing was perfect—very few people would really even get that reference, but we all busted out laughing. From then on, we always kept in touch. It seemed like every show I went to, and all the bands I hung out with, he would be there, and we would always have a great laugh and chat.

A handful of years later, I was working at Fender on the Jackson Guitars and EVH teams. David always kept in touch with me and Brian McDonald—even though he was working for Peavey, we were all friends. It wasn't like how so many brands are today, trying to kill each other because the industry is changing.

One day, David told me he was leaving Peavey and going to be back in Megadeth. I instantly said, 'Hey, man, let's bring you back onto Jackson,' as it was the most recognized brand he played. He came down to Jackson, and the David Ellefson Signature line was born. We would travel together for clinics, showcases, and whatnot, so we always had time for good talks. He always took the time to fill me in on the stories of my personal favorite thrash album of all time, Peace Sells, as well as family, business advice, and life in general.

David and I are very similar but also very different, and I think that is why I always love hanging out with him—having dinner, getting our kids tickets to Taylor Swift, and whatever else dads do. We are both family men first but manage to somehow support them through heavy metal. We have different spiritual points of vie, but we have never argued over it—always good honest discussions, without judgment or even a single word of negativity. We were actually having a great discussion on the way to Tucson when I had a blowout on the freeway, and he was right there, calm and collected, not worried about being late to the clinic or anything. In fact, we still made it on time, even after having to switch out cars with my wife.

A few years later, I left Jackson to go work for ESP. My band, Autumn's End, was on indefinite hiatus, and my job required me to commute back and forth to LA. There I was working with Frank Bello, who told me about his band with David, Altitudes & Attitude. Once again, here we are, hanging. Dinner and laughs. Time goes on, and in 2016, Autumn's End reforms with a new lineup [featuring drummer Jason Kowalski] and new music, and as we get things rolling again, David introduces me to Thom.

Let me tell you, Thom has been a blast—he's always in my corner and always finds the time to take a call, whether it's about my work, his work, my band, mutual acquaintances who are a disaster, or David himself. Quickly we became real friends. To make a long story short, we were rewriting all the music, and even though EMP were more than willing to put out what we had, we weren't ready, as our sound wasn't solidified yet.

Time goes on, and Dave and Thom acquire the Combat name to expand his label. Now please note that, as I mentioned earlier, Peace Sells is my favorite thrash album of all time, and as a kid my dream was to put out a record on Combat. And, lo and behold, I am on the phone with Thom and David, and Autumn's End is now working on a full length for Combat. Bingo! Here we all are again, making a dream come true.

It's crazy how this team and I keep working together. I have worked with hundreds of notable names in the music industry and become close friends with many, but Dave has always been there on my personal journeys. I don't believe in fate or destiny necessarily, but if it were true to me, then this would be the ultimate example of friends who are destined to be a part of each other's lives, as friends and in business. "

THOM HAZAERT "The year 2017 was an amazing one in the EMPire. The coffee company blew up; we put together the deals for our first signature artist roasts with Skid Row, Autograph, and Queensrÿche; we signed some amazing new artists to EMP, including Autograph, Madam X, Ron Keel; we released the new Mark Slaughter LP, Halfway There, and Doyle's As We Die; and we relaunched Combat. We also put together a huge line of signature products under the Ellefson banner: Combat Beer & Wine, Urban Legend, a coffee stout beer infused with Ellefson Coffee Co., a signature strap with GruvGear, an amazing new signature bass pedal with Kirk Hammett's KHDK, a full David Ellefson bass pedal board/processor with ISP.

But there was also a very sad side to 2017, as we lost one of our artists, the legendary Chuck Mosley—the original vocalist for Faith No More, who appeared on the band's first two albums, We Care A Lot and Introduce Yourself. We'd released Chuck's Demos For Sale in 2016 on THC, my little imprint label through EMP. It was a compilation of raw alternate takes and recordings from his debut LP with his band VUA, Will Rap Over Hard Rock For Food. And as a lifelong Faith No More fanatic, my name on that record is still, and will always be, one of my proudest moments.

When Chuck died there was such a massive and amazing outpouring of love and support for him, and it truly was amazing to see the influence he had. I just wish more people had gone that far out of their way to tell him how amazing he was, when he was still around to hear it.

On the cover of my copy of Introduce Yourself, Chuck wrote, 'Hugs to my Sugar Daddy. Love you man. We did it. Let's take a ride.' And we did.

RIP CHUCK MOSLEY, Dec 26, 1959–Nov 9, 2017. "

10

WHEN ROCK'N'ROLL GETS REAL

10.1 BILLION-DOLLAR BABIES

After we signed to Capitol Records in 1986, Megadeth were given a huge boost by Alice Cooper, who took us out on his *Constrictor* tour in early 1987. As I said earlier in this book, every artist needs a cheerleader to believe in them, and for us, it was Alice.

The irony of this story is one that really shows how life for me has come full circle, by me being able to be a champion for the band Co-Op, fronted by Alice's son, Dash Cooper. When we started EMP Label Group, my mission was to be able to help both young and established artists in our industry.

I had heard of Co-Op around my hometown of Phoenix, and I even had close family friends suggest EMP take a look at them. In many ways, it was Thom who really saw a clear vision in their music. He understood what they were aiming for, stylistically, and, although they were a young band, he got it. One day Thom called me to tell me how excited he was to be working with the band in the studio and developing them.

I think what I enjoyed most about them is that Dash was not just mirroring what he saw his father do but rather carving his own path with a more grungy and modern rock sound. Over the years, I've had a lot of musicians come up to me and tell me of Megadeth's influence in their lives, but I'm always impressed when the path they choose *doesn't* sound anything like Megadeth. For me, this is a real gift of speaking to someone's life but letting them take that influence and personalize it. This is true for pop, country, and even Christian artists who have claimed Megadeth as an influence!

At the time of the writing of this book, Co-Op have enjoyed three Top 10 singles on the Classic Rock radio charts, ('Old Scratch' hit #2), toured the USA, and garnering the praise of dear ol' dad on the *Nights With Alice Cooper* radio show, now in its fifteenth year of success on syndicated nighttime radio across the globe.

Alice & co. have been there to support me, Megadeth, and so much of our personal and professional lives for over three decades now. And as much as I regretted not doing the Cooper tour back in 2002, Alice and I recently discussed me playing bass with him and the Hollywood Vampires, the all-star band he plays in with Aerosmith's Joe Perry and legendary movie star Johnny Depp. Of course my Megadeth schedule didn't allow it, but trust me, if I could've, I would've said yes.

Throughout my life, there are repeated lessons and overtones of how if you say 'yes' and be prepared to help out whenever and wherever asked, life magically has a way of providing for one's needs. Watching things come full circle with Alice and Dash is a wonderful part of that equation.

ALICE COOPER ❝❝ *One thing that Dash's band has that I absolutely love is dynamics. I told them one time early on, when they had Mark and Court and everybody in the band. I said, 'Guys, right now you have great parts, but everybody is playing at the same time. You have no dynamics, it's one big solid line of blast, and I can barely hear the vocals.'*

The very next time I heard them play, they'd figured out how to make it dynamic. Where they'd go down to one guitar, doing a chug, with the vocals going, and they would come right in with a B-section, with everybody, and it was so powerful. And I said, 'Guys, you have no idea how hard it is to do that.' But they did it on every song. And they still do it. ❞❞

10.2 SO FAR, SO GOOD

In March 1987, our UK record label, EMI, wanted us to make our debut in Europe, which meant pulling us off the Alice Cooper US tour for two weeks. We made our splash at the famed Hammersmith Odeon in London. On our arrival in Europe, it was the first time we had experienced the effects of jetlag from overseas travel. That night, EMI wanted to take us out for the evening, and Deep Purple happened to be playing at the Wembley Arena, which was exciting, as guitarist Ritchie Blackmore had recently returned to the group, and they were supporting the hugely successful album *Perfect Strangers*.

This would also be the first time we tasted British ale, which has a higher alcohol content than most American beer. So much so that after a night of getting 'pissed,' Dave woke up in the middle of the night and actually *pissed* in my suitcase, mistaking it for the toilet. He and I were sharing a hotel room in London on that trip, and apparently jetlag and strong ale don't mix. It was a funny moment, though, and we still laugh about it to this day.

The next night, at the Hammersmith Odeon, we learned the show would be broadcast live on BBC radio. We also quickly learned that our guitars hadn't made it through British customs, so a handful of Fender and Gibson instruments had to be supplied in their place. At that time, we were playing high-performance metal instruments such as BC Rich and Jackson guitars, and clearly our replacements were unsuitable for the task. Fortunately, our guitars arrived just *moments* before we took the stage, and aside from detoxing from our usual heroin and cocaine use, which required massive amounts of alcohol to numb the pain, the show went off on time.

The next day we sailed off by ferry across the North Sea from Dover to the Netherlands. Our next show was going to be in Amsterdam, a city well known for its red-light district full of prostitutes and drugs, so we were very much looking forward to scouring the town upon our arrival. The seas were rough, though, and after much heavy drinking on the ferry, I remember going to my room to sleep it off until our arrival into Rotterdam the next morning. It was my first overnight boat trip, and, to make matters somewhat sketchy, the day before a ferry had actually capsized and most everyone on board had drowned! I guess that helped justify the excessive amounts of alcohol I consumed that night.

Once we arrived in Amsterdam, some of our gang set out to find drugs. One member of our party came back to the hotel after a few hours of scouring the area and told of a how a police officer pulled him off to the side of the road and actually scolded him—not for using drugs, but for using an old needle to inject them. Somehow we 'got well' (addict slang for using drugs not to get high but to feel 'normal'), and the show that night was interesting because during the day the city was so calm, but after hours the town lit up and was rowdy as hell!

This was also the first time I noticed how good the famed British Marshall guitar amplifiers sounded on the local 220 voltage circuits, which are standard across the UK and Europe. The tone was so rich and powerful, and it made me realize that our Marshall amps in the USA paled due to the 110-voltage across North America. We discovered the heart and soul of the *real* Marshall tone that had so inspired us.

For this tour, we shared a double-decker bus with the band Flotsam & Jetsam, with whom we also shared a manager. We knew them well, as they were often our support act when we played in their hometown of

Phoenix, Arizona. The Flotsam guys discovered where to buy the heavy-metal standard issue uniform of peg-leg stretch jeans at Kensington Market in London. All of our metal heroes from Iron Maiden to UFO wore them, and, now that we'd discovered them too, we bought an endless supply.

The tour left Amsterdam and graced Hamburg, Germany, before finishing in Paris, France. Keep in mind this was back in the days before the European Union and the standardized Euro currency. As a result, we had to go through immigration at each country's border. We had secured a large ball of hash on the tour, and as we went into Paris a member of the tour party was willing to shove the stash up his butt so as not to get searched and arrested. I'm not sure how he got it out—I didn't ask!—but once we were inside France, we lit up and smoked away. The things we did to quench our habits …

Coming back to the USA in early March, we were able to play the final date of the Alice Cooper tour in Long Beach, California. After that, we took a couple weeks to rest before heading over to Japan to make our debut appearances in Tokyo, Osaka, and Nagoya. We were greeted at the airport by fans and groupies. It was like everything we'd heard about KISS and The Beatles in their glory days. In fact, I recall arriving to the hotel in Tokyo and being whisked up to my room by a lovely young lady who was not only ready to take care of me for the night but also made my bed and had breakfast ordered to my room as I awoke the next morning. Now this was hospitality!

We felt like The Beatles in Japan. We had never experienced anything like this before. The Japanese were so kind, bringing us gifts each day while we attended lavish record-company dinners after the shows each night. Each day we traveled via the bullet train between cities and were treated like real rock stars. What was even more amazing was that at the shows, these fans would sing every word to every song, yet when you tried to talk to them back at the hotel, they couldn't really speak one lick of English! It was the first time I'd noticed how the lyrics and melody of our songs were something people everywhere could really resonate with, despite the language barriers. Over the years, I became keenly aware of how Megadeth are a band whose music and lyrics transcend all borders of culture, race, creed, religion, and politics.

•

Back in the USA that summer, we commenced the final leg of the *Peace Sells* tour with a run of shows that started in Miami and ended in Honolulu. By this time, drug use within the camp had escalated to monumental proportions. It was definitely taking its toll on our inner-band relationships, as well as our ability to write new songs, which we needed to get started on for the next album.

It was on this tour that we picked up Detroit native Chuck Behler as a drum tech and 'just in case' understudy to Gar. One day in Washington DC, Gar and Chris didn't show for soundcheck, so we started jamming some new song ideas with Chuck sitting in, one of them being 'Mary Jane.' To our amazement, Chuck played the song perfectly! It turned out he was paying attention not only to Gar but to the songs we were composing at soundcheck each day. It was that day that Dave and I made the decision that once the tour was over, we would fire Chris and Gar and bring in Chuck as the first replacement.

Once we got back to LA, we told Gar and Chris that they were out of the band, and immediately we went into rehearsals to finish composing the remainder of the next album. This was also the time I began to actively compose songs for the band. I had been a pretty good rhythm guitarist since I was about twelve years old, so now, instead of composing on bass, I began to write ideas on guitar. Bringing in riffs for 'Hook In Mouth' and 'Liar' was a huge accomplishment, and I credit a lot of it to the band just being Dave and me now, as the original guys, and also the fact that we were sharing the band apartment and spending a lot of time together, reshaping the new lineup. We were likeminded and synchronized. Making lyrical contributions to 'Mary Jane' and 'In My Darkest Hour' was another big milestone of my participation on the album, and gave me more validation in the creative department, beyond just playing bass.

We entered the Music Grinder studio on Melrose Avenue in Hollywood around late summer and began laying down the tracks for what would become *So Far, So Good … So What!* The title was suggested by our guitar tech at the time, referring to the mounting successes that often seemed to be internally overshadowed by lineup changes and the ongoing drug issues surrounding the band.

Producer Paul Lani had remixed the *Peace Sells* album at the suggestion of Capitol Records when we signed with them the previous year, and we retained him to produce *SFSGSW*. Paul was an experienced and seasoned engineer, but he was also quite smitten with the recent Def Leppard album, *Hysteria*, and wanted to model our sound on it. He recorded the drum kit with no cymbals, to achieve total isolation, and then went back and had Chuck record the cymbals on their own. That is one of the reasons why the album has such an odd sound to it.

As for recording bass, the previous albums were done with so little money that I just recorded on the fly. But now, we had a much bigger budget, so everything was now being done to much higher standards. That meant recording all of the instruments individually, as overdubs, which can be a very uninspiring method for our style of music. The fact that we were well rehearsed helped, but my mounting addiction to heroin and cocaine didn't help when it came to expediency. Cocaine makes you race, and heroin pulls you behind the beat. No wonder I could only record two songs per day!

The next issue was that were essentially now a three-piece band. The bar had been set by Chris Poland—the second guitar position in the band should be smooth and *legato*, juxtaposed with Dave's vicious and gutsy guitar playing. Now, Dave laid down his rhythm guitar parts and lead vocals, as well as his solos.

My good friend Jay Reynolds was the guitarist in the band Malice, who hailed from Los Angeles and were signed to Atlantic Records. Dave knew him as well, but Jay and I had become fast friends over music and our likeminded lifestyles. As buddies, we'd go out on the town to enjoy the Hollywood nightlife on a regular basis, with regular stops for drinks and girls at the infamous Rainbow Bar & Grill.

Meanwhile, after a few albums and some moderate touring, Malice were beginning to splinter internally, having not really made much money or got the necessary traction to make the grade on a major label. With that in mind, Jay indicated that he'd be up for the second guitar position in Megadeth.

Funny enough, Jay had previously invited me and Dave down to the studio to sing backing vocals on the Malice album *License To Kill*, along with the members of the LA band Black & Blue, which included future KISS guitarist Tommy Thayer. That night was also the first time we met producer Max Norman, who just a couple years later would go on to mix and produce several Megadeth albums.

JAY REYNOLDS 66 *I first met Ellefson [when] Megadeth played at the Country Club. I went to go see them play, and they were just fucking horrible. I was trying to talk to Dave, and he was just hammered, and then I wound up meeting Junior, and we got along like instantly. We were fast friends. I remember wanting to like them a lot but they just sounded horrible. But, you know, that was really early on.*

There was one guy in every band who was like the 'glue' guy, the Svengali, the dude who made it work, and we really all knew each other. So I would talk with

Blackie from WASP, Nikki (Sixx), or Robbin from Ratt, and I think David Ellefson definitely became that guy for Megadeth. Mustaine was obviously the talent, but Junior was always the guy that held everything together and was always trying to make stuff happen.

I remember before either one of our bands was signed, we would get our phone books out and exchange all the contacts we had in the music business. 'Do you know this guy?' 'Oh, you need to know this guy.' 'This guy's a great booker.' And we all put shows together. Malice played with everybody under the sun. We played tons of shows with WASP—we played with everybody from Metallica to hard-rock bands.

LA was so incestuous—everybody knew everybody else, and everybody knew what was going on with everybody else. So I got to be really good friends with both of those guys [Dave & David]. I stayed in touch with them, and we had really parallel courses, in terms of early Malice and early Megadeth. We would make an album and go on tour, and then they would do the same thing and come back, and then we would make an album and go on tour and come back. After Peace Sells, Malice had just toured on License To Kill, and we just couldn't stand our lead singer. He was just a miserable alcoholic, and he made the whole fucking thing, just, unbearable. And when I got back to Los Angeles, those guys [Megadeth] had just gotten back from their tour. And, you know, I was watching from afar, talking to them occasionally. They were starting to be successful. They had recorded Peace Sells for $15,000, and it got picked up by Capitol, and they remixed it or whatever, but that fucking record went gold [500,000 copies sold].

So I get back from the License To Kill tour, I'm sitting in my friend's house, couch-surfing in the Hollywood Hills, up in Laurel Canyon, and I get this call from Mustaine. He told me to come over, so I grabbed all my guitars, and I went over to their crappy apartment in Silver Lake, and they were like, 'Look, dude. We want you to be in the band. We want to hang out and jam with you for a couple weeks, and we'll see if it works.' And then began the insanity of just snorting drugs night and day and playing guitar twelve, fourteen hours a day. They told me if I wanted to be in the band, I had to make Chuck Behler a rock star. They were like, 'We hired the roadie, dude. And he's from Detroit. You gotta get him to shape up. And, by the way, go score me an eight ball or you're fired.'

When I joined the band, we jammed every day and night for, like, two weeks, and they said, 'Yeah. You're in. You got the gig.' So my first question is, 'What's the fucking deal?' I go, 'You guys all live in one apartment in Silver Lake. It's a fucking shithole. And no one's got a car except for Junior, who has the same van he moved out here in, that his parents gave him, and it's falling apart. You guys sold a lot of records. Where is the fucking money?'

They had a manager, and the accountant worked for him. The business of the band was just fucked. I'm just like, 'You guys are getting fucked, royally. Let's fire the management, let's fire the accountant, let's go for big time.' And I was like, 'Yeah, there's money out there like you wouldn't believe. You guys should be, like, fat right now. You should be buying houses and shit.' And this was news to them. They didn't have a fucking clue. Dave didn't want to fire the manager. He used to really talk up Dave, and send him, like, human skulls and Nazi postage stamps, all this weird stuff. Dave was resistant, but eventually he agreed.

So, we fire the guy, and we instantly have to find an attorney to get through all of this. We go meet with this big 'Hollywood' music attorney who was referred to us—he must have been, like, seventy-five years old. So we did this meeting with this dude, in his office in Beverly Hills, and we're all strung out completely by this time. After two weeks in the band I had snorted so much heroin that I was pretty much always high. Every day we'd bolt downtown and score, like, fifty balloons of heroin and fifty balloons of cocaine. It was ridiculous.

We go downtown, we cop all this dope, we're doing eighty down the freeway in this crappy car on the way to this meeting, and we're all snorting lines. So, we get to the meeting, and we walk in, it's this super-plush Beverly Hills office, we're all sitting out there, and the receptionist offers us coffee. So everybody says, 'Yeah … I'll have some.' Dave has like one sip of his coffee and throws up all over this attorney's desk.

But the funny thing is, when they got an attorney, and bank accounts, the band started getting money. And that was kind of a bad thing right there, because they were unsupervised. My idea was to go to, like, Ron Smallwood, or Doug Thaler, or Doc McGhee, get he some big-time management, get somebody to ride herd on this whole thing. Which I think eventually they did.

So here we go in the studio, and we're recording a fucking record, and everybody's just ... wasted. I mean, basically I was a hand-to-mouth, couch-surfing guitar player in Hollywood, with a drug habit. It just didn't pan out for me. I wish it had. It would've been cool. As a person, I would've fit in the band fine. I'm still good friends with those guys to this day. But jumping into speed-metal that quickly, I think my guitar playing fell a little short, and it didn't help that I was fucking wasted beyond belief. And I think the pressure of having to learn all this stuff, in that situation, in a short period of time, didn't help either. 🥁

As much as Jay was a dear friend to me, he was just not the right fit musically in Megadeth due to the complexity of the riffs and solos, which was quite different than the more power-metal stylings of Malice. In his place, Jay suggested his guitar teacher, Jeff Young, come in to lay down the solos, and then he would learn them for the tour.

A recent graduate of Musicians Institute in Hollywood, Jeff came to Music Grinder to lay down some solos toward the end of the sessions. He didn't really have the right look—he dressed more like a young surfer from Malibu than a thrash-metal rock star—but he laid down some impressive solos on tracks like 'In My Darkest Hour,' 'Liar,' 'Mary Jane,' 'Hook In Mouth,' and our cover of The Sex Pistols' 'Anarchy In The UK.' That was enough for us to invite him to join the band, as a world tour was being scheduled to support the new album.

JAY REYNOLDS 🎸*Jeff Young was my roommate. He was a GIT guy. And when I got hired to do the Megadeth thing, I literally told him, 'I gotta learn all these fucking* songs, and the new songs, and solos, in, like, two weeks.' I go, 'You learn all of Chris Poland's old solos, I'll learn all the songs, and we can compare notes.' So he was kind of my tutor—I had him help me figure all this shit out. It was tough dude. I wasn't, like, a speed-metal guy, I was an Iron Maiden, Judas Priest type of guitar player, so I had a huge learning curve jumping into this speed-metal thing.

And they called Jeff, 'cause Jeff was around, helping me with the parts, and the solos, and he was a great player. And Jeff hated that kind of music too. He was into Dokken, and really pretty hard rock with big vocals. He used to bag on that kind of stuff all the time before he got the offer to play in Megadeth. I'm like, 'This guy doesn't even like this kind of music, and he wears acid wash jeans, and you're gonna hire him? This isn't gonna last very long.' And even then his days were numbered.

I was hoping something would work out, because I loved the band, but I was so overwhelmed with the whole situation. And I think there was some outside resistance to the idea of having 'ghost' guitar players, especially in a band like Megadeth. So they fired me and ended up getting Jeff. It was the good old bad old days, we were all so fucked up it was a miracle we even survived that period. There's no perfect scenario for any of it. I think I even remember the day I got fired. Dave was heated, and yelling at me and Chuck, and he'd already threatened to fire us ten times a day, so I didn't take it that seriously, but when it came down to it, it's kind of a foggy period for all of us. I mean, who knows what the fuck actually happened ... 🎵🎵

Paul Lani did a mix-down of the *SFSGSW* album at Bearsville Studios in Upstate New York, but we weren't satisfied. It sounded too dry for the times, and we felt a more lively and atmospheric sound was needed to compete with the modern records of that day. Jeff Young knew Michael Wagener, who had risen to fame producing groups like Accept and Dokken, and had recently mixed the Metallica LP *Master Of Puppets*, so we call him in to remix *SFSGSW*.

Because Michael had largely defined the sound of the late-80s hair-metal records with his signature ambiance tones, we now went 180 degrees in the opposite direction and ended up with an album that was *too* slick.

As well as that, we were never really happy with the LP cover artwork. Instead of using the artist Ed Repka, who'd painted the amazing cover art for the *Peace Sells* LP, Capitol's in-house art department suggested we take a different direction on this new album. We went out to a dry lakebed north of Los Angeles and shot the existing photo of a guy dressed in our mascot Vic Rattlehead's new army-service uniform, holding a military rifle. What I remember is that the guy in the suit was *so* not the right fit, as he was came off looking coy and sheepish while trying to look menacing. It has prejudiced my interpretation of the album art to this day.

Meanwhile, the back-cover photos were shot on a short West Coast tour we did in November and December 1987 as a way to warm the band up for our upcoming support slot with Ronnie James Dio. The individual live photos were taken at a show we played at the Tacoma Dome, near Seattle. Once again, I remember being short of my usual supply of heroin and having to drink massive amounts of White Russians (vodka, Kahlua, and milk) to get through the show. That's probably why I have such a vengeful smile on my face!

JAY REYNOLDS ❝*I was there, dude, and I never got any acknowledgment whatsoever for being in the band. I rehearsed with these guys for two weeks, and we went right in the studio to record an album. We literally did the rehearsal studio maybe three or four times, and it was really just me and Junior. Junior and I just sat around and played guitar, day after day. And, he's a fucking great rhythm-guitar player, too. He would show me all the parts, and we'd jam and snort lines all day.*

Junior's one of those guys that no matter how high he got, how many drugs he did, he always maintained his shit. I was that way to a certain degree, too, but Ellefson really had it down.

Here's the thing. Dave Mustaine is the godfather of speed metal. He literally took all the New Wave Of British Heavy Metal shit, and fucking Motörhead stuff, and forged it into what became Metallica and Megadeth. Because he wrote the more influential of the first batch of Metallica songs, and taught James and Lars how to write songs. And then, out of spite, he formed Megadeth, and turned it into one of the biggest fucking bands of all time. He was so pissed off about getting kicked out of Metallica, he formed Megadeth, literally overnight. It was just, amazing. But the bottom line is this: Mustaine was the talent, Junior was the glue. They never would've survived, or existed, with David Ellefson. David Ellefson is the guy that made it all happen and held it all together.

It's a real miracle that anybody that was in the band lived, it's a real miracle that the band survived, and it's a real miracle that So Far, So Good … So What! even got made. 🗨

10.3 IN MY DARKEST HOUR

In 1988, we hit the road to support *So Far, So Good … So What!*, and it was during this tour that Nick Menza was brought in, by our soundman at the time, as understudy and drum tech for Chuck Behler. It wasn't so much that Chuck was raising any eyebrows, but rather that our soundman felt that his friend Nick might be a better candidate for the job.

Nick was brazen and bold, and he had no problem sharing his

opinions, which can definitely help you to survive in this business. However, it was clear to me that if he were ever to become a member of Megadeth, he would have to tone down his attitude and accept Dave as the band's leader and frontman, not try to compete with him. So, we let the scenario play itself out.

In January 1988, we kicked off a tour with Dio and Savatage, an up-and-coming metal band from Florida, the first of the three bands on the bill. We became good friends. The tour took us across North America and ended in Long Beach in March.

I made a comment in one of the major heavy-metal magazines that I was looking for a girlfriend, which got the fan-club mailbox whirling, with many young sweethearts across the country submitting letters to me in hopes of a 'date.' I was a good-looking young man with a career on the rise, and, as a well-raised chap from Minnesota, surely I was deserving of a good girl at some point in my life. Hell, I was even the 'Hunk Of The Month' in *Metal Edge* around this time!

Nick Menza's girlfriend, Stephanie, arranged for me to meet her friend Charlie after the final show of the Dio tour at the Long Beach Arena. Charlie was a pretty young woman who looked similar to the TV starlet Shannon Doherty, who was starring at the time in *Beverly Hills 90210*. She was making strides as an actress herself, and she seemed comfortable in the rock'n'roll circles, so I asked her out on a date. We hit it off, and our romance would continue for the next nine months.

Having had all my attention fully immersed in the band for the earlier years, it was nice to have what I could actually call a girlfriend—a relationship of my own, away from the band. I hadn't really had a steady girlfriend since moving to LA in 1983. I'd had plenty of dates, but now I was ready for a steady, and Charlie was it. From the beginning, though, she made it clear she was not okay with hard drug use, which forced me to hide my mounting heroin and coke habit from her.

We soon found an apartment in Central Hollywood and moved in together. We furnished the place together, too, and it felt like I had a real home base, a place to build a life away from the band. To me, it seemed most of the accomplished major-label rock stars had some type of home life like this in LA, despite their global fame. However, my trying to create this type of scenario caused problems inside the band, as it felt like it was creating a perception of having a life away from the band.

Additionally, being on tour while you're in love with a girl back home was incredibly difficult, so I brought Charlie out to see me on the road several times. Here the problems increased, creating even more separation between the band and me. Admittedly, bringing girlfriends on the road was tough with the lifestyle and schedule we had.

As the tour went on, we went to Europe, Japan, and back to the USA for one final leg before finishing off the campaign off with the huge Monsters Of Rock festivals in Europe with Iron Maiden, at Castle Donington and in Germany. By now, Charlie had discovered my heroin addiction, and she blew the whistle to my family and the band's management. As stunned and angry as I was at the time, I know in hindsight that she probably saved my life. She agreed for me to go to England to play the Castle Donington show with Iron Maiden, but once we got there, the severity of my addictions came to the surface with our agent and management, so we canceled the two remaining German festivals, and I went home to LA to enter a drug-rehabilitation clinic.

We had just switched to McGhee Entertainment, the largest managers in rock'n'roll at that time, with acts like Bon Jovi, Mötley Crüe, Skid Row, and Scorpions on their books. They made it clear to us that they didn't care if we partied as long, as we were productive. But if we couldn't produce music and tour, we had to get help, or we'd be dropped.

McGhee assisted me in entering the rehab after Donington, and I agreed to a ten-day program, but my heroin detox was so gnarly that I left after only three days. I knew what was on the line: my relationship with Charlie, our new management, and even the future of the band, all because of heroin. But that drug is so insidious. Once it's in your bones, it becomes incredibly difficult to kick.

Sure enough, Charlie left me, as she had promised she would if I didn't get clean. It was around this time that I met my wife, Julie. She was an integral part of the offices at McGhee Entertainment, and had just transferred from New York to their LA office. I stopped by the office one day to pick up my tickets to the MTV Awards, and we hit off immediately. A short while later, I asked Julie out for our first date. I was really good at hiding my addictions, and although she was aware of the drug use inside the band, I was clever at concealing the seriousness of my own use.

It was around this same time that Guns N' Roses guitarist Slash and I had connected, as he had just come home to LA from their hugely successful world tour supporting *Appetite For Destruction*. Slash and I were dedicated musicians who also shared similar interests in music and lifestyle. For the next several months, he and I would hang out almost daily, going over to each other's apartments to jam.

By February 1989, however, I had hit a new bottom, and I had to enter rehab a second time, this time at the Brotman Hospital in Culver City. Again, we were given a warning by McGhee Entertainment: if for any reason band members didn't complete our rehab stints successfully, they would drop us from their roster.

Two weeks later, those of us in rehab began to leave, against medical advice. Upon leaving Brotman, I went over to my dealer's apartment in Hollywood to cop some dope. Within hours, I was more strung out than ever, and I suddenly realized that my addiction was a progressive illness that would eventually kill me. There was no escaping it on my own. I was beat.

JAY REYNOLDS ❝*I was out of the band but we stayed great friends. I was the first one to say, 'You can stay here for a while until you get your shit together.' And the first thing I did was, I went in my bedroom, and I kicked it, cold turkey. [After that] I got a job and an apartment, but I really felt like I was a part of Megadeth. I was there, and I think I really influenced the band to get their shit together, in terms of really looking at the business.*

After that tour—I couldn't believe they survived that—they came home, and that's when they really started going off the deep end, as far as the drugs. They started going into rehab and trying to get clean. The worst part is, somehow or other, I ended up making all these drug connections, and I was still battling addiction off and on, and [although] I kicked it when I left the band, I fell right back into it. So I became, like, the celebrity fucking coke dealer for a little while. And those guys started coming and getting all their shit from me. There was just some crazy shit going on then. Anything could've happened. ❞

The next day, my guitar tech came over to my apartment—the one formerly cherished by me and Charlie, but now a drug den of inequity— to have 'the talk' with me about my addiction, and how he was also going to walk away if I couldn't get clean.

'You have everything millions of us musicians will never have, and you're just pissing it all away,' he told me. 'Getting help is a sign of strength, not weakness.' His words resonated with me. He had me hook line and sinker, and I knew he was right.

So back to Culver City I went, to enter Brotman a second time. Unfortunately, it was too late for McGhee Entertainment, who kept their promise and dropped us, issuing a statement to the music-industry trade magazines that they had parted ways with Megadeth.

Girlfriends were gone, management was gone, and by this time Jeff Young had been let go as well. Chuck Behler's position in the band hung in the balance, too. We were done. Completely sidelined. I lasted a few weeks in rehab, but by then I'd actually started using heroin in the hospital, brought in by another detoxing client. So I left treatment for a third time and began making the rounds to methadone clinics. Now I was taking cocaine, heroin, *and* methadone.

A couple of months earlier, before I entered Brotman the first time, Dave and I had reached out to a guitarist named 'Diamond' Darrell Abbott, from a band called Pantera, who I had met in Dallas the previous summer. That night, over drinks, Darrell (who later changed his affiliation to 'Dimebag') made a point to tell me how much our *Peace Sells* album changed his life. I remembered the encounter and mentioned it to Dave months later, once Jeff Young was out of the band and we were in search of a new guitarist.

We called Darrell up to invite him into Megadeth. He was thrilled with the offer but interjected that with him came his drummer, brother Vinnie. At the time, we still had Chuck as our drummer, so the offer was declined. Jeff Waters of Annihilator was also on the short list of guitar players, but he declined too, as his own band was on the rise. He and I would become dear friends years later, and we'd often talk about the 'what if,' had he joined back in that day. As a huge Annihilator fan, I'm happy for his success, and I certainly love his music, as I do with Pantera, too. I guess all things happen for a reason.

By summer of 1989, after several rehab stints, we knew it was time to change drummers. We also knew Nick Menza was chomping at the bit for an audition, so Dave asked that I go into a small rehearsal hall and give it a go. And so I did.

Nick was full of energy, bravado, and enthusiasm, but his tempos would always speed up. Chuck was super-solid with his tempos, but he was more reserved in his onstage appeal. Nick? Well, this was a whole new ball game. He had a contagious energy. His spirit and zest to be in the band was welcome and much needed. Plus he was funny, he was local, his physique was trim, and he flaunted himself like a rock star. He was fearless and shameless. In other words, he was the perfect next step. So we put him through rock school to learn the tricks of the trade with Megadeth.

With Nick in the fold, we commenced auditions for a new guitar player at the same rehearsal hall by Burbank Airport. We set out a list of three songs for each guitar candidate to know when he arrived. The criteria were simple: looks, chops, performance, and attitude. For most of the guys, we knew the minute they walked through the door if they were even worthy. Keep in mind, up to this point, Dave and I had auditioned dozens of failed singers, guitarists, and drummers, and by now we could read a guy before he even played a note.

In fact, for a couple guys, I don't think we even made it all the way through the first song; Dave and I would reach back and turn off our wireless belt packs and quietly set our guitars down, leaving the new guy, Menza, to do the dirty work of delivering the news to the candidate that *it wasn't going to work out, but thanks for coming down.*

During this period, a hungry young manager named Ron Laffitte would call on me regularly, vying for a chance to manage the band. He knew his way to Dave was through me, as I was the VP to Dave's President of Megadeth. Ron was a reasonable man, and he instinctually understood Dave, Megadeth, and our genre. He'd been the tour manager for Armored Saint on their 1984 tour with WASP and Metallica. From there, he had taken several jobs under big-name managers, one being Rod Smallwood, whose clients included such notable fellow Capitol Records artists WASP, Poison, and of course Iron Maiden.

I finally got Dave to take a meeting with Ron about managing Megadeth. Soon, Ron was engaged to manage the band. He knew we needed to get back in the game, and he brought us the opportunity to record Alice Cooper's 'No More Mr. Nice Guy' for SBK Records, as part of the soundtrack to a new Wes Craven film, *Shocker*. We entered the Record Plant in LA with famed songwriter and producer Desmond Child, who had penned #1 hits for Bon Jovi, Alice Cooper, and more. The three-piece lineup of me, Dave, and Nick somehow got the track recorded, despite the incredible addiction still ravaging the band. We then shot a music video for the song with director Penelope Spheeris, who we had met in 1987, when we re-recorded our cover of Nancy Sinatra's 'These Boots Are Made For Walking' for her film *Dudes*, which featured actor Jon Cryer (now best known for *Two And A Half Men*), Red Hot Chili Peppers bassist Flea, and Fear singer Lee Ving. Penelope had more recently directed the video for 'In My Darkest Hour,' and had included us in her film *The Decline Of Western Civilization Part 2: The Metal Years*.

By now, the industry was full of sober rock stars, and bands like Megadeth, with our hard drug use, were just not going to be tolerated any longer. Ron had just the right amount of candor and desire to set the sober ball in motion for us.

One day, I came back from visiting my drug dealer, and Ron was there with Dave in the kitchen of our apartment. I broke down in tears and told Ron how bad things were with my drug use. Looking me straight in the eye, he said, 'If you really want help, I'll do everything I can to help you.'

'Yes,' I replied sincerely. 'I want help.' From that moment on, Ron set out to get a drug counselor and a team to help me clean.

I discovered a doctor in the LA area who was having some success detoxing addicts with a new drug called Buprinex, which was similar to today's Suboxone. It is injected into the fat of your buttock or stomach with a small needle. I began the process, but I needed a good kick in the pants to get serious about it.

Ron's senior management partner called me into his office to have a sit-down talk with me. 'You HAVE to be clean to be in the band now,' he told me. 'If you use, you lose, and you will be replaced.'

Wait a minute … what?! I couldn't believe what I was hearing—and from a new manager! I think I was more hurt that the managers were now doing the dirty work.

•

It was during the initial process of getting clean that we shot the music video for 'No More Mr. Nice Guy.' It was clear they wanted Dave as the star of the video, and that Menza and I were merely going to be backing musicians on this one. It was also around this time that a new business manager and accountant were brought in to establish new directives in our legal and business matters.

It was clear that Ron was guiding us on a new path: everyone had to be clean, and we needed to be a team. I get it. But I also know the feeling of being *told* to get sober; none of us like to be told we are doing something wrong, especially with drugs and alcohol, and even more so when our lifestyles seemed to be one big party. Now, the party was over, and we were turning a corner with the band, becoming a global business and brand. As much as I resented the manager telling me this, I knew he was right. It was time for me to turn the corner and get clean.

As I've said elsewhere in this book, in hindsight, and with over twenty-nine years of sobriety and more than thirty-five years into this monster we've built called Megadeth, I have come to understand my place in the group and be increasingly comfortable in it. I've also come to understand addiction as an illness. Part of my recovery is recognizing that I'm called on to be a steward of goodwill for the band, the fans, and others in the business around us. I'm not perfect, but it's a mission of purpose in a super-cool vehicle to glorify and celebrate this amazing heavy-metal legacy we have built together.

MARK SLAUGHTER ❝❝*I met Dave through an ex-girlfriend of all things—Charlie. He was living with her, and she said, 'Hey, come by.' So, I went over, and he's like, 'Hey, I'm Dave. How's it going?' Or Junior, as he introduced himself. So we talked, and, he's a very likeminded person, we're very close in age, and, on that side of it, he was very articulate, very well spoken. I thought, Whoa, this guy seems like he's got it all going on.*

Fast-forward a little bit later, Megadeth were recording at the Enterprise, and Dana and I were mixing The Wild Life. I saw Junior there, and I saw Mustaine, and we played them 'Times They Change,' and David was like, 'Oh, that's so killer,' and it was just kind of one of those things. It's funny because Megadeth is one of those things—a very heavy-metal band that's just a staple at the top. And we both were kind of from the MTV era of metal bands, but on very different ends of the spectrum. To me, it was all about songs. So, it was just kind of in a different vein, and a different mindset, but we had mutual appreciation for each other's talent.

The other thing is, at that time, Mustaine was about to have a child, and we talked a little bit, and the next thing you know they were coming through Vegas, and I went down and saw them at the Thomas & Mack, and they were fucking great.

A lot of people don't know this, but Nick Menza actually auditioned for Slaughter. He was actually in the running, but Blas was more of the … Tommy Lee, hair-band, or whatever you want to call it. We're entertainers, not just players. And Blas was the perfect drummer for Slaughter. Nick Menza was great, he was just very serious with, like, start the song, get to the end of the song, and kick ass in-between—he just had this drive that was more than this young, twenty-one, twenty-two-year-old kid that was playing with us.

For whatever reason, Megadeth and Slaughter just had a very parallel course. Here's another thing that a lot of people don't know. Vinnie Vincent Invasion was on the Alice Cooper tour, first, and then we left and went over to Iron Maiden. On the same tours, Megadeth started with Iron Maiden, and then they went over to Alice Cooper. So we basically switched tours. And it's funny, I've never, in Slaughter, or Vinnie Vincent Invasion, played with Megadeth. The closest I got was playing in the MTV Rock N' Jock Baseball Game with Sam Kinison—Mustaine played the National Anthem, and I played shortstop.

We were running in the same circles of headliners, but we never played together. We were on the Bill & Ted Soundtrack together, all over MTV … despite all the differences, the paths were very similar. And I don't think those guys would go home and listen to a Slaughter record, as much as I never went and really immersed myself in the Megadeth stuff.

Tim [Kelly] was our resident metalhead, he was all about Metallica and Megadeth and Queensrÿche. Anybody who had a great guitar player, that's what drove him. Slaughter did some heavier, more 'metal' stuff on our records, and we realized, as much as that was what we came from, that wasn't really what our audience was looking for. But from the beginning, I've always had so much respect for Megadeth, and David personally, and that's never changed. 🗡🗡

THE NEXT LEGACY

11.1 MINNESOTA NICE
11.2 BASSTORY
11.3 DAVID ELLEFSON DAY

11.1 MINNESOTA NICE

My dad was a strong businessman. He ran a major farming operation that had been in our family since about 1886, and he would suffer no fools when it came to music as a career. He and I would butt heads on occasion about how the entertainment business was more unorthodox than most other businesses, to which he would often exclaim, 'Your business is nothing but a bunch of shysters and conmen.' The truth is, I couldn't argue that! But if you want to be in the circus, you have to become one of the animals. That's just how it is.

As a result, I've always felt inclined to step up and oversee business matters with every band I've been in. I was never comfortable just 'being the bass player.' I knew there was a complex business behind it all, and that success didn't just happen because a band had a look or a sound, or could write a song. Someone was at the helm. Elvis had Colonel Tom, Led Zeppelin had Peter Grant; there are always those guys who have a firm handle on how to cast a vision and see it through.

Some of the more embarrassing moments in my adult life came when my mom, dad, and older brother, Eliot, would come to visit me in Los Angeles, and Dave and I were pretty much homeless and squatting with anyone who would let us in. We weren't malicious about it—we were desperately trying to build a band and make a couple bucks to eat, and then we'd be on our way. But for my upper-middle-class family to see me living like this, it was not exactly a 'call home to mom' kind of moment. But it was the reality of building Megadeth.

245

Having to call my mom and dad and tell them about my drug addictions were not exactly proud moments either. I remember calling them from Brotman Medical Center in Culver City in February 1989 to ask them to come out to see me during family week in one of my three stints in rehab, when I was trying to get cleaned up from booze, cocaine, and heroin.

It was the same year Metallica lost the Grammy for 'Best Metal Album' to Jethro Tull. As sad as that was, it was even sadder to see Metallica and Guns N' Roses racing up the charts while Megadeth were sidelined due to our drug habits. Fortunately, I got clean and sober in March 1990, just before we recorded the *Rust In Peace* album. Everything changed once I got clean, and the band was on a new footing of one hundred percent abstinence and sobriety throughout the 1990s.

Although my dad didn't really understand the addict mentality, I was able to really have a great relationship with him upon my sobriety. In fact, in my four years sober before he passed away on April 2, 1994 (also my wedding anniversary), Dad and I got to have some amazing telephone conversations about life, philosophy, and even faith. As it turns out, he sat on committee boards at church, helped found the Jackson County Historical Society Museum (where I have a large display of Megadeth achievements, and where the Mary Jane Terwilliger headstone resides), and was a friend to everyone in the Jackson community.

Dad got to see me buy my first home in Scottsdale, own nice cars, and become a respectable member of society. That was all the result of getting sober and fully embracing the Lord's gift of music and leadership that He put upon me.

Although my dad didn't get to see Julie and me get married, I know he would have been proud. He loved Julie—especially her healthy cooking—and he told my mom, 'I hope David and Julie take care of each other'—meaning he hoped that I would marry her. Having your parents approve of your spouse is so critical. As the saying goes, 'When two get married, six get married,' meaning the in-laws are now part of the family, too!

We decided right up front that we didn't want our family to be part of the circus of rock'n'roll. In Julie's previous professional life, she'd enjoyed incredible success with some of the biggest rock acts in the world, including Bon Jovi, Mötley Crüe, Scorpions, and Skid Row, but now she was retired from that and had moved on to the 'raising kids' business.

Every day I see our family grow, I'm eternally thankful that I've been able to support my family with my dream of playing music, and to provide the stability for that has allowed Julie, Roman, and Athena to carve out their paths, too. Today, Roman is the keeper of the facts on all things, having just graduated college with his bachelor of science degree in business administration, while Athena is pursuing a degree in nursing and medicine at one of our state universities. She also has a terrific musical gift of perfect pitch and synesthesia, whereby she sees colors to music, but although she could have pursued music professionally, she saw enough of the rough spots in my career that she'd rather just enjoy it and not have her livelihood depend on it. Smart girl!

I think, in the end, my dad would proud of me and Julie and our two wonderful kids. Julie has done an amazing job, dedicating her life to them while I've been away on tour for so much of our marriage. We have a strong bond in our house, and we chalk our successes up to my sobriety and that we have God at the center of our family. Not in a crazy religious kind of way, just a simple *remember who runs the show around here* kind of way. I guess having a strong family backbone and a common-sense religious upbringing are among the perks of being raised in the cornfields of Minnesota!

11 11.2 BASSTORY

In 2015, just before I recorded my bass parts for the *Dystopia* album, I was invited to do a spoken word tour of Australia to support my then-recent autobiography, *My Life With Deth*. Not quite sure of the curriculum and flow of spoken word, I chose to bring my bass with me so that, if nothing else, I could revert to a sort of bass clinic with stories from my book.

As the *Dystopia* tour wound down with festival shows across South America in November 2017, it appeared that most of 2018 (if not some of 2019) would be time off the road to begin making a new Megadeth album. As a result, I began contemplating ways to fill my calendar during this downtime.

One phone call with Thom and his creative wheels were already turning. First, he suggested we write this book you now hold. Then he suggested the concept of Basstory. It would be modeled on my spoken word tour and include storytelling around the riffs and music that defined my career. Additionally, it would encompass my bass clinics I had been doing for endorsers like Jackson guitars and Hartke amplifiers, with aspects of the master classes I had done at educational facilities like Berklee College of Music in Boston, Massachusetts.

THOM HAZAERT ❝*For a couple of years, I had been encouraging David to bring more of the spoken-word-style engagements he did in Australia to the USA. He had done a few, several years ago, but wasn't sure it was a viable concept. I* encouraged him, as I usually do, and explained over and over that it was a very different time in his career, and Megadeth's, even from a few years ago, with the Grammy, and the huge success of Dystopia, but he still wasn't convinced. But I knew this was important to build, as a part of David's legacy, and, in hindsight, I guess I was right.

So I kept on him, and eventually I broke him down, as I tend to do, and around it we built the entire Basstory concept, which initially grew from social media posts David had been doing, finding photos of his old basses and gear, and posting them with the hashtag #everybasshasastory. But with David, the stories go so far beyond the basses. There are so many fascinating aspects to his personal journey, and the Megadeth story, that I knew fans would love to hear. Melody Myers, our personal design wizard, took some incredible Mike Savoia photos and built the imaging that would come to define Basstory, and quickly it took on a life of its own.

David summed the whole thing up one night on the mic at one of the shows when he said, 'Basstory is kind of like a bass clinic, only you can buy T-shirts and drink beer.' And, in the simplest common denominator, it is. But it's so much more.

We enlisted our friend James Rivera from Combat/EMP recording artists Helstar, with whom David also did a record as Killing Machine, to perform with David on some of the shows in an impromptu jam session, and, in the Midwest, Combat artists Wrath and Green Death (who we appropriately dubbed 'Green Deth') opened and closed the show with killer renditions of classic Megadeth songs with David.

The East Coast US leg ended every night in an all-star jam with Bumblefoot and our friends (and EMP Artists) Dave Sharpe and Christian Lawrence of Dead By Wednesday, which spilled over into a Florida run, culminating in a star-studded Basstory at the Brass Mug in Tampa during our PBX-Playback Independent Music Expo featuring myself, David, Christian, and Dave from Dead By Wednesday, Head from KoRn, Troy Sanders of Mastodon, Jason Bieler of Saigon Kick, Kyle Sanders of Hellyeah, Bumblefoot, Dirk Verbeuren, and more.

As a fan, getting to see David in that intimate club environment was the closest I, *and many of those fans, will ever get to seeing Megadeth in a tiny club. And getting to perform with him night after night was one of the most mind-blowing experiences of my life. We joked on the road the whole time about how it was like the Killing Is My Business tour, and in many ways it was. It was our way to get back out and really connect with David's fans, in a way that in a machine as big as Megadeth is usually damn near impossible. But that's been my mission with David as long as we've worked together, and I think why the fans support what we do as much as they do. We came home to the new issue of Bass Player magazine, featuring David and Frank Bello on the cover, with a feature about Altitudes & Attitude, talking about EMP and David's hugely successful Basstory tour. Apparently, we did something right.* 🗣

The difference between Basstory and a standard clinic is that we were going to take it into the nightclubs and concert halls across the USA, instead of music stores, with support from bands on the EMP Label Group and Combat rosters. This would allow the fans to experience a more concert-like atmosphere with merchandise, VIP meet-and-greets, alcoholic beverages, and the like.

The concept became even more fitting as we rounded the corner into 2018 and Megadeth management launched the '35 Years Of Megadeth' campaign, which celebrated the studio, live, and greatest-hits album releases of the past thirty-five years of the group. As we tightened up the concept for Basstory, we also launched the Ellefson Touring Agency, also known as ETA. This booking agency would offer nonexclusive booking agents from around the world to help our EMP artists (and non-EMP artists) get on tour to support their releases.

The first tour was for the boss man himself (me), allowing me to help get the logistics tightened up as we began to approach other legacy and newbie artists about joining the ETA roster. When we first launched EMP Label Group, we quickly discovered the frustration many of our artists were having with getting on tour to support their new releases. Thom mentioned that a booking agency should become part of our all-inclusive wheelhouse of music-industry offerings to serve both the artist and the label by assisting our artists to get out on the road and tour.

Live music and touring is still a profit center for most any artist willing to hustle and live within their means. Selling EMP CDs and the artist's own merchandise at the merch table can still pay the bills on the road, even when nightly performance guarantees are minimal.

The first night of Basstory, in Portland, was the acid test in a nightclub, in front of fans and concertgoers who were probably as inquisitive about the concept as we were. Initially, I played along to some backing tracks on my laptop, before inviting musicians from one of the support bands to join me for the closing numbers. The concept worked, and thus launched a new method of storytelling-meets-clinic around the world.

To this day, I'm still referred to as 'the ambassador' and 'the keeper of the facts' for most things inside the Megadeth camp. Basstory became a perfect outlet for me to keep Megadeth's history alive and well in our downtime making studio album number sixteen, and also keep my own connection to the fans relevant and current. The irony being that, sometimes, our greatest path forward is to go back in time and visit our past.

As the years click by, the more I'm seeing that even the youngest of our fans want to go back to the start and discover the songs, history, and stories of our earliest years. As Thom predicted, Basstory became the perfect vehicle to do just that!

11.3 DAVID ELLEFSON DAY

For over a year, Thom had been hinting that something big was in the works back in Jackson. The Ellefson Coffee Co. store launch had made headline news around the world in 2017 and got the wheels turning back in my hometown, while only a month later, Megadeth had won the 'Best Metal Performance' Grammy for the title track from *Dystopia*. Suddenly, I was a hot commodity back home in a way that I had never experienced in all my years since I moved away in 1983, even with the fame of Megadeth all those years later.

As we wrapped up the Iowa Rock 'n Roll Music Association festivities over Labor Day weekend of September 2018, we took a casual stroll back through the town of Jackson, only thirty minutes north of Okoboji, Iowa, just over the Minnesota border. We dropped in to Kat's Hog Heaven, which of course now houses Ellefson Coffee Co in Jackson, and as we sat there with the owner, Donnie Schoenrock, he confirmed with Thom that their two years of planning was coming to fruition; that the proclamation for the official David Ellefson Day had been approved by the city of Jackson! We agreed on October 9 as the official day and set the plans in motion for the inaugural event only a month later.

We launched Basstory in the Northwestern US in mid-September, followed by a handful of dates in Texas, for which I was joined by my good friend, Helstar vocalist James Rivera. The next week was a five-day run of Midwest dates across Illinois, Wisconsin, and Minnesota. David Ellefson Day would be that same week, just a few days before Basstory launched across six countries in Europe.

Obviously, the prestigious honor of having a day named after me on the calendar was an exhilarating moment in my life. It is also an honor usually granted only to dead presidents and religious figures, so it seemed to me that this was a moment not just to bask in my own glory but also to create an opportunity to utilize this day for something bigger and find a way to truly give back. So we formed the David Ellefson Youth Music Foundation, a nonprofit 501.c3 corporation designed to encourage, support, and inspire the next generation of musicians by raising funds and making contributions to public and private schools and organizations in need of funding for their music-education programs.

The first foundation initiative was right there in Jackson. What better place to start giving back than in the very place where many of the roots of my career were planted? My endorsers at Jackson Guitars and Hartke amplifiers and even Eddie Van Halen's EVH brand donated guitars, basses, and amplifiers to the Jackson School district band program, with an additional commitment for further support.

With the foundation established, we began looking for likeminded allies, and we didn't have to look very far, as we were quickly introduced via our friends in the Grammy mothership, the Recording Academy, to the Grammy Music Education Coalition, a nonprofit arm with a similar mission. We had a few conversations, and it was a natural fit.

Within a few days, we had signed on as a partner, which culminated in an amazing panel discussion in December 2018 at our PBX Playback Independent Music Expo event in Tampa, where the director of the Grammy Music Education Coalition, Lee Whitmore, joined us all the way from Boston, alongside the Recording Academy's Florida director Kenny Cordova, Brian 'Head' Welch of KoRn, producer Toby Wright, and Guns N' Roses and *Rust In Peace* producer Mike Clink, who also served as a Grammy trustee for over a decade.

For over an hour, moderated by Thom, we discussed the highs and lows of winning (and not winning) Grammys, and all the amazing work done by the Recording Academy, MusiCares, and the Grammy Music Education Coalition, and how it all tied into what we were now doing with the David Ellefson Youth Music Foundation. As cool as it had been to be a Grammy *nominee* all those years, *winning* a Grammy seemed to thrust me and our brands into a much more advantageous position to partner on initiatives that could benefit so many more people.

As a kid, I thought fame was something to be flaunted—to be worn as a badge of self-glorified accomplishment. But here I was, at fifty-three years of age, humbled by the altruistic doors opening before me. Suddenly, it all became clear: submission to God over all these years was paying off in ways I could never have comprehended when I was younger. As a teenager, sitting in the classroom at Jackson High School, I daydreamed of going out to Hollywood to become a big rock star and then coming home to flaunt it in everyone's face. But here I was, on my special day, humbled by the honor. Instead of prideful boasting, I felt a responsibility to give back and help those whose dreams may be crushed under the weight of financial cutbacks in school music programs—the very programs that gave me a foundation in my own musical path.

It's ironic that my sobriety and spiritual mentors over the years used to say things to me in my twenties like, *One day, you'll have the power,* and *The Good Lord got you sober not to help yourself, but to be in a position to help others.* Suddenly I knew what they meant. A day under my name was really a day under His name … not a day for me, but rather a day to give back to those who believed in and supported me. For that, I'm forever thankful to the fine folks of Jackson, and the faithful members of *Team Ellefson.*

EPILOGUE
MAY IT GO WELL WITH YOU!

❝If all you do in your life is only for you, then your life ends when you die. But if you offer your life and talents for others, then your life carries on after you pass. It's called legacy. **❞**
AUTHOR UNKNOWN

At the end of my books, I always feel a need to review, recap, and summarize the point of writing the book in the first place. In this case, this book was intended not only to tell the story of my own life these past few years but also to demonstrate my realization of how precious life is and how big it really becomes when we serve others with our resources.

In my previous book, *My Life With Deth*, I shared quite a few thoughts and experiences regarding my spiritual quests and yearnings during my life up to that point. So much so that at one point I had to decide if the book was going to be a religious story about a rock'n'roll guy, or a book about a rock'n'roll guy who had a tendency toward spiritual seeking. I chose the latter.

After *MLWD* was published, I finished up a year of seminary education at the St. Louis Concordia Seminary. As much as I prefer hands-on, real-life learning, that year of SMP schooling was rewarding. The online classroom allowed me to do the work as I traversed the world on Megadeth's *Th1rt3en* tour that year. I must say, it was a bit challenging, walking offstage at 2am in Istanbul to join an online classroom for two hours, or waking up at 4am in Thailand to do the same.

It did allow me to pursue a minister license, whereby I can now '*marry 'em and bury 'em*'—in other words, I can legally officiate weddings and funerals. I've also done a few baptisms in the church as well. It's quite an honor to do these things. You realize, in that moment, that you are helping shape another person's spiritual quest. Although I haven't presided over any funerals yet, speaking at my brother Eliot's funeral taught me to look hard and wide for the meaning of life and death. I know there are many Psalms on the subject, but I found it best in 2 Corinthians 5, which refers to the struggle of our frail earthly bodies.

Overall, the seminary experience opened my eyes to a greater understanding of the Christian faith in which I was raised, as well as other world religions I frequently come into contact with in my travels as a global performer. I soon put it together that people learn what they learn as a result of their upbringing, customs, and traditions, and that a nation's politics, religions, and culture are intertwined and cannot be separated into individual components.

My view as a musician is that it is wise to appreciate that when foreign countries invite you to perform for them, you are their guest, and any political and religious ideals should stay with you internally. To me, that is just common sense. Or maybe I should say uncommon common sense, especially in this time of such great divisiveness in America, when certain news outlets like to label us as either 'liberal' or 'conservative.'

Really? To me, we are all slightly liberal (music, the arts, thrill-seeking) as we are also conservative (family, finances, safe neighborhoods). There is no black and white on this matter. In fact, the longer I get on in my years, the more I've found most of it is about living somewhere in the gray areas, those which aren't so ironclad.

Maybe instead of *gray areas* I should say the areas between black and white—that's where the colors exist. For me, that's where the greatest exploration and discoveries happen. This ideal helps me so much when I travel, when the best-laid plans of mice and men can some days unravel by the minute. Plan as you might, sometimes life just shows up looking a little different. The weather changes your plans, your luggage goes missing, or simply you're simply just not in the mood for it today—even being a rock star. Such is life.

Despite our own faults, it's easy to expect others to be perfect. When they stumble, we cast them into the great lake of fire and claim, 'How could they do this? They had everything to live for.' Nowhere is this truer than in the US news media. But wait a minute: aren't all of us subjected to the sinful nature? Shouldn't we be surprised, then, if we do *anything* right? Again, it's about viewing life through a new lens.

That's probably my greatest takeaway from my year of seminary. It taught me that because of the sinful nature (*born of the devil*, if you will), we will always tempted to move away from good (God), and thus we fall short of our Creator's chosen ideal for us. We just can't help it, because we are weak in the flesh, and evil is stronger than any of us. But here's the catch: our Creator (or your interpretation of that deity), the one that put us here on the planet, isn't just messing with us; rather, He has our back to get us through the quagmire of the human condition. He is bigger than all of it. So as much as we will continually fall prey to sinful thoughts and actions, there is One greater than us who presides over us all, granting us forgiveness to help us move past our transgressions.

As I heard a trusted friend say one day, 'I'm convinced God always gives us just a bit more than we can handle, so we have to rely on Him!' BOOM! So, next time you see or hear of someone doing something bad, I challenge you to view it through a different lens. Instead of *expecting* them to do right, just know they are also tempted by the darkness, just like you are. Despite their best efforts to do right, people often stumble and fall.

When we forgive our neighbor, it's because the Creator doesn't keep score with us, so we have no authority to keep score with our neighbor, either. It can be quite liberating to come to realize this, although I'm certainly not perfect at it. But the seminary did frame it in a new way for me.

In the end, I'm realizing, after fifty-four good years on the planet, that I probably won't be doubling my age anymore. I guess that's why they call it 'over the hill.' But, as much as I feel young, act young, and hopefully emit a youthful energy, the energy to try and control things starts to fade away as we age. Thank you, God! Hopefully, it's from wisdom gained out of experience. And probably a bit of, *Who the hell has the energy to fight this fight, again?*

Just when I thought *surrender* meant giving up, I was taught that it also means to come over to the winning team. Hmmm. Maybe the uncommon common sense is in discovering joy by letting go. Take control and be controlled. Or let go and live in peace. Some days are easier than others.

I never set out to be a record-label mogul, but when I began to help new and classic talent get their music out to their fans, I quickly realized what the importance my life's work as an artist can be, to be the wind in their sails. Signing some of personal favorite bands, like Sword and Doll Skin, and friends old and new like Mark Slaughter, Autograph, and Ron Keel—as well as discovering new artists like Green Death, Archer Nation, Symbolic, and Semblant—has brought a renewed sense of my purpose in the music business. It's reminded me that trust and reputation have a value beyond money.

I never set out to have a coffee company (there's plenty of good coffee down the street), but when I can help bring people together over a good cup of joe, it makes the venture just that much more special. Even more so, as we set out to create 'artist roasts' for our friends in the music community, we are blessed to be able to continue to spread goodwill with fans and musicians everywhere. I remember the day when sex, drugs, and rock'n'roll were the communities I hung out in. Who would have thought that coffee—the drink that wakes you up rather than knocks you out—would set the course for new horizons?

Now, looking back on the amazing whirlwind of things we've accomplished these last few years, and looking forward to 2019 and beyond, I am beyond thankful for all of the blessings of opportunities and achievements. All the more so with the support of dedicated fans and friends around the world. I can't wait to see what's coming next.

In closing, I want to thank you again for taking time to hang out with me through the pages of this book. I have been blessed with a good life. Even more, you have been very gracious to me over the years as a musician, and I am privileged to play my songs for you each night. I've been blessed to be part of something much bigger than me, first through life-changing musical endeavors and now through exciting new business ventures.

To me, there is no better gift than being able to turn my love of music into a lifestyle that further transcends our time here on the earth.

Be prepared, be agreeable, and say *yes* to opportunity. These seem to be the vital ingredients that make it all work. Sometimes, success isn't found in the result, it's found in the journey.

May it go well with you!

TIMELINE
BY THOM HAZAERT

NOVEMBER 12, 1964 David Warren Ellefson is born in Jackson, Minnesota. (I tried to find something else exciting that happened on this day—maybe another celebrity birth?—but apparently David is the most famous person born on that day. It was a Thursday, which apparently was relatively uneventful. But what if I told you that, in 2020, you will be able to use your 1964 calendar again, as the dates will be identical? You're welcome.)

NOVEMBER 8, 1975 Thomas Lawrence Hazaert is born in Green Bay, Wisconsin. Seems like nothing else all that interesting happened that day, either. But in dog years I would be 192.

MAY 25, 1983 David Ellefson and Greg Handevidt graduate from high school and move from Jackson to Los Angeles to attend the Guitar Institute of Technology, aka Musicians Institute. Neither ends up at GIT, however. Instead, they move into an apartment downstairs from a guy who says he was in some band called Metallica. Megadeth form later that month, and less than a year later they'll sign to Combat Records.

JUNE 12, 1985 Megadeth release *Killing Is My Business ... And Business Is Good* on Combat Records. The band then launch their first US tour with labelmates Exciter. The #1 rock song on *Billboard* is 'Tough All Over' by John Cafferty & The Beaver Brown Band. We don't know why either.

NOVEMBER 1985 Megadeth play with Slayer at the legendary NYC venue L'Amours.

FEBRUARY 1986 Megadeth play at NYC's Irving Plaza, where they are approached by Capitol Records A&R Tim Carr, who later signs the band to Capitol.

APRIL 1986 While still signed to Combat Records, Megadeth begin work on *Peace Sells ... But Who's Buying?* The title track would first appear on *Combat Bullets* in 1986.

SEPTEMBER 9, 1986 *Peace Sells ... But Who's Buying?* is released by Capitol Records. The band tour with King Diamond and play two shows of a planned five-date run with Motörhead. Shortly thereafter, they make their European debut at the Hammersmith Odeon, and support Alice Cooper on the *Constrictor* tour. Thom Hazaert will eventually buy *Peace Sells* on cassette from a neighbor who's stopped listening to metal. Later, this becomes pretty relevant.

JULY 1987 Megadeth perform their final dates in support of *Peace Sells*, with support from Over Kill and Necros. These are also the band's final shows with Chris Poland and Gar Samuelson.

AUGUST 1987 Megadeth begin work on *So Far, So Good ... So What!* Chuck Behler and Jeff Young are announced as the newest members of the band. In Green Bay, twelve-year-old Thom Hazaert anxiously awaits the album's release. And puberty.

260

JANUARY 1988 Dio, Megadeth, and Savatage embark on a tour of North America.

JUNE 17, 1988 Megadeth appear in the Penelope Spheeris documentary *The Decline Of Western Civilation Part 2: The Metal Years*.

AUGUST 1988 Megadeth wrap up the *So Far, So Good … So What!* world tour at Castle Donington in the UK, with Iron Maiden as headliner. (Other bands on the bill include KISS, David Lee Roth, Guns N' Roses, and Helloween.)

JUNE 1989 Nick Menza joins the ranks as Megadeth's new drummer, replacing Chuck Behler. Later that summer, the band enter the studio to record a cover of Alice Cooper's 'No More Mr. Nice Guy' for the Wes Craven film *Shocker*. Eventually, the space-time continuum would converge in a weird *Back To The Future* sort of way, leading to the creation of this book.

FEBRUARY 1990 Megadeth recruit guitarist Marty Friedman as their newest member, as they enter the studio with producer Mike Clink to record the seminal album *Rust In Peace*.

SEPTEMBER 1990 The *Clash Of The Titans* tour embarks across Europe, with co-headliners Slayer and Megadeth. The powerhouse bill is rounded out by Testament and Suicidal Tendencies.

OCTOBER 1990 Megadeth join Judas Priest on their *Painkiller* tour of North America.

JANUARY 1991 Megadeth give their first performance in South America at Brazil's famed Rock In Rio festival.

MAY 1991 *Clash Of The Titans* North America begins with co-headliners Slayer, Megadeth, and Anthrax. Seattle newcomers Alice In Chains are the opening act.

JANUARY 1992 Megadeth enter the studio to record *Countdown To Extinction* with producer Max Norman. It will hit stores on July 14, debuting at #2 on *Billboard*. In April, the Rodney King riots devastate parts of LA, leading to a citywide curfew.

SEPTEMBER 19, 1993 Megadeth relocate to an undisclosed location in Phoenix, Arizona, leading to the city being temporarily renamed.

JANUARY 1994 Megadeth begin work on *Youthanasia*, once again with *Countdown To Extinction* Producer Max Norman. The album is released on November 1, with a world tour to follow.

APRIL 2, 1994 David Ellefson and Julie Foley get married in Maui, Hawaii.

OCTOBER 1994 Megadeth are the first band on the internet, as Capitol Records launches the first ever band website, *Megadeth, Arizona*.

FEBRUARY 2, 1996 Roman Ellefson is born.

JUNE 1997 Megadeth release their seventh studio album, *Cryptic Writings*, produced by Dann Huff.

JUNE 1998 Ozzfest begins, with Megadeth, Tool, Limp Bizkit, and Ozzy Osbourne as the featured acts.

OCTOBER 23, 1998 Athena Ellefson is born.

AUGUST 31, 1999 The Megadeth album *Risk* is released—the first of two to feature drummer Jimmy Degrasso, who replaced Nick Menza the previous year.

JANUARY 2000 Al Pitrelli replaces Marty Friedman as Megadeth's guitarist.

MAY 2001 Megadeth release *The World Needs A Hero* on Sanctuary Records.

FEBRUARY 2002 Megadeth disband due to Dave Mustaine's arm injury.

MARCH 2002 The live double-CD and DVD set *Rude Awakening* is released.

SEPTEMBER 2004 Dave resurrects Megadeth and releases *The System Has Failed*, the first of three albums to not feature Ellefson. Former guitarist Chris Poland contributes solos to the record.

FEBRUARY 2010 David Ellefson re-joins Megadeth for the *Endgame* world tour, as part of the twentieth-anniversary celebrations for *Rust In Peace*.

MAY 2010 The Big Four—Metallica, Slayer, Megadeth, and Anthrax—play their first stadium dates together.

FALL 2010 Slayer, Megadeth, and Anthrax join forces for the *Jägermeister Music Tour*, a throwback to the *Clash Of The Titans* lineup.

SUMMER 2011 Frank Bello and David Ellefson begin their Hartke-sponsored dual-bass clinics.

APRIL 2012 The Big Four play Indio, California. The first Metal Masters event takes place, featuring Ellefson, Frank Bello, Charlie Benante, and Mike Portnoy.

JUNE 2012 The Mayhem tour begins, with headliners Disturbed, Godsmack, and Megadeth.

SEPTEMBER 2012 Megadeth release *Th1rt3en*, their first studio album to feature Ellefson in over a decade.

JUNE 2013 Megadeth release *Super Collider*.

OCTOBER 2015 Metal Allegiance debuts on the maiden voyage of the Motörhead Motorboat Cruise.

MARCH 2015 Megadeth enter the studio with Chris Adler and Kiko Loureiro to begin recording the Grammy Award–winning *Dystopia* album, which will be released in January 2016. (This is the first time Thom Hazaert sees his name in a Megadeth album, and he subsequently buys a copy for his mother. She is not a fan.)

SEPTEMBER 8, 2015 The *Shocker* Special Edition Blu-ray is released by Scream Factory, featuring Thom Hazaert's short documentary about the soundtrack. Ten days later, Metal Allegiance's self-titled debut album is released on Nuclear Blast Records.

APRIL 2016 EMP Label Group forms and puts out its first release, by the Arizona-based band Doll Skin.

OCTOBER 2016 Ellefson Coffee Co is launched.

FEBRUARY 2017 Megadeth win their first ever Grammy Award for 'Best Metal Performance,' for the title track from *Dystopia*.

APRIL 2017 Ellefson Coffee Co. hosts the grand opening of its first retail location in Jackson, Minnesota.

SEPTEMBER 2017 David Ellefson is honored by the Iowa Rock 'n Roll Music Assication's Hall of Fame.

OCTOBER 9, 2018 Today is proclaimed David Ellefson Day in his hometown of Jackson, Minnesota.

NOVEMBER 2018 Megadeth begin recording the follow up to Grammy Award–winning *Dystopia*.

JANUARY 18, 2019 Altitudes & Attitude's debut album, *Get It Out*, is released on Megaforce Records, featuring David Ellefson and Frank Bello (Anthrax).

ACKNOWLEDGMENTS

DAVID ELLEFSON WOULD LIKE TO THANK

My wife Julie and our two children, Roman and Athena. My partner Thom Hazaert, who pushes me, guides me, encourages me, and is always at the ready for all things Ellefson. My agent Matthew Hamilton for helping my literary ambitions become reality. Tom Seabrook and the staff at Jawbone Press.

Additional thanks to Donnie Schoenrock, Melody Myers, Jon Romanowski, Jeff Cary, Mike Tempesta, Ira Cary Blanco, Jack Knight, Jordon and Nathan Ellefson, Mary Hunt, John Aquilino, Randy Walker, Pamela Trepanier, Steve Conley, Dale Steele, Steve Smith, Al Pitrelli, Dave Small, John Davis, Jon Bjorgaard, Jeremy DaPena, Steve Smith, Bob Goheen, the members of Doll Skin (Alex Snowden, Nicole Rich, Meghan Herring, and Sydney Dolezal) and their families, Keith Rowley, Ron 'Bumblefoot' Thal, Christian Lawrence, Dave Sharpe, Ben McClane, Ron Bienstock, Jill Michaels, Edwin Hsu, Chris Poland, John Dallmus, Randy Spencer, Jack Tillery, Cory Brennan, Chris Shields, Bob Johnson, Brad Furhman and all at 5B Artist Management, Alex Diesel and Merchlive, Mike Tempesta and all at Fender/Jackson, KHDK, Buck and Shelley at ISP, Jon-Paul Hutchins, Hannah Romberg, Paul Waggoner, Toby Mroczek, Alex Gilbert, Tony Bass, Will McCrum, Mike Peterson, Jeff Powers, Scott Bird, Scott Borgerson, Patrick Ritchie, Bill Elevens, Richard Paine, Don Hanson, Bryan Evenson, Scott Borgerson, Scott Bird, Andy Somers, John Becker, Shauna O'Donnell, Shaunna Heth, Tim Binder, Bob Chiappardi, Ron Laffitte, Missi Callazzo, Mike Monterulo, Jay Ruston, Ryan Greene, Richard Easterling, Mike Portnoy, Alex Skolnick, Mike Clink, Max Norman, Toby Wright, Rich Ross, Kyle Bailey and all at Replay Guitar Exchange, Chuck Behler, Jeff Young, Danny Hill, Danny Wimmer, Gary Spivak, Mike Ransom, Mike Gaube, Mark Abbatista, Adam Mott, Chris Rakestraw, Fred Kowalo, Willie Gee, Mike McGee, Alice Goldstein, Drew Fortier, Stephen Shareaux, Justin Lessman, Jamie West, Susan Reiter, Amerika Hall, George Horhay, MasterSound Tampa, Greg Carlson, Jeff Yonker, The Neuenschwander Family, KKOJ FM, Tod Decker, Brad Altman, Brian Lew, Harold Oiman, David Plastik, Brad Schmidt, Bobby Gustafson, Maria Ferrero, Jerome Haultier, Ed Pugliesi, Steve & Linda Handevidt, Enrique Abeyta and *Revolver* magazine, Loudwire, BraveWords, Wrath, Green Death, Helstar, Arise In Chaos.

The Recording Academy (Marc, Kenny, Mo). Lee Whitmore and the Grammy Education Coalition. The Iowa Rock 'n Roll Music Association Hall of Fame. The Hall of Heavy Metal History. To all my life-long friends, family and supporters in The City of Jackson, Minnesota.

All the people who so graciously gave of their time and contributions to the book, including: K.K. Downing, Dan Donegan, Brian 'Head' Welch, Randy Kertz, Chris Adler, Jimmy Degrasso, Frank Bello, Kiko Loureiro, Dirk Verbeuren, Kristian Nairn, Alice Cooper, Brian Slagel, Mark Menghi, Juan Garcia, Greg Handevidt, Chris Cannella, Dash Cooper, Mark Tremonti, Mark Slaughter, Bradley Schmidt, Ron Keel, Jay Reynolds, and Jason McMaster.

And, finally, to Dave Mustaine for being my running buddy for over thirty-five years … we still have the best stories at the party!

THOM HAZAERT THANKS

My family, Reilly and Jenna Hazaert, Barbara Alger, Melody Myers, my partner David Ellefson for letting me be a part of his amazing story, Julie, Roman, and Athena Ellefson, Alice Cooper, Dash Cooper, Sheryl Cooper, Alex Diesel, Haggis, and Merchlive, Matty Bluntz, Kristian Nairn, Mark Tremonti, Dan Donegan, Brian 'Head' Welch, Daryl 'DMC' McDaniel, Drew Fortier, Doug Esper, Jack Tillery, Bam Margera, MasterSound Studios Tampa, Max Norman, Jimmy DeGrasso, Eddie Ojeda, Frank Hannon, Dirk Verbeuren, Kiko Louireiro, Jody Glisman Best, all at the Syndicate, Jason Hillery at Midwest Communications, Katherine Turman and *Nights With Alice Cooper*, Bumblefoot, Ron Keel, Mark Slaughter, Jason McMaster, Madam X, Symbolic, Archer Nation, Mike Clink, Chuck Mosley (RIP), all the EMP and Combat artists, past, present, and future! And most of the people David thanked. You know who you are.

Huge thanks to Joel McIver for passing me the torch. It was an honor and a privilege. Thanks for giving me such huge shoes to fill.

Extra special thanks: Mark Manzke, Big Metal Al, Matt Mosley, Karmen Keith, Andrew Southern, Christopher Cusack, Nigel Rozier, Johan Stromqvist, Je Block, Shawn Rattlehead, Valentin, Kaloyan, Vantsislav, Sten Meijer, Derek Allen (Rest In Peace Ryan Greathouse), Flava Dave Turnham, Stuart Brown, Michelle 'DethAngel' Coulter, Jason Sandgoat, Steve Prziborowski, Erik Bigalke, Anita Gongola, Mark Cardoza, Steve Libby, Stu McGill, Tim Boyles, Omar Baig, Amy C. Scott, Josh Brant, Rob Bolender, Amerika Hall, White Dream, and Lucas Engel.

JOIN THE #EMPIRE

davidellefson.com
ellefsoncoffeeco.com
grillingismybusiness.com
emplabelgroup.com

combatrecs.com
mylifewithdeth.com
morelifewithdeth.com